# Fighting the British

This book is dedicated to the following members of our family
who served during the Napoleonic Wars:

*Jean Antoine Wilkin, 10th Cuirassiers*

*Georges Wilkin, 10th Cuirassiers*

*Jean Lambert Wilkin, Train d'artillerie*

*Jean-Joseph Wilkin, 15th Cohort 1st Company*

Four brothers, four deserters.

# Fighting the British

## French Eyewitness Accounts from the Napoleonic Wars

*Bernard Wilkin & René Wilkin*

Pen & Sword
**MILITARY**

First published in Great Britain in 2018 by
**PEN & SWORD MILITARY**
An imprint of
Pen & Sword Books Ltd
47 Church Street
Barnsley
South Yorkshire
S70 2AS

ISBN 978-1-47388-081-8

Typeset by Concept, Huddersfield HD4 5JL.
Printed and bound in England by TJ International Ltd, Padstow, PL28 8RW

Pen & Sword Books Limited incorporates the imprints of Atlas, Archaeology, Aviation, Discovery, Family History, Fiction, History, Maritime, Military, Military Classics, Politics, Select, Transport, True Crime, Air World, Frontline Publishing, Leo Cooper, Remember When, Seaforth Publishing, The Praetorian Press, Wharncliffe Local History, Wharncliffe Transport, Wharncliffe True Crime and White Owl.

For a complete list of Pen & Sword titles please contact
PEN & SWORD BOOKS LIMITED
47 Church Street, Barnsley, South Yorkshire, S70 2AS, England
E-mail: enquiries@pen-and-sword.co.uk
Website: www.pen-and-sword.co.uk

# Contents

# List of Illustrations

# Acknowledgements

The authors would like to thank all who have helped to produce this book. We are particularly grateful to the employees of the *Archives Générales du Royaume*, the *Bibliothèque Nationale de France* and the *Service Historique de la Défense*. We would also like to thank Sébastien Dubois (*Archives Générales du Royaume*), Timothy Baycroft (University of Sheffield), Maude Williams (University of Bochum) and Thierry Lentz (*Fondation Napoléon*). Let us not forget the readers of *Fighting for Napoleon* and those who have shared their enthusiasm for the period with us. As always, we need to express our gratitude to Rupert Harding at Pen & Sword, without whom this book would not exist.

The support of our family proved essential in overcoming the many frustrations associated with producing a book. We cannot thank enough Alexis Wilkin, Adélaide Blavier, Philomène Wilkin and Basile Wilkin. We are also extremely grateful to Phileas Wilkin, our three-year-old dictator, who makes his father and his grandfather proud.

# Introduction

## Understanding the French Perspective

Lower-ranks of the French army are rarely given a voice in British and American studies of the Napoleonic Wars. This fact alone provided a strong incentive to work on our previous book, *Fighting for Napoleon*. With the advent of social and cultural history, understanding common soldiers has become an essential part of contemporary military studies.[1] Their experiences can open new doors and bring historians to a new level of understanding. The success of our first monograph clearly signalled that not only professional researchers but also a broader English-speaking public were eager to explore the lives of French rankers during this violent period of history. Presenting *Fighting for Napoleon* at various conferences in Britain gave us a chance to communicate with our readers. It soon became clear that many were particularly interested by the Franco-British aspect of the Napoleonic Wars. We were asked several questions about how French soldiers perceived the British military and how this vision evolved from 1793 to 1815. The notion of hatred between the nations was also commonly raised. Moreover, our overview of British prisons and the treatment of French prisoners in England and Scotland triggered several debates. Ultimately, we saw this curiosity as an invitation to write a new book on the struggle between French and British soldiers during the Napoleonic Wars.

The fight against France from 1793 to 1815 is not entirely understood in Britain. It is clear that its memory lives in our environment and is deeply rooted in our urban and rural communities. Trafalgar Square and Waterloo Station, two places among thousands of others christened after famous battles of the time, are silent reminders of the European struggle for power. Unfortunately, clichés and shortcuts are also commonplace. Today, Nelson and Wellington are overwhelming figures. Hundreds of public houses bear their names and countless publications describe their adventures. While they are rightly remembered as talented leaders, they overshadow other important

---

1. Testimonies of soldiers of enemy nations of Britain in other conflicts are becoming more common in English. See, for example, for the First World War: Benjamin Ziemann and Bernd Ulrich, *German soldiers in the Great War: letters and eyewitness accounts* (Barnsley, 2010).

British commanders who fought the French with distinction in various parts of the globe. Likewise, Trafalgar and Waterloo are too often used to illustrate the fight against France. These battles were undoubtedly fundamental but cannot be understood without a broader perspective. The British intervention in Egypt, the Calabrian expedition and the assaults against Boulogne-sur-Mer, to list only a few operations, were also crucial episodes. As the title *Fighting the British* suggests, this book is entirely dedicated to the battles between French and British soldiers. With the exception of two peace interludes in 1803 and 1814–1815, the British fought the French continuously from 1793 to 1815. The war began on 1 February 1793 as a clash between competing European powers inspired by fundamentally different ideologies. The French Republic had not only executed Louis XVI on 21 January 1793, sending a strong message to foreign monarchies, but also refused to evacuate her recent conquests. Following years of conflict, William Pitt's resignation led to the 1802 Peace of Amiens. This short interlude failed to appease either side. The war resumed in 1803 and only finished when France was restored to a non-threatening European position in 1815. It should be remembered that the conflict was not exclusively an external matter for Britain. When Thomas Paine published his *Rights of Man* in 1791–1792, he brought home radical social and political ideas inspired by the Revolution. Likewise, the failed French attempts to support republican rebels in Ireland were fascinating episodes in a long-lasting internal struggle. Readers must therefore remember that the operations covered in this monograph happened within a wider context. Several other nations made vital contributions to the war effort against France and Napoleon. This fact is important not only to understand the global nature of the conflict but also to appreciate the psychology of the French military. For French soldiers, Britain was one enemy nation among many others. A crucial British victory like Trafalgar might have made an impression on the French public but was not seen as a turning-point by the population or by the army. It should be remembered that just over a month after Nelson's triumph at Trafalgar, the French won decisively against the Austrians and the Russians at Austerlitz. Moreover, state propaganda was omnipresent and made sure to turn British successes into minor setbacks.[2] In fact, the French regarded diplomatic and economic international influence as the main danger associated with Britain. As this book will demonstrate, French soldiers knew little about Britain. Most had never met British people before the conflict and had no clue about their culture or language. They always talked about the 'English', even when mentioning Welsh, Irish or

---

2. A fact mentioned in our previous book: Bernard Wilkin and René Wilkin, *Fighting for Napoleon* (Barnsley, 2015).

Scottish soldiers,[3] and associated them with a set of clichéd characteristics such as greediness and dishonesty.

*Fighting the British* is built on a large body of primary sources written during the Napoleonic Wars. Hundreds of letters and personal diaries of French soldiers were consulted and carefully selected. Official after-action reports and proclamations, sometimes far more detailed than any form of correspondence, are also included. These primary sources are unequal in terms of quality and present specific problems, which need to be understood. Letters were often written over long periods of time by mostly young un-educated men. Less than 38 per cent of them knew how to read or write and illiterate soldiers usually relied on their educated friends to correspond with their families.[4] Low-ranking men sent letters to keep in touch with their relatives but also for more pragmatic reasons. Darkening their situation to evoke pity, French soldiers almost systematically asked their parents for money. On the other hand, letters were rarely written for posterity and are among the only surviving primary sources detailing the experiences of the lower ranks in the French army. Diaries written during the wars were also useful for the redaction of this monograph. They were often kept by more educated men, mainly young officers, who understood that they were wit-nessing a unique period of history. Narcissism and exaggerations are common issues with private journals, but they are also rich in details and are untainted by post-war reconstructions.[5] Official after-action reports are equally inter-esting and enlightening but must be received with a healthy amount of scepti-cism. Surviving officers of a lost battle were often keen to blame the defeat on their dead colleagues. Reports were their only hope of justifying their own actions, and sometimes saving their military careers. Proclamations are also problematic. Aimed at civilians or soldiers, they were overwhelmingly designed for propaganda reasons.

This book attempts to cover a long and difficult period of history. As such, there are inevitable gaps in the archives. In a few cases there was no other choice but to use memoirs and souvenirs written after the conflict to com-pensate for the lack of surviving documents. The memoirs featured in this book were mostly written soon after the fall of the French Empire. The authors of *Fighting for Napoleon*, acknowledging how fragile and unreliable memory can be, have voluntarily prioritised those authored before 1830.

---

3. A mistake still commonly made in France and Germany even today. Even when the com-plexities of Great Britain are understood, the French word 'Anglais' is so popular that it is used by virtually everybody.
4. René Wilkin, 'Le remplacement militaire dans le département de l'Ourthe', in: *Bulletin de l'Institut archéologique liégeois*, CXII (2001–2002), p. 275.
5. Unless they have been reworked after the Napoleonic Wars, which is not uncommon.

Memoirs are obviously far more suspicious than other sources. We found several occasions where the writers had plagiarised other sources or wrongfully claimed to have served in places where they had never been. We should highlight that we have not attempted to cover every single campaign and battle fought between the French and the British. There were hundreds of smaller operations and incidents, both at sea and on land, of minor importance. While minor battles are undoubtedly interesting from a historical point of view, they are rarely mentioned in primary sources.

This book is divided into six chapters. The first investigates the Revolutionary Wars, concentrating mainly on the siege of Toulon where Bonaparte made a name for himself, and the expedition to Egypt. Despite the annihilation of the Egyptian expeditionary corps, this chapter will argue that Bonaparte managed to both raise his profile and benefit from the adventure. It will also be demonstrated that the French blamed the defeat on General Menou rather than on British-Ottoman military superiority. The second chapter concentrates on major naval combats. Looking at the battles of the Nile and Trafalgar, it will be argued that both defeats were once again explained by the lack of leadership on the French side rather than by British superior planning or experience. Chapter 3 investigates the French expeditions to Ireland of 1796 and 1798, the aborted invasion of Britain and the British campaign in Calabria. These operations will highlight how ideological the war between France and Britain could be. Playing on republican feelings in Ireland, the French tried to spread revolutionary ideas to hurt the British. On the other hand, the British used the monarchy and traditional catholic feelings to inflame Calabria. The camp of Boulogne-sur-Mer, as this chapter will show, was also highly significant. Events such as the first military distribution of crosses of the Legion of Honour contributed to Napoleon's aura and guaranteed the army's devotion. The following chapter is interested in the Peninsular War. This long and complex campaign began as an attempt to enforce the Continental System but became a trap for the French army. It will be argued that the French never understood Wellington's tactics and too easily dismissed him as a poor commander. French soldiers, however, learned to respect British discipline and bravery under fire. The fifth chapter studies the invasion of the south-west of France in 1813–1814, the Hundred Days and the occupation of the country by the Allies. The presence of British soldiers on French territory was met with both curiosity and hostility. After the battle of Waterloo, veterans looked bitterly at the occupiers but were forced to admit that the British usually behaved better than did the Russians or the Prussians. Chapter 6 looks at the controversy surrounding French prisoners in Britain. The historiography, especially in France, has traditionally presented British camps and prison-ships as extreme places where captive soldiers died in great numbers. This chapter will argue against this and show that the British, although initially unprepared for large influxes of enemy soldiers, took major steps to improve their circumstances. It will be demonstrated that British prisons were tough but nonetheless offered acceptable conditions of detention. As stated in our previous book, several volumes would be needed to do justice to the Franco-British conflict and to the many topics approached in this book. We invite the reader to look at the bibliography for further reading.

Bernard Wilkin & René Wilkin
February 2017

*Chapter 1*

# The Revolutionary Wars and the First Napoleonic Campaigns

## The Siege of Toulon

The War of the First Coalition marked the beginning of a long-lasting struggle between the French and the British. After the fall of the Girondins and the rise of the Jacobins at the National Convention, several parts of France turned against the Revolution in June 1793. Important cities in the south, such as Marseille and Nîmes, followed the path of insurrection. The Convention reacted by sending the Army of the Alps, led by General Carteaux. This force recaptured Avignon in July 1793 and Marseille a few weeks later on 25 August. Stories of the bloody reprisals following the capture of Marseille encouraged the royalists to surrender the city of Toulon to Admiral Hood, the commander of an Anglo-Spanish squadron. Apart from the failed siege of Dunkirk, this was the first important contribution made by Great Britain to the War of the First Coalition.[1] Republican forces, eager to punish the city of Toulon for what they perceived as an unthinkable act of treason, began the siege on 8 September 1793. François-Michel Royer[2] had fought as a lieutenant for the Republic since 1792. In a letter to his parents, he described the capture of Marseille, the role played by the British and the early phase of the siege:

> The camp of Toulon, army of Carteaux, 17 September 1793, year 1 of the French Republic
>
> Dear father and mother,
> I have not received an answer to the letter that I have written to you and the difficult circumstances in which we were forbade me from writing again. However, you must have received my letter from Arles.

1. Jennifer Mori, 'The British Government and the Bourbon restoration: The occupation of Toulon, 1793', in: *The Historical Journal*, 40 (1997), pp. 699–719.
2. François-Michel Royer was born in Thonon on 13 January 1770. He worked as a librarian in Switzerland before joining a Swiss regiment in the French army and the National Guard. He was transferred to the *Légion Allobroge* as a lieutenant on 20 August 1792. He became a captain in 1794 and was sent to the 27th *demi-brigade légère* in 1797. He continued serving and became commander of a battalion in 1813. Royer fought during the campaign of France and was an officer of the Legion of Honour. His date of death is unknown.

You could not believe how badly we have suffered; never sleep in a bed, always exposed to the weather, no tent, and, more often than not, no supplies. It is happy for us that it is not raining and, since I left you, we have seen no rain. The sea breeze is also against us. Well, this is nothing as long as the righteous cause triumphs.

You have probably heard of the progress of our Legion, which distinguished itself everywhere. Before leaving Marseille, we had many fights in L'Isle, Avignon, Lambesc, Salou, Orgon and Septèmes, which is the last city before reaching Marseille.

The Legion attacked Marseille without being ordered to do so. Doppet[3] was commanding us. The army came forward to help and our artillery began to fire. Despite being outnumbered by the enemy, we took three strongholds, one after another, one on the mountain. This victory and the capture of their cannon took them by surprise.

During the action, Marseille was occupied by the aristocrats, who bombarded the patriotic area of the city for twenty-four hours. But, having heard of the routing of their whole army, they fled either by sea or towards Toulon.

The next day, we entered Marseille and were welcomed by shouts of 'Long live the Republic! Hurra to the Allobroges!' Having entered Marseille long before the army, I cannot describe the joy of the people: all embraced me and, due to my role, said: 'Here are the liberators!'

After having stayed for a while to revive their courage, we took the road for Toulon. But what a surprise to hear that the perfidious inhabitants of Toulon had opened their doors to the English and the Spanish! This did not discourage us: we strode towards Toulon. I was in the vanguard with three hundred men; we arrived at Ollioules, a little town about a mile from Toulon. As soon as we arrived, the municipality organised our accommodation and ordered its citizens (I say 'citizens', I mean 'traitors') to let us drink as much as we wanted to. Why did they do that? To slit our throats during the night. But we did not fall into the trap.

The commander of the column wanted us to stay in the city, but our captain, who commanded the Allobroges, told the commander that we were in front of the enemy and we should not stay here. From there, he brought us further and the volunteers of the Basses-Alpes, who formed the vanguard with us, stayed at the gates of the city.

What had the municipality done during that time? It had ordered the English to fight us, which happened at four. There were many soldiers in

---

3. François Amédée Doppet was a French general from Savoie who served under the orders of Carteaux before becoming commander of the Army of the Alps. He later served on the Council of Five Hundred but retired and died in 1799.

the city and the English fell on us, as did the people, who fired at us from their windows. We were forced to retreat: we lost two cannon and six of our men were killed; eighteen English were killed and a captain. We came back to the army, expressing our indignation at this rebellious city.

The next day, we advanced with a more imposing force and, despite enemy fire, we took the dangerous narrow pass of Ollioules, occupied by the English and the Spanish. We chased them up to the gates of Toulon. Ollioules was sacked and eight houses burned. The enemy lost many men and four carts of wounded that were trying to reach Toulon. We captured six Spanish soldiers and a captain.

We are currently in front of Toulon. The cannon have not stopped firing on the 18th and 19th of this month. Toulon is one of the most fortified cities and I think many men will lose their lives; we are probably going to be there all winter.

[...] The general promised us that the Legion would go back to our department after the peace of Toulon. But when will that peace happen? Fortified places are impossible to capture and they fire at us from all sides.

I ask you, my dear parents, to tell me what happened in Savoy. And we will see each other again soon? My brothers and sisters are well and they send their regards to you and to all the family. I hope you will send news soon; I learned that my brother was in Nantes. Why did you not send me his address?

Louis XVII was proclaimed [King] in Toulon.[4]

If the city of Toulon had indeed proclaimed Louis XVII king at the end of August, François-Michel Royer had no reason to be so pessimistic about the outcome of the siege. Indeed, the French Republican army held in its ranks a talented and ambitious artillery captain named Napoleone di Buonaparte.[5] Well connected to prominent political figures such as the younger brother of Maximilien Robespierre, Bonaparte had a clear idea of how to capture the city. He tried to present his plan to General Carteaux but was dismissed. The young Corsican officer did not give up and used his connections to be appointed artillery commander of the Republican forces. Following this promotion, he ordered different batteries to bombard the fort of Malbousquet, a major obstacle to the capture of the city. Carteaux was replaced as commander of the siege by General Dugommier on 11 November 1793. Dugommier, a professional soldier, immediately recognised the value of Bonaparte's plan

---

4. François-Michel Royer, 'Impressions d'un Allobroge devant Toulon', in: *Carnets de la Sabretache: revue militaire rétrospective* (1899), pp. 146–9.
5. He later adopted the French version of his name, Napoleon Bonaparte.

and issued orders for it to be followed. The systematic bombardment of strategic positions forced the British to attempt a sortie on 23 November. A French counter-attack prevented the British from succeeding and led to the capture of General O'Hara. Napoleon, who took part in the counter-attack, wrote a letter to Edme Henri Victor Dupin[6] to tell him about the incident:

10 *frimaire* year II [30 November 1793]

Ollioules

[...] On the 10th, at five in the morning, the enemy sent six thousand men, commanded by the English General O'Hara, governor of Toulon, and pushed aside our forward posts before reaching the battery. They neutralised six cannons out of twenty-four. At this moment, our forces arrived. General Dugommier fought with the courage of a true republican. We took the battery and captured the English General, who suffered an arm wound; we pursued the enemy with our bayonets in their backs. We killed four to five thousand men and captured a great number of them, including a Spanish colonel, an English major and a great number of officers of lower rank. The cannon of the *Convention* were repaired soon enough to increase the confusion of their retreat.

Our soldiers, carried away by feelings of indignation, went immediately to Malbousquet. We chased them from the heights; we destroyed a fort that they had started building; we took a great number of tents; we destroyed what we could not carry away ...[7]

On 16–17 December the final assault began. An anonymous French Count,[8] fighting for the royalists inside the city of Toulon with the British, described the chaos of the attack:

Anyway, I was at a forward redoubt on the west side the same night our fate was decided on the other side. A bit before the day, we were ordered to leave our post and retreat to the city. Once we arrived, I heard of this disastrous project to order a general evacuation: my despair was easy to understand. I ran to gather my friends, who forced me to replace my uniform with a costume of pillage and disorder. This happy precaution saved my life. The enemies within were starting to shake the city and

---

6. Edme Henri Victor Dupin was born in 1743 and died in 1802. He was a lieutenant-colonel in the engineers.
7. Napoleon Bonaparte, *Correspondance générale publiée par la Fondation Napoléon. Tome I: les apprentissages, 1784–1797* (Paris, 2004), pp. 148–9.
8. This anonymous Count had military experience, for which reason the British gave him a position in the artillery during the siege of Toulon. He later fled to London, where he published a narration of the siege in 1794.

threatened to cut off our retreat. We hurried to gather our most precious belongings and went to the port. There, I witnessed the worst spectacle that the earth might have endured. A fire had destroyed all the ships, the stores and the arsenals. The explosion was so loud that nature itself seemed disturbed. It was impossible to distinguish the sky or the earth and the sea was only a field of fire: this was a picture of hell. It was hard to distinguish objects and distances and the heat of the atmosphere was hard to endure, but this was little compared to what I still have to write. [. . .] The republicans had already captured most of the right side of the city. The fire was, for them, a target and they rained down bombs and grenades on us. The Allies on the left side, warned that the insurrection was spreading behind them, fired at the city to hold back the malcontents and to protect the boarding. But there was a revolt in the arsenal and in the city; everybody fired at everybody. Disorder was everywhere in the port and fear forced people to retreat to that place. We could see from all sides furniture piled on the embankment, groups of men and women running and hitting each other. Shouts filled the air and screams were making this horrible spectacle more atrocious.

[. . .] This was the awful scene when I arrived near the dock, carrying a child in my arms and dragging several lost women. I jumped into a departing ship; as soon as we had moved, I felt something impossible to describe. Suddenly, I was violently thrown on my seat; it felt like struggling in a fire. [. . .] I learned that it was the explosion of a ship, which killed many people and probably my friends too. I have been unable to find them.[9]

Three days after the assault, a report about the capture of Toulon was written by a man named Morisot, who was at the time serving with the army of Italy. Fighting for the Republicans and eager to demonstrate his political conviction, Morisot included several exaggerations. His letter mostly highlights the role played by the British in the defence of Toulon but also describes an unusual act of kindness:

Solliès 30 *frimaire* [year] 2 of the French Republic
Army of Italy directed against the rebels of Toulon

I will tell the fortunate story of our armies against the rebels of the infamous city of Toulon, which will soon endure well-deserved punishment.

9. Comte de C***, *Séjour de dix mois en France, par un émigré, qui n'avoit pu sortir de Toulon en décembre 1793, & ne s'est sauvé de France que par l'élargissement des prisonniers de Paris, en août 1794* (London, 1794), pp. 20–6.

For days, we made ready for a great assault against Fort Pharaon. Our soldiers were only waiting for the order [to attack]. They proved it when the generals ordered the assault during the night of the 26th to the 27th. They climbed the redoubt like cats. They managed to enter but, unfortunately, were unable to stay long. They were pushed back violently and suffered two hundred casualties, mostly from the regiments of Aquitaine and Dumaine. Once the combat was over, we heard the voice of a wounded man, who was dying and shouting: 'Comrades, I am sad to die, I will not have the pleasure to die for my country, to help beat the enemy. But what makes me feel better is to scream from the redoubt, Long, Long live the Republic!' We were forced to retreat and had lost all hope because of this redoubt. But Paul Barras[10] and the generals had another plan for a second assault. They ordered all the inhabitants of the surrounding area to go to the redoubt and they had to bring all their tools to trace a path, which could be used to carry up small cannon. It was soon done and, having carried the cannon up during the night of the 27th to the 28th, Paul Barras and the generals ordered a second assault. Our soldiers, always brave, did not hesitate to climb the mountain where they had suffered the day before. (I forgot to say that Paul Barras and the generals were leading the columns.) But what a surprise to see that, once we had arrived at the redoubt, there were only two of our soldiers there who had been wounded the day before. They told us how accommodating the English were. First, they asked them if they were hungry or thirsty. They laid them on mattresses and used the surgical art with as much care as possible. When the decision was made to leave the redoubt, they said: 'Comrades, we have to leave you. Tomorrow, your people will be here and they will continue to treat you as required by your unfortunate predicament.' After having evacuated our two wounded, we saw that the English had spiked our cannon. But two hours were enough to repair three of them, which we used to fire at the city. The English were still holding two small forts lower than the Pharaon and they fired back. The generals and Paul Barras would have been hit if they had not been sitting down. I went for a walk near the battlefield and saw our troops going forward. I heard loud screams in the city, and even shots, and everybody assumed that they were fighting. Indeed, that was the case. Finally, the English left Toulon but refused to take anybody with them. And many people drowned while trying to reach their ships. They were

---

10. Paul Barras was commissioner to the French army during the Revolutionary Wars and later became one of the Directors of the Directory, the executive power of France. He was removed from office and retired when Napoleon Bonaparte took over. He died on 29 January 1829.

unable to leave and we have already shot twelve officers and imprisoned all soldiers. The English left much wheat in Toulon.

Joy is on every face and we see that everything protects the Republic. And having witnessed all these fortunate things, we believe that we are invincible – the English abandoned this place where we were expecting to lose thirty thousand men and we entered Toulon without losing one man, except for those wounded the day before ...[11]

This important document demonstrates how vital the artillery was for the siege of Toulon. It also suggests that the French were far less hostile towards British soldiers than they were towards royalists and other enemies of the Republic. Domestic opponents were hated while foreigners were regarded largely with disdain. Interestingly, there is no mention of Bonaparte in any testimony written by lower-ranks in the weeks following the siege of Toulon. Despite having played a decisive role in the capture of the city, the future emperor was yet to gain fame and become known by ordinary soldiers. This point is illustrated by the following letter, written by Antoine Baudet[12] to his mother. This document is one of the few surviving letters sent by professional soldiers serving in the French army before the Revolution:

From Lacerant, 22 December 1793, year II of the French Republic
My dear mother,
This [letter is] to give you news. All is very well, thank God. I hope the same for you. Your previous letter told me that my little sister is dangerously ill. This upsets me a lot. You want me to be by your side to help. You need to know that this is not possible as long as the war continues. No leave is granted. We fight here, in the mountains, days and nights in the snow, and rain up to our ears. Some of our men left for the siege of Toulon. Marseille, we took it during the last days. Two to three hundred men were killed, sixty wounded. After that, we entered Toulon with our drums and cannon. The English, the Spanish and the people from Piedmont left Toulon with their ships. Before leaving, they burned most of Toulon. They left men in the fort of Lamarque. They blew up another one. This is how they retaliate. They left four hundred cows, three thousand sheep, stocks of flour and many of their cannon when leaving. You should see the mountain of prisoners we have. Last month, we took about fifteen hundred men ...[13]

11. Anonymous, 'Le siège de Toulon 1793', in: *Carnet de la Sabretache: revue militaire rétrospective*, 116 (1993), pp. 47–8.
12. Antoine Baudet joined the 11th regiment of line infantry on 4 July 1784 and continued serving until the Revolutionary Wars.
13. Jérôme Croyet, *Paroles de grognards* (Paris, 2016), pp. 64–5.

The end of the siege of Toulon was followed by the bloody suppression of supposedly royalist elements. Hundreds of people were shot in the city centre and many trials were held during the following months. Napoleon Bonaparte had been wounded in the thigh by a British sergeant during the final assault and was not involved in the suppression. Days after the end of the siege, he was promoted to the rank of brigadier general and was sent to the Army of Italy. This episode was not of major importance to the Revolutionary Wars but it became significant for Bonaparte's career. Toulon offered him an opportunity to prove both his valour and his leadership and opened the doors to a senior position in the army. Had the British sergeant killed Bonaparte instead of wounding him during the final assault, history would have been very different. However, Bonaparte healed quickly.

Meanwhile, the French and the British continued fighting during the next years. In 1794 the soldiers of the French Republic besieged the city of Nijmegen in the Netherlands. A soldier named François[14] reported the following anecdote:

> On 8 November 1794, instead of firing grapeshot at us, they [the British] used large coins, which we found entertaining to collect while running to encourage the enemy to fire even more. At that time, we were receiving only paper money [and] were therefore grateful to the English for providing coins. I was able to pick up 287 of them, which later proved very useful. Some of us were very badly wounded, and those who were hit by those coins almost invariably died.[15]

That year would prove crucial for Napoleon Bonaparte. His association with Robespierre landed him in trouble during the Thermidorian reaction of July 1794, but he somehow managed to be acquitted. He became a national hero the next year when he crushed a royalist insurrection in Paris. On 12 *vendémiaire* year 4 of the Republic (4 October 1795) Parisian troops of the National Guard refused to recognise the decrees of the National Convention and destroyed symbols of the republic. The Convention asked General Jacques Menou to deal with the situation, but his timid reaction failed to impress the royalist rebels. The next day General Bonaparte took over.

---

14. Jean Charles François was born in Picardy on 19 June 1777. He volunteered at the age of fifteen in 1792 and fought at Valmy. He became a corporal in 1793 and was wounded the same year. He was again wounded in 1796. He left for Egypt in 1798 and fought there for the following years. He continued to serve in the French army after the campaign of Egypt and fought at Austerlitz, Jena, Eylau and in Spain. He eventually rose to the rank of captain. He retired on 3 August 1824 and died in 1853.

15. Charles François, *Journal du capitaine François dit « le dromadaire d'Egypte »* (Paris, 2002), p. 110.

Despite being outnumbered by the royalists, he repelled an assault using grapeshot, not a common sight in the streets of Paris, and then launched a cavalry charge led by Joachim Murat. The deaths of more than three hundred attackers destroyed royalist hopes and saved the Convention. Bonaparte became a hero and was given command of the Army of Italy on 2 March 1796. He proved equally competent during the following campaign when he crushed the Austrians and forced them to sign the Treaty of Campo Formio on 18 October 1797. The First Coalition was dead and the French Republic was unchallenged on the continent.

## The French Campaign in Egypt

Following the end of the War of the First Coalition in 1797, the French Republic had only one major enemy left: Great Britain. In 1798 General Bonaparte offered to lead an expedition to Egypt to establish a permanent French presence there and threaten British India. Officially, the French intended to bring freedom to the population and expel the despotic Ottomans.[16] The Directory, the executive power of the French Republic, agreed with Bonaparte's plans and allowed the young general to gather 35,000 soldiers during the spring of the same year. The Directory was obviously interested in defeating the British but was equally eager to send an ambitious and charismatic military leader far from mainland France. The soldiers were gathered months in advance but were left in the dark. They knew that they were about to face British soldiers but they did not know where. Naturally they concluded that the day had come to fight the British in their own country, as François explained:

> 28 April 1798: staying in Avignon … We are told that the army is gathering on the side of the Mediterranean sea and that a maritime expedition is being prepared in Toulon. This army will be commanded by General in Chief Bonaparte. A proclamation from the Directory says that we need to finish the war in London. All of us are looking at the Channel and are eagerly waiting to punish those proud Britons on their land. Their perfidy and tyranny at sea were making Europe miserable.[17]

The expeditionary corps left Toulon on 19 May 1798. Most soldiers still did not know where they were headed. Louis-Joseph Bricard's diary explained:

> Newspapers and men said many things about the expedition; some said: 'it is for Sicily'; others: 'we are going to Malta'. Those who were more

---

16. Zeinab Abul-Magd, 'A crisis of images: The French, Jihad, and the plague in Upper Egypt, 1798–1801', in: *Journal of World History*, 2 (2012), p. 315.
17. François, *Journal du capitaine François*, p. 197.

educated said that we were to land in Sardinia, Naples, etc. Finally, others said that we were going to Egypt and, from there, to India.[18]

Bonaparte's reputation was already growing when the army left for Egypt. Bricard wrote:

> General Buonaparte arrived and soldiers were very satisfied to learn that he was our commander. The squadron was under the orders of Admiral Brueys; sailors did not seem happy to be led by this admiral.[19]

Not everybody was convinced by Bonaparte. François Bernoyer,[20] a tailor working for the French army, travelled with him to Egypt but was shocked by the general's arrogance. He wrote the following letter to his wife while crossing the Mediterranean:

> On board the *Patriote*, 9 June 1798
>
> My dear friend,
>
> [...] There is here, my dear friend, the strongest discipline and, near the general, everybody observes the strictest etiquette: we try to replicate the old customs of the court and this looks so ridiculous that it seems as if we are observing a great lord in the middle of a Spartan camp. I do not know if Bonaparte adopted this system to improve his aura or his reputation, but he is wrong because nothing distinguishes a man more than his love for his country and his love for Freedom ...[21]

Many Frenchmen had never been on a ship before. Edouard de Villiers du Terrage,[22] an engineer following the expedition, was not so pleased with life on board:

> As soon as I arrived, I realised how boring a sailor's life was. We were served at the table. I sleep in a hammock suspended five feet high; the string on the side of my head broke and I fell, fortunately without being hurt.[23]

---

18. Louis-Joseph Bricard, *Journal du canonnier Bricard, 1792–1802, publié pour la première fois par ses petits-fils Alfred et Jules Bricard, avec une introduction de Lorédan-Larche* (Paris, 1891), p. 297.
19. Bricard, *Journal du canonnier Bricard*, p. 301.
20. François Bernoyer was born on 24 December 1766 in Avignon. He served as a tailor for the French army in Italy and the Expedition to Egypt. He later served as a tailor for the King of Holland, Louis Bonaparte, in 1807. He survived the Napoleonic Wars and died after 1837.
21. Christian Tortel and P. Carlier, *Bonaparte de Toulon au Caire d'après 19 lettres de François Bernoyer* (Paris, 1996), pp. 32–3.
22. Edouard de Villiers du Terrage, born on 25 April 1780, was an engineer and became famous for writing the *Description de l'Egypte* with other scientists.
23. Edouard de Villiers, *Journal et souvenirs sur l'expédition d'Egypte: 1798–1801* (Paris, 1899), p. 19.

On 11 June the French force invaded Malta, then under the control of the Knights of Malta, to secure a rear-base and protect the French fleet from British ships. Despite being chased by the Royal Navy, General Bonaparte and his men came in sight of Alexandria on 30 June. In a letter to his brother, a French translator named Pierre Jaubert[24] explained how the Royal Navy failed to intercept the French fleet:

> Aboukir, 20 *messidor* year VI [8 July 1798]
>
> My dear brother,
> We are, my dear Jaubert, in Egypt. [...] The English fleet has been unlucky. It missed us near Sardinia and then missed the convoy of Civita-Vecchia, made of 57 ships and carrying 7,000 men from Italy. It arrived in Malta five days after we had left and went to Alexandria two days before us. It must be assumed that it went to Alexandretta, thinking that we would land there to invade India ...[25]

The invasion of Egypt began on 1 July 1798. François Bernoyer reproduced a proclamation, written by Bonaparte, justifying the expedition and explaining its goals to the army:

> From Alexandria, 19 *Messidor* year VI [7 July 1798]
>
> My dear friend,
> [...] A proclamation that Bonaparte had printed while on board the *Orient* was given to us. I reproduce it here.
> Soldiers!
> You are about to take part in a conquest of the greatest importance to civilisation and world trade. You will deal the most certain and terrible blow to England, while waiting to deliver the fatal blow. We will have a few tiring marches, we will fight battles, we will succeed in all our operations, destiny is on our side.
> The Beys and the Mameluks, who favour exclusively English trade, who have covered our traders with misfortune and tyrannised the inhabitants of the Nile, will cease to exist in a few days. The people with whom we will fight are Muslims. The first article of their faith is this: 'There is no other god than God, and Mahomet is his Prophet.' Do not contradict them. Behave with them as you have behaved with the Jews and the

---

24. Pierre Amédée Jaubert was born in Aix-en-Provence on 3 June 1779. Fluent in Arabic and Turkish, he took part in the campaign in Egypt as a member of the Commission for Art and Science. He later served Napoleon in different diplomatic missions and died in Paris on 28 January 1847.
25. Loredan Larche, *Correspondance intime de l'armée d'Egypte interceptée par la croisière anglaise* (Paris, 1866), p. 10.

Italians. Treat their Muftis and their Imams well, as you have done with Rabbis and bishops. [...] You will find here customs that are different from Europe: we need to get accustomed to them.[26]

The Egyptians had never seen such a large army and the country had last been conquered by the Ottomans in 1517. However, for most of the French soldiers, landing on African soil was a necessity rather than a glorious moment. Captain Jean-Baptiste Vertray,[27] of the 9th half-brigade, explained in his diary why he was happy to leave the ship:

As for myself, I was very willing to disembark as I was suffering from sea-sickness. Combat on the ground is nothing in comparison to the tortures that sailing imposes on those who are not accustomed to difficult weather, especially on such frail ships as those we were on. I was happy to see the coast and was wishing for the moment I could get my appetite back.[28]

The news of the French arrival forced many civilians to flee to the country-side. Horatio Nelson had tried to warn the Mamluk warriors about the French landing and had even told them where to expect an attack but his advice was ignored. The Mamluks were confident in their strength and believed that their cavalry would crush the French soldiers.[29] On 21 July 1798 the French and the Ottomans fought each other at the battle of the Pyramids. Six days after this encounter Captain Guillot, of the 25th half-brigade, wrote:

From the headquarters at Cairo, 9 *thermidor* [27 July 1798]

I hurry, my very dear mother, to let you know about the arrival of the French army, to which I am honoured to belong, in Alexandria, Egypt. [...] Finally, we arrived near Cairo on the fourth of this month. The whole enemy army was armed and waiting for us but, with our usual impetuosity, we attacked them. After three-quarters of an hour the enemy had three thousand dead on the battlefield; the rest, unable to flee, jumped into the Nile, a river as strong as the Rhone, and, as a result, they either drowned or were shot while in the water. After such a victory, we entered Cairo and were the masters of the whole of Egypt ...[30]

26. Tortel, *Bonaparte de Toulon au Caire*, pp. 74–6.
27. Jean-Baptiste Vertray was born in Lallaing on 3 February 1774. He served as a captain in the 22nd company of the 9th half-brigade and later in the Imperial Army. He was later made an officer of the Legion of Honour and died in Autun on 17 November 1853.
28. Jean-Baptiste Vertray, *L'armée française en Egypte, 1798–1801: journal d'un officier de l'armée d'Egypte* (Paris, 1883), pp. 29–30.
29. Robert Tignor, *Egypt: a short history* (Princeton, 2010), p. 197.
30. Larche, *Correspondance intime de l'armée d'Egypte*, p. 32.

This crushing demonstration of military superiority allowed the French to occupy Cairo. The two defeated Ottoman commanders, Ibrahim Bey and Murad Bey, were forced to retreat to Syria and Upper Egypt to organise the resistance. In Cairo Bonaparte found a luxurious palace for himself but left his soldiers in far less pleasant conditions. Even a high-ranking man like General Dominique Dupuy[31] was horrified. He wrote to a friend on 11 *thermidor* year VI [29 July 1798] that 'this city [Cairo] is atrocious. The streets are plagued with piles of rubbish; the people are horrible and stupid.'[32]

The French did not keep the upper hand for long as a British intervention soon changed the course of the campaign. As will be explained in the next chapter, Nelson destroyed the French fleet at the battle of the Nile on 1–2 August 1798. The annihilation of the French navy was a strategic disaster, leaving the army stranded and isolated in Egypt. In addition, supplies and communications were also intercepted by the Royal Navy, as explained in this letter, written by a French soldier named Jacques Pistres, and ironically captured by a British ship:

> Cairo 29 *thermidor* year VI [16 August 1798]
>
> I eagerly avail myself, my dear friend, of the opportunity afforded me by one of our officers, who has thrown up his commission and got leave to retire, to write you this letter, in the hope that it will be more fortunate than the one which I sent you from Alexandria, the frigate by which it was sent having been taken by the English ...[33]

Bonaparte knew that this difficult situation was threatening his army's morale. Proclamations were printed and officers acted as propagandists. A good opportunity to cheer up the French soldiers came when news surfaced of the Irish rebellion of 1798. In May 1798 the United Irishmen, a group influenced by the French Revolution, rose up against British rule. In August of the same year a thousand French soldiers landed at Kilcummin and joined the rebels. They were defeated a few weeks later but the chaos was exploited in Egypt. Louis-Joseph Bricard explained:

> On 25 *fructidor* [year VI, 11 September 1798] the general-in-chief let us know that he had heard very favourable news from Europe. [...] There was a revolution in Ireland and the army of patriots had eighty thousand men. A formidable convoy of muskets sent by the French had arrived. This insurrection was inevitably going to bring peace with England.[34]

---

31. Larche, *Correspondance intime de l'armée d'Egypte*, p. 111.
32. Larche, *Correspondance intime de l'armée d'Egypte*, p. 62.
33. Larche, *Correspondance intime de l'armée d'Egypte*, p. 116.
34. Bricard, *Journal du canonnier Bricard*, p. 331.

However, peace was nowhere near. Despite Bonaparte's orders to treat the Egyptians correctly, French soldiers did not understand local customs and managed to upset the populace. Moreover, heavy taxes were imposed to support the French presence. These elements together led to a revolt in Cairo in October 1798. Religious leaders called for jihad against French soldiers and used Islam as a rallying banner. This insurrection was easily crushed but the violence upset the previously Francophile elements of Egyptian society. The mood also changed on the French side. Soldiers and scholars, previously indifferent or favourable to the Egyptian population, began to voice their hostility and saw civilians as agents of the British. François Bernoyer betrayed his anger in the following letter to his wife:

> From the island of Roudah, 30 *Nivôse*, year 7 [9 January 1799]
>
> My dear friend,
> [...] The Ottoman Court knows perfectly well the fanaticism of the Egyptians, reputed to be one of the most extreme of the whole Orient; they used this stupid credulity to serve the English cause: all means were good to fulfil their goals, even the most disgusting. They are not afraid to renounce justice and humanity to fulfil their guilty ambitions and insatiable avidity. They abandoned thousands of subjects to pain and misery. Their plan of attack demonstrates their hypocrisy.[35]

To make Egypt a viable French colony, Bonaparte launched an operation to capture Syria. According to François Bernoyer's letters, most French generals disagreed with Bonaparte's plans. Enemy forces based in Syria were too formidable for the small French army. French generals tried to dissuade Bonaparte but nothing worked:

> From Cairo, 30 *Pluviôse*, year 7 [30 March 1799]
>
> My dear friend,
> [...] On 19 January a letter from General Marmont came to Alexandria and told Bonaparte that the English fleet, reinforced by two ships, one Turk and the other Russian, had started bombing the city. Despite this attack, the expedition to Syria designed by Bonaparte was maintained. However, he assembled his generals to know what they thought of this expedition: three-quarters disapproved but only General Lagrande was brave enough to speak out loud in these words: 'I do not pretend to understand the views, the projects, or which political reasons encourage our general-in-chief to embark on such an expedition to Syria. However, may I be permitted, my General, to express my fears based on my little

---

35. Tortel, *Bonaparte de Toulon au Caire*, p. 138.

experience, which forces me to speak out. You want to attack the Pasha of Acre, afraid that he might do the same here. To do so, you will need to reduce the troops in all our garrisons here to form an army of at least fifteen thousand men. You will only be able to leave a handful of brave soldiers here. To guard this immense city [Cairo], you will expose them to the furore and the fanaticism of a considerable population. Let us suppose that you only want to capture Acre; it is 180 leagues distant, half of which is in the desert with impracticable paths. I know that our enemy is not trained in the art of war; if he was, he would only have to wait for us in the desert. Then, our defeat would be certain, even if our army was twice as big! Moreover, we would have to besiege all the forts on our way. [. . .] You must know that the English and the Russians are allied to the Turks: they would supply all sorts of things to defend Syria.'

[. . .] All the generals rallied behind General Lagrange but Bonaparte was firmly sticking to his first plan. His usual tactic was not to wait for the enemy but to go forward.

[. . .] Despite the great faith I have in the military talents of General Bonaparte, I doubt that this expedition will be a success because I notice that generals do not get along together. May this expedition not be fatal to us. Farewell![36]

The expedition went ahead and by 18 March 1799 the French army was close to Acre. The siege of the city would soon become a major thorn in Bonaparte's side. Sergeant Jean François was serving in the army marching towards Syria and took part in the attempt to capture Acre. His diary includes lengthy sections about the siege, with several mentions of the role played by the British:

On 19 [March 1799], we arrived with the whole army to besiege Saint-Jean-of-Acre. We continued to build positions until the 26th. Several assaults were launched until 1 April, but without decisive result.

We lacked supplies and had only bad water. To make our critical situation worse, our stock of ammunition was getting low. The generals invited the soldiers to collect cannonballs fired by English ships or by the besieged garrison to renew our stock of ammunition. They promised to pay for these cannonballs, depending on the size, twelve, nine, eight, six or four *sous*. In a single day, we brought thousands of them into our depot. I was collecting them with my friends, rather to show off than for the money. [. . .] I was keen to look for perilous situations, having at the time more than eighty-three *louis* [gold coins] and my friends had as

---

36. Tortel, *Bonaparte de Toulon au Caire*, pp. 152–3.

much. It was, for most of us, a distraction and a pleasure to go on the shore to taunt the English; as soon as we noticed that they were ready to fire, we lay on the ground and, as soon as the salvo had passed, we ran to pick up the cannonballs, despite the fire. Quite a lot of soldiers were killed in this manner, but we needed something to fight with.

François' account was probably exaggerated but not entirely untrue. French soldiers, lacking supplies, were indeed encouraged to collect cannonballs. Bonaparte soon realised the complexity of the task ahead. Acre's garrison commander, Jezzar Pasha, refused to surrender the city, and was assisted by a Royal Navy flotilla led by Commodore Sidney Smith. Combined Ottoman-British efforts were able to contain the French assaults. Sergeant François took part in several attacks and counter-attacks. Undoubtedly a brave man, François was also a natural-born braggart who could not resist embellishing his adventures in his diary:

[...] On 3 [May 1799], we launched an assault. We took a tower and killed many enemies; my company lost seventeen men, including two sergeants and a corporal.

[...] On 6, at five in the morning, after having been on guard duty for the night, we saw the enemy. He was attacking several points of the line. We took our weapons and, without using covered paths, we rushed into the trenches, [where] we found ourselves mixing with these enraged Turks. I killed a few and was noticed by General Lagrange. After three-quarters of an hour of hand-to-hand combat with the bayonet, the Turks retreated and we held the trenches, from where we continued to shoot at the enemy. That day, I was convinced that I had cheated Death; it had missed me in this terrible combat and I was sure to be invulnerable. I climbed on the top of the trench and, helped by two friends who loaded my muskets, I shot again and again. I was completely exposed to enemy fire from the rampart. I was hit by eight bullets, but only two bruised my right thigh. I remained there for an hour and fifteen minutes, despite the orders of my chiefs and my friends, and used seventeen packs of cartridges.

At 2 in the afternoon, we came back to the camp. As soon as I arrived, General Marpande asked for me. I went to meet him; he congratulated me and told General Reynier, who wrote a very flattering letter. I was promoted to the rank of sergeant Major of the 3rd company of the 3rd battalion of the 9th and, the next day, was mentioned in dispatches of the army.[37]

37. François, *Le journal d'un officier français*, pp. 30–3.

The siege of Acre was a costly episode for both sides. In early May the French managed to breach the walls and enter the city, only to discover a second set of fortifications. The soldiers who went through the breach were trapped between the outer and inner walls.[38] François reported a tragic story involving Commodore Smith:

8 May 1799

We learned during the night that two hundred courageous soldiers led by General Rambeaud[39] had entered the city. Having realised that they were cut off, they decided to fight to the last man, knowing the barbaric Turkish custom of killing prisoners. They took a mosque and fought like lions against the tigers led by the butcher Djezzar [Jezzar Pasha, the Ottoman commander]. Our brave General Rambaud and several of his valiant men had already died and the mosque was about to be assaulted when Commodore Smith arrived with a detachment of English to save this handful of brave men. He convinced them of how pointless it was [to die] and they agreed to surrender.[40]

This story was also reported by François Bernoyer, who insisted on the fact that Sidney Smith, 'this friendly officer, saved the life of two hundred men'.[41] By 10 May it had become clear that the city would not fall. French soldiers were hit hard by hunger and cold, and the plague ravaged their camp. More than 2,000 Frenchmen died during the siege of Acre. On 21 May the siege was raised. Sergeant Bricard, who was in Egypt with the rest of the army, heard frightening rumours about the siege's aftermath:

A few days later, we received more news. The army had stopped the siege of Acre to return to Egypt. This time, details of the dangers and the pain endured by our troops were frightening. We learned that the general-in-chief, after having sacrificed quantities of our brave men, saw how disgusted our soldiers were and abandoned the project of taking the fortified city. It required a lengthy siege and a bombardment that we were unable to organise, having no artillery or ammunition and being forced to collect cannonballs fired by the English.

The army left on 3 *prairial* in the morning, leaving behind numbers of unfortunate wounded Frenchmen, as well as plague victims. These circumstances offered the most atrocious sight. Plague continued its

---

38. Margaret Chrisawn, *The Emperor's friend: Marshal Jean Lannes* (Westport, 2001), p. 55.
39. General François Rambeaud, born on 20 May 1745, was indeed killed inside a mosque during a last stand on 8 May 1799.
40. François, *Le journal d'un officier français*, p. 39.
41. Tortel, *Bonaparte de Toulon au Caire*, p. 172.

carnage on the road. Those who were attacked by it were left on the sand, waiting for a cruel death brought by the Arabs.[42]

Plague was a great source of misery and terror. Even French doctors were scared of it and sometimes refused to examine its victims. Edouard de Villiers du Terrage reported the following incident in his diary:

> Bonaparte heard that the chief pharmacist in Alexandria, Royer, refused to treat plague victims; he immediately ordered the following: 'Royer will be dressed as a woman and paraded on a donkey in the city while carrying a sign: he is unworthy of being French, he is afraid to die. He will be imprisoned after and then sent to France.'[43]

The French position in Egypt was compromised. Bonaparte, realising that there was no hope for the campaign, and eager to follow his own agenda in France, left the country on 22 August 1799. His departure was a terrible shock for the men left behind. Sergeant Bricard was clearly upset when he wrote the following entry in his diary:

> On 6 [*fructidor*], at the beginning of the day, we were surprised to learn that General-in-Chief Bonaparte, followed by his headquarters, including Generals Berthier, Lannes, Andréossy, Murat and Marmont, had arrived between Alexandria and the fort of Aboukir at night. Reaching the shore, where ships were waiting for them, the general-in-chief ordered his headquarters and his men to embark on the frigates. These orders were immediately followed and, when they left, they were pleased to hear from Bonaparte that they were travelling back to France. All the horses were brought to Alexandria.
>
> In the morning we were hurt to see our brigs and frigates leave; everybody was petrified. A departure organised like an escape in such critical circumstances, the Mediterranean controlled by the enemy, Egypt threatened from all sides and, to make things even worse, our salary left unpaid. Soldiers grumbled, and everybody was fearing the worst for this army.[44]

Bonaparte's conduct angered more than one soldier. Years after the expedition, navy officer Joseph de Bonnefoux[45] wrote:

---

42. Bricard, *Journal du canonnier Bricard*, p. 365.

43. Villiers, *Journal et souvenirs sur l'expédition d'Egypte*, p. 93.

44. Bricard, *Journal du canonnier Bricard*, p. 376.

45. Joseph de Bonnefoux was born to a noble family in Béziers on 22 April 1782. He joined the French navy and became an officer in 1799. He served on board the famous *Belle Poule* but was captured by the British in 1806. While in England, he tried to escape four times and finally came home in 1811. Bonnefoux resumed his career after the Napoleonic Wars and wrote various books. He died in Paris on 14 December 1855.

The morale of our crews and our passengers was very much affected; it was said that Bonaparte did not care much for the Army of Egypt and was only there to demonstrate something and, indeed, it was legitimate to think so.[46]

Charles Lasalle[47] was also visibly shaken by Bonaparte's departure but tried to put things in perspective in a letter to Division General Dugua:

Egypt, 24 *fructidor* year VII [10 September 1799]

The departure of General Bonaparte was the last straw and made my stay in Egypt even more difficult. [...] They talk in various ways about the departure of our general. Some (and I think they are silly) only see treason; others, and they are in the majority, see it as a ray of happiness: he will fetch reinforcements, or peace will come and we will go back to our dear fatherland ...[48]

Other soldiers were able to get out of Egypt in time. Lieutenant François-Paul Berthier,[49] who served in the artillery, was sent home a few weeks before Napoleon left Africa. As soon as he arrived in France, he described his Egyptian campaign to his sister in the following letter:

Aix 23 *Vendémiaire* year 8 [15 October 1799]

My dear sister,

I am back in France after a difficult journey. [...] We arrived at the main fortress of Egypt on 4 *messidor*; there was not much resistance. We took a city named Rosette and Alexandria and its defending forts.

From there, we travelled about 45 miles in Egypt and found the Mamelouk army waiting for us on the side of the Nile. We were stopped and fought for nearly twelve hours. We lost a few men but won the battle and we chased them up to Cairo, their main fortress. From there, we arrived at their camp on the ninth. We did not spare them and attacked them as soon as we arrived. It was a very hot battle. However,

---

46. Emile Jobbé-Duval, *Mémoires du Baron de Bonnefoux* (Paris, 1900), p. 79.
47. Antoine Charles Louis de Lasalle was born in Metz on 10 May 1775. He fought with the Army of Italy and in Egypt. He later rose to the rank of general but was killed at the battle of Wagram on 6 July 1809.
48. Charles Lasalle, 'Lettre du chef de brigade Lasalle au Général Dugua', in: *Carnet de la Sabretache, revue militaire rétrospective* (1895).
49. François-Paul Berthier, born in Barraux on 26 November 1772, joined the army in 1789 and served in the artillery. He fought during the siege of Toulon and in Italy and Egypt, where he was promoted to the rank of lieutenant. He was later awarded the Legion of Honour but was badly wounded in Spain in 1808 and sent to a non-combat unit. Berthier died on 13 January 1856.

we won after two hours and took their cannon and fortresses, around 150 cannon. The enemy's defeat was almost like drowning because those who did not throw themselves in the water were killed during the fight.

From there, we had a few skirmishes in the desert against these enemies called Arabs.

The army left to besiege Acre during the month of *Pluviose*; we stayed there for two months to take this city but we failed to take it. The army turned around and went back to Cairo in good shape.

After a month of rest, we had to go back for an expedition named the battle of Aboukir where the Great Turk sent around 24 thousand men which we beat in 24 hours without taking any prisoner except for those who were in the fort, taken three days after.

Three or four days after this battle, General *Bonnaparte* [sic] ordered us to embark for France, but with only some of his guides because our departure was rushed. We only heard of our travel when we set foot in the boat; we left behind everything we had, clothes as well as money, which were useful in that moment.

Despite this, we are now in France in good health, after much travelling and tiredness. I am very well and I hope to see you soon to kiss you and to tell you everything I can. I salute you and kiss you with all my heart.[50]

With Bonaparte gone, General Jean-Baptiste Kléber was appointed commander of the French forces in Egypt. Kléber was angry, as he had not been told that Bonaparte intended to leave or that he would be left in charge. Kléber had no faith in victory and immediately planned a general retreat out of Egypt. He agreed with Sidney Smith the convention of El-Arish – concerning the evacuation of the French army – on 24 January 1800. However, it soon became clear that the British had no intention of ratifying the convention. Attacked and outnumbered by the Ottoman army of Yussuf Pasha, Kléber led the French army at the battle of Heliopolis on 20 March 1800. That day, 11,000 French soldiers crushed 40,000 Ottomans. This brilliant victory allowed the French to retake Cairo and put an end to the revolt. However, General Kléber was murdered by a Muslim opponent on 14 June 1800. Subsequently General Jacques-François Menou was appointed commander of the French expeditionary force. Far less popular than his predecessor, Menou was left in an impossible position. Outnumbered and without supplies, he faced a powerful British-Ottoman offensive. The crucial blow came when a

---

50. Berthier, 'Lettre d'un lieutenant de l'artillerie des guides', in: *Carnet de la Sabretache: revue militaire rétrospective* (1896), pp. 446–8.

British army, led by Lieutenant General Ralph Abercromby, landed at Aboukir on 8 March 1801. The French army moved towards Alexandria and arrived in the city on 20 March. The next day the French and the British fought the battle of Alexandria (also known as the battle of Canope). Sergeant Bricard took part in the fighting and witnessed the disaster:

> On 30 *ventôse*, the French army moved. Half-brigades, which had already suffered in previous battles, were ordered to attack the enemy in his camp. Resistance was strong; the enemy camp was full of cannon, far superior to our artillery. Everything suggested that this would be a difficult day. But who could have predicted that they [the French commanders] would do so little for our battalions' courage. They were fired at but did not shoot back!
>
> [...] During this deadly fight, the infantry, instead of being used to force the enemy position, stayed in formation under English fire. We were riddled with cannonballs and grapeshot for three hours without being able to shoot back.
>
> After having suffered considerable losses, the French army was ordered to retreat to its initial position. The enemy, who also suffered serious losses, retreated to his camp.
>
> [...] It was said that General Lanusse,[51] while severely wounded and receiving encouragement from General Menou, answered: 'Go! I am fucked and your colony too!'
>
> This terrible battle brought consternation to the French ranks. Such a considerable loss of soldiers, officers and generals made it impossible for the army to fight another battle. The generals were disunited and this was a growing source of concern.[52]

The battle of Alexandria was indeed a disaster for the French. Menou was overwhelmed, attacks were not coordinated, and so many generals had died that the French soldiers were left without leaders. The British won a decisive victory but paid a high price: Lieutenant General Abercromby was badly injured and died on 28 March 1801. After this costly defeat, the French were forced to retreat to Alexandria, which was promptly besieged by the British. French officers, such as Captain Vertray, were divided and openly voiced their opposition to General Menou:

> The army had no faith in General Menou; after the defeat of Canope, protests were voiced. A great number of officers said openly in

---

51. François Lanusse, born on 3 November 1772, fought during the Revolutionary Wars. He was promoted to the rank of general in 1796 and died during the battle of Alexandria.
52. Bricard, *Journal du canonnier Bricard*, pp. 455–6.

Alexandria that General Reynier should have been appointed commander and it was still perhaps time to do so.[53]

A month later the French captured Bulaq. The aftermath of the siege led to a
number of bloody episodes. The animosity between the French and British
soldiers was more than obvious. French soldier François testified:

> 14 April 1800: During the capture of Bulaq, we recognised English
> officers among the rebels and French deserters among the dead. Captured
> Europeans were shot without trial. Among the few prisoners that I per-
> sonally took, I recognised an Englishman by his accent. To be certain,
> I spoke to him in Arabic but he was unable to answer. Then I asked: 'Are
> you English?' He answered half in German, half in English. Convinced
> that he was really an Englishman, I blew his head off. That way, I demon-
> strated my hatred for this nation, the cause of all our problems.[54]

The Egyptian expedition did not consist entirely of soldiers; 167 scientists
and scholars, including mathematicians, chemists, naturalists and others went
with it to study various aspects of the country. The crumbling discipline of
the French army after the British victory at Alexandria on 21 March 1801
triggered serious conflicts among the members of the *Commission des Sciences
et des Arts*. One of these scholars wrote the following entry in his diary:

> Rahmanié, 21 *germinal*, year IX [11 April 1801]
>
> When the convoy arrived from Rahmanié, we were told that we had lost
> Rosetta. At four in the evening, on the 19th, we had no doubt that the
> enemy was on the move and, at five, the place was evacuated. Three
> thousand Turks and a thousand English took it without resistance. They
> either ignored the tower of Aboumandour [on the left side of the Nile] or
> had no time to position their cannon on top of it. Had they done so, the
> whole convoy would have been lost. They only destroyed an armed
> barge. The retreat was so precipitate that we left everything in the city.
> Troops retired to Métoubis, barges and little avisos [dispatch boats]
> retreated to here in Rahmanié.
>
> Here, everything is in the open, no forward camp, no troops. This fort
> is cluttered and defenceless. We expect the enemy any time soon and
> there is no general to face him. The place is commanded by a brutal man,
> both rude and ignorant, named Lacroix,[55] promoted to chief of the

---

53. Vertray, *L'armée française en Egypte*, p. 172.
54. François, *Journal du capitaine François*, p. 375.
55. Mathieu Lacroix, born in La Rochefoucauld on 29 September 1761, fought in the armies of
    Louis XVI before the Revolution, later serving the Republic. He was promoted to the rank

fourth [half-brigade] by General Menou. He became furious when he saw us arriving from Cairo and threatened to send us back there with our hands and feet bound. He was unable to read the passport of General Belliard, presented by citizen Fourrier,[56] and said that he had been given a bunch of whores and scientists, for whom he had no use. We endured his insults patiently, but when he said that we could not leave for Alexandria, we asked citizen Cavalier, chief of the dromedaries. This person put as much kindness and efficiency into helping us as the other had poured insults and stupidity. He promised to take the Commission of Arts to Alexandria, escorted by the dromedaries, despite the orders of the Commander.

[...] During the night, as we were preparing to leave, many soldiers used the chaos of the situation to steal from our tents. Rozière[57] had brought his boxes of mineralogy outside his tent. [...] He found his boxes forced, the samples of Mount Sinai, Mount Bavam, Syène, Cosseir, etc., etc., taken to the beach. Soldiers were throwing them at each other while making jokes about scientists. 'These scientific rascals, they said, have trunks weighing as much as gold but there are only rocks inside.' 'If we could only use them as musket stones.' And at the same time, they hit them and broke them in little pieces. Others said: 'It is for these stones that these wretched scientists forced us to climb mountains, etc., etc.' In the middle of this, Rozière and his friends were unable to intervene. They would have risked being murdered by the soldiers. The officers were quiet and a few smiled. However, I must admit that only a few soldiers were involved in this violence. A few officers even came to bring order but the bravest were unable to silence the bad elements, or rather the bandits who had broken the boxes. It would not have been wise to punish them; these criminals were capable of anything.

A few soldiers, on the other hand, helped us collect the minerals. We managed to find a few but they had been stepped on, and were cracked, the crystals were broken, etc., etc. This is the kind of brigandage that is tolerated by Lacroix at the camp of Rahmanié. His rude words of yesterday among his soldiers probably caused this ...[58]

---

of brigadier general of the 4th half-brigade of light infantry during the campaign of Egypt. He later served in Austria, Poland and Spain and was made a baron in 1811. He died on 21 July 1822.

56. Joseph Fourrier, a surveyor.
57. François Michel de Rozière, a French mining engineer who later became a professor.
58. Anonymous, 'Fragments d'un journal d'un savant de la Commission d'Egypte', in: *Carnet de la Sabretache: revue militaire rétrospective* (1936), pp. 309–10.

The city of Cairo was taken in June. The siege of Alexandria lasted until September 1801, when it was decided to surrender the city to the British. Edouard de Villiers explained how:

> 10 *fructidor* [28 August 1801]. The war council decided to surrender the city, despite Menou, who claimed that he wanted 'to be buried below the ruins of the city'.[59]

The British agreed to use the Royal Navy to repatriate French soldiers to Europe. Under the treaty, the French scientific commission was also forced to hand over its Egyptian antiquities, including the Rosetta stone. General Menou wrote the following letter to General John Hely-Hutchinson, the British commander in Egypt:

> Army of Orient 19 *fructidor* year XI [6 September 1801]
>
> I have in my possession a stone, found in Rosetta, which carries three types of different writing. It is my property, but I really wanted to offer it to the Republic once back in France. Do you want it, General? You may have it because you are the strongest and I will not be displeased to say in Europe that my property has been taken from me by the English general. You were lied to when they told you that this stone was on board the *Oiseau*. It had been all along in a warehouse. I had it brought to my house, I will take it out and you can take it as you please.[60]

The French soldiers were sad to be defeated but also greatly relieved to leave Africa. The Egyptian expedition had been a difficult experience in a foreign and unknown country. Captain Vertray was one of the soldiers who survived the campaign and was repatriated by the enemy:

> This news was welcomed by the army. Nostalgia tormented those who were homesick but we had suffered so much and had despaired of seeing our homeland again that we were happy to leave Egypt. We made ready for departure and were ready to embark. [...] on 20 *thermidor* year IX, we arrived at Aboukir and on 21 [8 August 1801], we were embarked on English ships, which left in the evening. Our crossing was made in good conditions; the thought of our return to France made seasickness less painful. When we saw the coast of France, soldiers could not contain their happiness. Songs were sung on the deck, where games had been organised.[61]

59. Villiers, *Journal et souvenirs sur l'expédition d'Egypte*, p. 308.
60. François Rousseau, *Kléber et Menou en Egypte depuis le départ de Bonaparte* (Paris, 1900), p. 424.
61. Vertray, *L'armée française en Egypte*, pp. 182–3.

Sergeant Bricard was also evacuated by the British. Unsurprisingly, he hated the food served on board:

> We finally came close to Aboukir, where a prodigious quantity of English and Turkish ships were waiting for us. We embarked on the English ship the *Braakel* with our weapons. We were welcomed by the officers, who invited us to dine with them.
>
> [...] We received the same rations as the English; peas, bacon, salted beef or boiled; either one or the other; of everything, not much and badly cooked. These meals were so poorly made that I was unable to eat them. We also received a mediocre portion of bad biscuits and white wine.
>
> [...] On 12, an officer of the 4th half-brigade died on the bridge; he was the fourth Frenchman to die on board as a result of the poor meals and the lack of support.
>
> [...] On 18 [*vendémiaire* year X, or 10 October 1801], with indescribable joy, we entered the port of Toulon. To make things better, we were told that we were now at peace with England and with the Ottomans.[62]

The expedition to Egypt failed to threaten British India and was responsible for the loss of nearly 30,000 men. The Royal Navy played a decisive role early in the campaign. Nelson's audacious victory at Aboukir Bay cut off the French and left them at the mercy of the Ottomans. Ravaged by the climate and by plague, the French managed to hold on against all the odds. They fought for three years in Africa, but were finally forced to surrender when the British intervened on land. This clear defeat did nothing to damage Bonaparte's reputation, however. Supported by propaganda, the ambitious general managed to advertise his Egyptian victories in mainland France while blaming others for any reverses of fortune. Confident and popular, he was able to become First Consul and successfully negotiated peace with Britain in 1801–1802. What remained of the French army in Egypt was repatriated by the British, but they left behind a taste for social change. In the years following the expedition a wave of modernisation hit Egypt and led to the country's independence. In Europe, the Egyptian campaign also left a lasting legacy: orientalism and a taste for Egyptian aesthetics influenced both art and science.

---

62. Bricard, *Journal du canonnier Bricard*, pp. 474–80.

*Chapter 2*

# War at Sea

## The Battle of the Nile

As seen in the previous chapter, the French expeditionary corps left Toulon
for Egypt on 19 May 1798. The Royal Navy came close to intercepting the
French fleet but ultimately failed to prevent the landings by General
Bonaparte's men at the end of June. Once the city of Alexandria was captured,
the French Admiral François-Paul Brueys d'Aigalliers took his ships to
Aboukir Bay, some twenty miles from Alexandria. Horatio Nelson, leading
the British fleet, searched for the French fleet for more than a month. On
1 August 1798, the *Alexander* and the *Swiftsure*, scouting for Nelson, finally
sighted the enemy ships near Alexandria and followed their trail to Aboukir
Bay. By four in the afternoon, the *Alexander* and the *Swiftsure*, leading the
other British ships, had the French fleet firmly in their sights.[1] Lieutenant
Antoine Jequart, aboard the *Guerrier*,[2] described in a series of reports[3] written
days after the battle how the British approached the Bay of Aboukir:

> At two [in the afternoon], the English army[4] was spotted, the watchman
> above our mast counted twelve ships west north west, three miles from us
> and sailing east. [...] At three, two other ships were also spotted west.
> They were regrouping with the first [squadron of English ships], at a
> distance of about two-thirds of a mile. The number of ships spotted was
> therefore fifteen, including fourteen warships and a brig. They were led
> by a *germe* [Egyptian ship], a native ship, sailing the same way.[5]

Ensign Bachelon, on board the *Guerrier* with Lieutenant Jequart, also saw this
Egyptian ship:

1. Ian Germani, 'Combat and culture: imagining the Battle of the Nile', in: *The Northern
   Mariner/Le Marin du Nord*, 1 (2000), pp. 53–72.
2. The *Guerrier* was a 74-gun ship built in 1753. She was captured by the British during the
   battle of the Nile but burned soon after.
3. These reports were first examined in: Karen Nakache, 'Des marins français à Aboukir:
   témoignages', in: *Cahiers de la Méditerranée*, 57 (1998), pp. 207–33.
4. Lieutenant Jequart uses the term army but he means navy. This is a common mistake.
5. SHD AM: 1A2 210. Dossier des vaisseaux perdus à Aboukir. Report by Antoine Jequart,
   1798.

The brig *Railleur* was outside the harbour and chased the *jerme* [the Egyptian ship] in front of the English army [navy] by firing several shots to force her inside the harbour, which she seemed to do. However, the English brig also intervened and she [the Egyptian ship] fled and the *Railleur*, unable to catch up, returned to the harbour.[6]

Soon after this incident, the French Admiral Brueys gave his orders to the fleet. An anonymous officer aboard the *Aquilon*[7] recalled:

[...] Our general ordered the army to raise the flag and to stand ready for combat. This was done immediately.[8]

The officers of the *Conquérant*[9] confirmed those orders and remembered others in their report:

1. All hands aboard ship to battle stations and ready to fight
2. To rig the topgallant mast
3. To remain at anchor and fight, and finally to send a rope to the ship *Spartiate*, and receive one from the *Guerrier*, in front of us.[10]

In fact, Admiral Brueys was unsure about the best course of action. He initially intended to engage Nelson's fleet but was convinced by his officers that the French did not have enough men aboard the ships to man the guns. When the British admiral slowed his fleet at four in the afternoon, Brueys thought that Nelson was not willing to risk a battle in the evening and was waiting for dawn before engaging the enemy. The French admiral might have hoped to escape during the night. However, the British fleet began its battle approach soon after. Brueys, now aware of the immediate danger, prepared his ships for action. The fighting began late in the afternoon. The British formation approached and engaged the enemy vanguard, composed of the *Guerrier*, the *Conquérant*, the *Spartiate*[11] and the *Aquilon*, in order to cut the French line. The French rear-guard, hampered by an unfavourable wind, witnessed the beginning of the battle without being able to intervene.

---

6. SHD AM: 1A2 210. Dossier des vaisseaux perdus à Aboukir. Report by Bachelon, 1798.
7. The *Aquilon* was a 74-gun ship. She was launched in 1789 and captured by the British during the battle of the Nile. She was renamed HMS *Aboukir*.
8. SHD AM: 1A2 210. Dossier des vaisseaux perdus à Aboukir. Report by an officer of the *Aquilon*, 1798.
9. The *Conquérant* was a 74-gun ship launched in 1746. She was captured by the British during the battle of the Nile and demolished in 1802.
10. SHD AM: 1A2 210. Dossier des vaisseaux perdus à Aboukir. Report by the officers of the *Conquérant*, 1798.
11. The *Spartiate* was a 74-gun ship launched in 1798. She was captured during the battle of the Nile and later fought on the British side during the battle of Trafalgar.

Ensign Beaussier, on board the *Conquérant*, described the first minutes of the battle:

> At around half past five, the enemy ships were within the range of our guns and our general ordered us to open fire. The *Guerrier* began and then the *Conquerans* [*Conquérant*].[12]

The British managed to create and exploit a gap in the French formation. The speed of the attack was such that it took the French aback and delivered a severe blow. One officer on board the *Aquilon* described how the fire from three different ships killed most of the crew and the captain:

> Commander Thévenard[13] ordered the few men who remained on the top mast and those who were in the 18 battery to go to the lower deck to man the battery of 36. [...] At eight, a cannonball took both legs off *Citoyen* Thévenard and he died a few moments later.[14]

The situation was no better on the *Conquérant* whose 'captain was badly wounded, hit by a musket ball in the chest'.[15] By nine, the French vanguard was defeated and most of its ships captured. The *Guerrier* was almost entirely destroyed by British guns:

> We lost all our masts and they all fell on the port side, covering several of our guns on the second deck. Soon after, we lost all the remaining guns on the second deck. We were forced to abandon it and gathered everybody on the top deck. At half past nine, we lost more guns and had no hope of saving the ship, considering our critical position with three ships fighting us, one on the side and the two others in the front and behind. We were also fired at by muskets and fireworks and they fell on us and killed and wounded a great many of our men and disabled our guns.[16]

---

12. SHD AM: 1A2 210. Dossier des vaisseaux perdus à Aboukir. Report by Beaussier, 1798.
13. Antoine René Thévenard, born in 1766, served in the French Navy for the Republic and became a captain in 1793. He commanded the *Wattignies* in 1795 and led the naval division of Saint-Domingue the next year. He commanded the 74-gun *Aquilon* during the battle of the Nile and was killed during the action.
14. SHD AM: 1A2 210. Dossier des vaisseaux perdus à Aboukir. Report by an officer of the *Aquilon*, 1798.
15. SHD AM: 1A2 210. Dossier des vaisseaux perdus à Aboukir. Report by the officers of the *Conquérant*, 1798.
16. SHD AM: 1A2 210. Dossier des vaisseaux perdus à Aboukir. Report by men of the *Conquérant*, 1798.

Ensign Sornin[17] was also on board the *Guerrier*. He witnessed the capture of his ship and the destruction of the French admiral's ship, the *Orient*[18]:

> We fought, despite the position of strength of the enemy, until half past nine. For more than an hour, they shouted at us to surrender but our captain never answered. He hoped to keep them busy to allow our best ships, which were in the middle of the formation, to crush or sink several enemy ships, which would have made us the masters of the battlefield. However, the worst turn of fate for the Republican army happened when fire engulfed the ship *Orient* at nine in the evening. Ships behind us stopped firing and we had no hope left. All our guns were dismantled, on both decks, and our captain welcomed an English officer on board who took our ship.[19]

The French admiral's ship had indeed caught fire at around nine in the evening. The British saw an opportunity to destroy her and fired into the blaze. Ensign Berhelot was on board the *Orient* during her final moments:

> A moment after, I noticed, thanks to the reflection of light on the sea, that the ship was on fire, but, confident in the crew's ability to stop it, I encouraged the men who served the guns of 36 to stay as courageous as they had been.[20]

Moments later, Berthelot was forced to jump into the water to save his life. Admiral Brueys, wounded twice earlier in the battle, had already been killed by a cannonball when an explosion finally destroyed the *Orient* at around 10 in the evening. More than a thousand crew members died during this episode. Captain Jean Trullet[21] saw the explosion from the *Guerrier*:

> I saw the fire on board the *Orient*, and the flames were progressing fast. The enemy stopped firing after an explosion took this unfortunate ship at around 11 in the evening.[22]

---

17. Ensign Sornin was captured by the British during the battle and taken aboard the *Culloden*.
18. The *Orient* was a 118-gun ship launched in 1791. She was the flagship of the French fleet during the battle of the Nile. Hit by British fire during the battle, she exploded in the evening.
19. SHD AM: 1A2 210. Dossier des vaisseaux perdus à Aboukir. Report by Sornin, 1798.
20. SHD AM: 1A2 210. Dossier des vaisseaux perdus à Aboukir. Report by Berhelot, 1798.
21. Jean Trullet, born on 15 April 1755, joined the French Navy in 1770. He rose to the rank of captain in 1777. He commanded the *Guerrier* during the battle of the Nile and was captured by the British. He served again from 1803 but retired in 1810 and died in 1819.
22. SHD AM: 1A2 210. Dossier des vaisseaux perdus à Aboukir. Report by Jean Trullet, 1798.

Ensign Mathieu also witnessed the destruction of the flagship from the *Mercure*[23]:

> At around 11 in the evening, the *Orient* blew up and the explosion was so frightening that terror spread among the crew.[24]

The middle of the French line was also in contact with the British. Lieutenant François Talon, on board the *Franklin*,[25] was under heavy fire:

> At around eleven, we had three ships on us and, the captain having been wounded, *Citoyen* Martinet took charge, being the only officer not wounded. All the ships ahead of us had stopped firing and we were heavily damaged and many of our people were out of action. The great mast had fallen and the spanker was down too. It was impossible to cut the ropes because the admiral's ship was burning on our rear and we would have endured the same fate. Considering our unfortunate position, and to avoid the same fate befalling our crew, *Citoyen* Martinet came on the top deck, where I was, and ordered fire to stop.[26]

In fact, the destruction of the *Orient* sealed the fate of the French fleet. The battle continued during the night and early the next day, but in vain. At dawn, French officer Mille realised the extent of the defeat:

> We saw that all ships from the *Franklin* to the *Guerrier* had been captured by the enemy and all the others had stopped or were drifting far from the line. The ships *Tonnant*[27] and *Thimoléon*[28] were fighting against three enemy ships. Three others came and fought the *Heureux*[29] and the *Mercure*.[30]

Julien François, a French civilian who had joined the expedition to Egypt, saw the sea battle from the city of Alexandria. He was clearly bitter when he wrote the following letter to his wife:

---

23. The *Mercure* was launched in 1783 but was captured by the British during the battle of the Nile.
24. SHD AM: 1A2 210. Dossier des vaisseaux perdus à Aboukir. Report by Mathieu, 1798.
25. The *Franklin* was launched in 1797 and fought at the battle of the Nile. She was captured by the British and served under her new name, *Canopus*, until 1887.
26. SHD AM: 1A2 210. Dossier des vaisseaux perdus à Aboukir. Report by François Talon, 1798.
27. The *Tonnant* was an 80-gun ship. She was launched in 1789 but captured by the British during the battle of the Nile. She served during the battle of Trafalgar and was broken up in 1821.
28. In fact the *Timoléon*, commanded by Captain Tullet.
29. The *Heureux* was a 74-gun ship.
30. SHD AM: 1A2 210. Dossier des vaisseaux perdus à Aboukir. Report by Mille, 1798.

Alexandria, 12 *thermidor* year VI [30 July 1798][31]

[...] I have to stop here my dear Julie. The English, made to look more competent by the stupidity of our own navy, cannot do anything against us. The ports of Alexandria, defended by several cannon and by nature itself, would only offer death and shame to this enemy who, I repeat, is only formidable when facing the ignorance of our navy. Imagine that our squadron was positioned to face the English three or four to one: such stupidity was unmissable to an enemy who has made the sea his element.[32]

Louis-Joseph Bricard[33] heard rumours about the battle. He relayed the mood in his diary:

At around noon, a rumour circulated saying that the English squadron had been totally destroyed. The ships that we had seen explode and those currently burning were theirs. This news pleased us greatly. We longed for peace and everybody was congratulating our Navy. However, at six in the evening, this joy turned into sadness. Everywhere we heard that 'our fleet does not exist any more: all is lost, burned or sunk by the English!' This terrible blow left everybody in a state of disarray; we looked at each other and everybody kept quiet. This loss was so considerable that we had trouble believing it.[34]

Edouard de Villiers du Terrage, encountered in the previous chapter, watched the battle from the shore. He was also convinced that the French had won, before hearing further news:

2 August. [...] In the evening, we are told that the French have won; that two ships have exploded; that two others have sunk; the rest will be taken, except one who managed to flee, but she is pursued. Our joy is great. This news is brought by a small boat sailing the Nile, but it is not official. We wait for Brueys' dispatch to Bonaparte.
3 August. What a change! I ask if yesterday's news is confirmed. I was answered: 'We have no fleet any more.' My first thought was that the wind had blown away the French and the English, but someone contradicted me: 'Everything that was said about the English yesterday is

---

31. This date is interesting since the battle of the Nile happened on 1–2 August 1798. In fact, French soldiers and civilians usually took days or even weeks to finish a letter and often added several paragraphs about recent events.
32. Private collection.
33. See Chapter 1 for a biography.
34. Bricard, *Journal du canonnier Bricard*, pp. 321–2.

applicable to us.' The ship that blew up on 14 in the evening is the *Orient*. The *Artémis* blew on 15 in the morning.[35]

The battle of Aboukir left all the French soldiers and civilians in a state of shock but did not trigger a general feeling of hostility against the British. For example, François Bernoyer heard that the British had taken good care of the wounded from both sides:

From Cairo

My dear friend,

[...] The vast floating blaze, all that remained of the *Orient*, left both squadrons in a sort of stupor. For more than fifteen minutes, they were immobile, halted by consternation, but suddenly combat resumed. Its outcome was the total loss of our squadron. After their victory, the English took the whole day to rescue the wounded without distinction: ours were transported with great care to the hospitals in Alexandria.[36]

The battle of the Nile was a disaster for the French. The destruction of the French fleet left the Mediterranean Sea to the British and played a significant role in Napoleon's failure in Egypt. The Republican army, isolated, fought on for another two years. The French expeditionary corps finally surrendered to the British on 31 August 1801 and the survivors were brought back to France by British ships.[37]

## From Egypt to Trafalgar

The resounding defeat at Aboukir left French navy officers deeply divided. Louis Lejoille,[38] in charge of the 74-gun *Généreux* on 1 August 1798, criticised Pierre-Charles Villeneuve and his handling of the rear division at Aboukir Bay. Lejoille accused the future commander of the French fleet at Trafalgar of having fled the action too early. Serving under Villeneuve's command, Lejoille continued to complain in his personal correspondence during the following months:

---

35. de Villiers, *Journal et souvenirs sur l'expédition d'Egypte*, pp. 58–9.
36. Tortel, *Bonaparte de Toulon au Caire*, p. 99.
37. Andrew Lambert, 'The glory of England: Nelson, Trafalgar and the meaning of victory', in: *The Great Circle*, 28 (2006), pp. 3–12.
38. Louis Lejoille, born in Saint-Valery-sur-Somme on 11 November 1759, came from a family of sailors and served on a ship from the age of seven. He became a lieutenant in the French navy in 1793 and distinguished himself in the following years. He took part in the battle of the Nile, during which he fought against the *Bellerophon*. Lejoille was killed on board the *Généreux* during an exchange of fire with a fort in Brindisi (Italy) on 9 April 1799.

Corfon, 22 *fructidor*, year VI [8 September 1798]

My dear brother
You will see from my two other letters, based on my diary and the letter
written after leaving Bequiers, how unfit General Villeneuve was to lead
men otherwise driven by honour and their love for their country. This is
even worse! General Villeneuve, to our great surprise, took the road used
by merchants who fear corsairs to go to Malta and has, despite the wind,
continually followed the coastline of Barbarie, despite the lack of supplies and fresh water on board. He was aware that an English squadron of
six frigates was between Malta and Candie. He preferred to go to Malta
and risk disarming our guns because of the lack of supplies rather than
risk a fight by taking another road, where we could have found something to capture, either a warship or a merchant. You should know that
our two ships and our two frigates were the best of the army …[39]

The battle of the Nile had dealt the French a severe blow but their navy
remained operational. Its ability to transport large numbers of troops was
tested just a few years later. Indeed, the War of the Second Coalition took a
turn for the worse for the Austrians, Neapolitans and Russians in 1801.
Forced to sign separate treaties with France, they left Great Britain isolated in
her struggle against the French Republic. The French and the British finally
agreed on a preliminary peace agreement in London on 30 September 1801,
followed by the Treaty of Amiens in March 1802. First Consul Bonaparte
took this opportunity to mount an expedition to the Caribbean colony of
Saint-Domingue to crush the independence movement led by former slave
Toussaint Louverture. Some eight thousand French soldiers left Brest on
board forty-six ships on 14 December 1801. More would follow later. During
the first months the French army recaptured several strategic points but
the expedition soon faced a deadly enemy: yellow fever. The disease killed
thousands of men, including the commander of the expedition, General
Charles Leclerc. At the same time the uneasy peace between France and
Britain turned sour. After months of tension, Britain finally declared war on
France in May 1803. This new conflict meant new dangers for the men
stationed in Saint-Domingue. In his personal diary Sergeant Major Philippe
Beaudoin[40] of the 31st half-brigade explained how he learned about the con-
flict when he witnessed a naval battle:

39. Louis Lejoille, 'Documents inédits sur l'expédition d'Egypte', in: *Carnet de la Sabretache:
revue militaire rétrospective* (1936), p. 305.
40. Philippe Beaudoin was born in Batilly-en-Gâtinais on 20 June 1775. He volunteered for the
3rd battalion of Loiret on 10 September 1792. He fought during the Saint-Domingue
expedition and fell in love with a local woman, who was later murdered when the French

9 messidor year XI [28 June 1803] near Môle-Saint-Nicolas [north-western coast of Haiti]

Battle at sea between the heavy frigate *La Poursuivante* (commanded by Viomest [Jean-Baptiste Willaumez]) and two English ships. We climbed to see them, thinking that it was a celebration, but we were really surprised to see an English ship (named *Hercule*) approaching the frigate and firing as soon as they approached the Cap-à-Fous.

Then we saw the ship's cannonballs hitting the shore; this made us suspect a war against England. The frigate, being pushed too close to the shore, changed direction and aimed to rake the ship [*Hercule*]. This last one, fearing the frigate, changed direction and ran away. The frigate destroyed her rudder but, having not enough men to board, wisely returned to Môle. She lost forty men killed and wounded, and the frigate was riddled with holes. [The crew] disembarked and told us that we were at war with England.[41]

Beaudoin left Haiti for France at the end of 1803. Unfortunately for him, the captain of his ship made a crucial mistake which led to the capture of the whole crew by the British navy:

In the morning [15 April 1804] we saw a convoy of eleven ships. The second-in-command told the captain that it was an English convoy and added that we ought to head in another direction. The captain refused, saying that these ships were Spanish. The second tried again and again to convince him but we carried on. At around ten, the captain said: 'I can see now that they are English and we should have turned.' The second-in-command replied: 'Do whatever you want. It is too late now. Even if we head in another direction, they will catch up with us in two hours.' This is exactly what happened.

As soon as we turned, a frigate followed us. An hour and a half later, she caught up with us, fired at us, checked our flag and replaced her Spanish flag with an English one. The second-in-command told the captain: 'You are putting me in jail and you will pay for that.' Then, she [the British frigate] fired a volley at us but fortunately did not injure anybody. We lowered our flag. Then they took all the officers and non-commissioned officers without much ceremony, hitting us with the flat of their sabres. They took us on board the corvette *L'Ecosse* and left us for

---

left. In 1804 Beaudoin was captured by the British while at sea and remained a prisoner of war until 1812. He died of illness on 25 February 1864.

41. Philippe Beaudoin, 'Carnet d'étapes du sergent-major Philippe Beaudoin', in: *Carnet de la Sabretache: revue militaire rétrospective* (1909), p.219.

twenty-four hours without water or food. Luckily, we were transferred to a merchant ship named *Gassie* ...[42]

Beaudoin's tale was a reminder that French navy captains were far less competent at sea than their British counterparts. Indeed, several experienced French navy officers had been executed or had fled during the Revolution. However, Napoleon, who had plans to conquer Britain, needed his ships to protect the invasion fleet. In October 1805 the French and Spanish fleets in the Mediterranean were ordered to escape the British blockade and sail to Brest to clear the Channel and protect the expeditionary corps. However, Admiral Villeneuve's French fleet was intercepted by Nelson on 20 October.

The battle began the next morning, close to Cape Trafalgar. Captain Jean Lucas[43] commanded the French ship of the line *Redoutable*, which engaged HMS *Victory*. Days after the battle he wrote the following report:

Report to his Excellency the minister of Marine and of the Colonies, by M. Lucas, ship captain, officer of the Legion of Honour, on the naval battle of Trafalgar between the combined fleet of France and Spain under the orders of Admirals Villeneuve and Gravina and the English fleet commanded by Admiral Nelson, and particularly on the combat between the *Victory* of one hundred and ten guns, commanded by Admiral Nelson, the *Téméraire* of the same power and another ship, a two-decker, against the *Redoutable*, of which S.M. [*Sa Majesté* or His Majesty in French] had given me the command.

Although the loss of the *Redoutable* is part of one of the worst defeats undergone by the combined fleets of France and Spain in the bloody battle of Trafalgar, the role of this particular ship, I believe, deserves a distinguished place in the annals of the French navy.

I owe it to the memory of the brave men who died in the terrible fight or went down in the remains of the *Redoutable* when she sank. I owe it also to the glory of the small number of those who survived that inexpressible slaughter to bring under the notice of your Excellency a picture of their exploits. [...] Nothing can match the ardour of such heroes when I announced to them that we were going to attack the English admiral. Even the intrepid Nelson could not have died against more noble enemies so worthy of his courage and of his grand reputation. I will not try to explain the movements of the two armies during the

42. Beaudoin, 'Carnet d'étapes du sergent-major Philippe Beaudoin', pp. 627–9.
43. Jean Jacques Etienne Lucas was born in Marennes on 28 April 1764. As a young officer he fought in the American War of Independence. He later fought during the Revolutionary wars and eventually gained fame for his role at Trafalgar. He was captured after the battle and died in Brest on 29 May 1819.

whole of the action. I was only able at intervals to discern the ships in my immediate neighbourhood. I will only mention the manoeuvres preceding the assault and those ending this miserable battle but I will include all the details of what took place on board the *Redoutable* against the ship *Victory* and the *Téméraire* of a hundred and ten guns, and another ship, a two-decker, of which I do not know the name or the power.

On 20 *vendémiaire* year XIV [12 October 1805] the combined fleet left the bay of Cadiz, carried by a southern wind, weak at first but then cold and strong. The fleet was composed of thirty-three ships, eighteen French and fifteen Spanish, with five frigates and two French brigs.[44]

Aspirant Julien Houssart[45] wrote a battle report for Admiral Villeneuve two days after Trafalgar. He described the day preceding the battle:

28 *vendémiaire*, year XIV [20 October]

[...] At seven in the evening, the *Hortense* signalled the discovery of a few ships who might belong to a squadron or fleet.

We could see ahead of the army [navy] rockets and coloured signal flares.

At quarter to nine, the brig *Argus* passed by the stern to bring a warning message to the admiral, from Admiral Gravina, that the ship *Achille* was aware, at the end of the day, of eighteen English ships in the wind and in front of the army [navy].

At nine, we saw the signal to make ready for battle on board a ship of the observation squadron. This signal was immediately relayed to the whole army [navy] by gunshot and fires. [...] During the night we saw enemy fire and sails.[46]

Jean Lucas also saw enemy signals on 20 October 1805:

[...] I told the admiral I could see an enemy squadron or fleet. It did not seem far away and the ships of this squadron were sending a great quantity of signals, remarkable for their beauty and for their colours. At around nine in the evening, the admiral ordered battle formation.[47]

44. A. Parès, *La bataille de Trafalgar: racontée par le commandant Lucas* (Toulon, 1914), pp. 9–23.

45. Julien Houssart was attached to the staff of Admiral Villeneuve and served on board the *Bucentaure*, the French admiral's ship. He survived the battle and was captured by the British.

46. Julien Houssart, 'Copie du rapport de combat de Trafalgar écrit le surlendemain, à bord du «Neptune» anglais et remis à l'Amiral Villeneuve', in: *Carnet de la Sabretache: revue militaire rétrospective* (1905), pp. 291–8.

47. Parès, *La bataille de Trafalgar*, pp. 9–23.

On the day of the battle Julien Houssart was able to count the enemy ships:

> At dawn, the frigate *Hermione* spotted 33 sails, including 27 ships. Frigates were ordered to recce the enemy.[48]

Captain Jean Lucas gave more details:

> [...] On 21 [October 1805], at the beginning of the day, we saw the enemy west-south-west. The wind was quiet but the sea was still choppy. The combined fleet was spread west-north-west, its ships were very dispersed and seemed to form only one line. The enemy was also without order but was manoeuvring to rally. Its power was then understood and we saw twenty-seven ships, including seven three-deckers, four frigates and a schooner.
>
> At around seven in the morning, the admiral ordered our ships to form a line of battle in the natural order. [...] I left the position held during the night and changed tack to take my place in the line of battle, which was far away. At eight, I managed to reach my position and at nine the enemy had formed two columns. [...] The admiral judged that the enemy wanted to attack our rear-guard and ordered the fleet to turn.[49]

Julien Houssart watched the British ships approach the French formation:

> The enemy force split into two columns. One went towards our centre and the other to our rear-guard. The one on the right had eleven ships and the one on the left sixteen, including two ships that went on the right. [...] The enemy was closing and seemed to move to cut the rear of the line behind the *Santa-Ana* and the *Sma-Trinidad*.[50]

The French opened fire soon after:

> [...] At around eleven in the morning, both enemy columns approached our fleet, one column preceded by a three-decker, the *Royal Souverain*, commanded by Rear-Admiral Collingwood, and the other by the *Victory* of the same strength, commanded by Admiral Nelson, and the *Téméraire*, also one hundred and ten cannon, to attack the centre of our formation.
>
> At eleven thirty, the ships of our rear-guard fired at the *Royal Souverain*. This ship fired at us from far away but I did not want to answer. [...] The column led by Admiral Nelson was nearing our line of battle. The three-decker's following ships manoeuvred to surround the French admiral's ship. One of them tried to go astern. As soon as I saw

---

48. Houssart, 'Copie du rapport de combat de Trafalgar', pp. 291–8.
49. Parès, *La bataille de Trafalgar*, pp. 9–23.
50. Houssart, 'Copie du rapport de combat de Trafalgar', pp. 291–8.

this, [...] I ordered the bowsprit on the stern of the *Bucentaure* to be prepared, ready to sacrifice my ship for the defence of the admiral, and I told
my intentions to my officers and the crew, who answered by screaming
'Long live the admiral! Long live the commander!' while playing drums
and fifes. I was with my officers inspecting our cannon and everywhere
I found brave men burning with impatience to start the action. A few told
me 'Commander, do not forget to board them.' At eleven thirty the
entire enemy fleet hoisted its colours. The flag on the *Redoutable* went up
in an imposing manner, fifes and drums saluting the flag, the soldiers
presenting arms.

The enemy column, which was headed against our centre, was within
range of *Bucentaure*'s guns and her crew started firing. I ordered a
number of gun captains to go up on the forecastle and told them that
many of our ships fired poorly, their shots too low. I ordered them to aim
for the masts and, above all, to aim well. At eleven forty-five the first
battery of the *Redoutable* opened fire and cut the foretopsail yard of the
*Victory* and cheers and shouts were heard all over the ship. Our fire was
intense and in less than ten minutes the same ship lost her mizzen-mast,
foretopsail, and main topgallant mast. I was so close to the *Bucentaure*
that they called me several times to say that I was going to ram them.
Indeed, the bowsprit of the *Redoutable* touched the crown of the flagship's
stern, but I assured them they had nothing to be anxious about.[51]

The crew of the *Bucentaure* were in a far more precarious position. Julien
Houssart wrote:

It was very quiet and the smoke was enveloping us in such a manner that
we were blind and unable to do anything. [...] The leading enemy ship
had a hold on us. The *Sma-Trinidad* was downwind and was about to hit
us. We called her but she did nothing. We had to stay in our position,
and endure a few more volleys, to avoid crashing into her. The *Redoutable*
was so close that our portside hit her.[52]

Meanwhile, the *Redoutable* was within range of the *Victory*:

The damage done to the *Victory* did not affect the daring manoeuvre of
Admiral Nelson. He persisted in trying to break the line in front of the
*Redoutable*, threatening to board us if we opposed. The great proximity of
this ship [the *Victory*], followed by the *Téméraire*, instead of intimidating
our crew, only increased their courage and, to demonstrate to the

51. Parès, *La bataille de Trafalgar*, pp. 9–23.
52. Houssart, 'Copie du rapport de combat de Trafalgar', pp. 291–8.

English admiral that we did not fear boarding, I had grappling irons made fast at all the yardarms.

The ship *Victory*, having failed in passing astern of the French admiral, boarded us, dropping alongside and sheering off aft in such a way that our poop lay alongside her quarter-deck. From this position the grappling irons were thrown on board her. Those at the stem parted, but those forward held, and at the same time our broadside was discharged at close range. This resulted in horrible carnage. We continued to fire at each other for some time. We had to use rope rammers in several cases, and fire with the guns run in, being unable to bowse them, as the ports were masked by the sides of the *Victory*. At the same time, elsewhere, by means of muskets fired through the ports into those of the *Victory*, we prevented the enemy from loading their guns, and before long they stopped firing on us altogether.

It would have been such a day of glory for the *Redoutable* if she had only had to fight the *Victory*! In the end, the batteries of that ship, unable to resist us, stopped firing. I realised that they were getting ready to board us; the men were gathering on the forecastle. I had the trumpet sounded, the agreed signal for boarding with our divisions. They came up with such order, officers to the head of their men, that it seemed like an exercise. In less than a minute our decks were swarming with armed men, who spread out on the poop deck, in the rigging, and in the shrouds.

A heavy exchange of musketry fire followed, in which Admiral Nelson fought at the head of his crew. Our fire became so rapid and was so superior that we reduced that of the *Victory* in less than fifteen minutes. We threw more than two hundred grenades on board. The decks were covered with dead and wounded and Admiral Nelson was killed by the firing of our muskets.[53]

There is little doubt that Admiral Nelson was indeed killed by a crew member of the *Redoutable*. Many British and French specialists have tried to identify the man who pulled the trigger but the task has proved almost impossible. However, one name often crops up in the historiography. The narration of the battle offered by Sergeant Robert Guillemard in his book *Mémoires, souvenirs: mémoires de Robert Guillemard* is a popular one in France.[54] The author claimed to have served on the *Redoutable* and to have fired the shot that killed Nelson. Unfortunately, the book is widely suspected of being a work of fiction. In fact, there is no evidence that Sergeant Robert Guillemard

53. Parès, *La bataille de Trafalgar*, pp. 9–23.
54. Robert Guillemard, *Mémoires, souvenirs: mémoires de Robert Guillemard* (Paris, 1826).

ever existed. Jean Tulard, the renowned specialist of the Napoleonic Wars, denounced the book as a fake.[55] But whoever killed the British admiral, it did not save the *Redoutable*. Lucas' report offered an intense picture of the continuing battle:

> The upper deck of the *Victory* was evacuated and the ship ceased firing. But it proved difficult to board because of the motion of the ships and the elevation of the third battery. I ordered the supports of the main yard to be cut so as to use it as a bridge. *Aspirant* [midshipman] Yon and four sailors, using the anchor of the *Victory*, climbed on board and told us that there was nobody left in the batteries. But just as our brave fellows were rushing to follow them, the ship *Téméraire*, which had noticed that the *Victory* was not fighting any more and was inevitably going to be captured, came down under full sail on our starboard side, firing at us with all her guns.
>
> It would be impossible to describe the carnage produced by this murderous broadside. More than two hundred of our brave men were killed or wounded. I was also wounded, but not seriously enough to leave my post. Unable to do anything against the *Victory*, I ordered the remaining crew to join the batteries and to fire at the *Téméraire* all our remaining guns. This order was executed.
>
> However, we had suffered so much and we had so few guns that the *Téméraire* fired back to great advantage. Soon after, another ship, whose name I do not know, placed herself across the stern of the *Redoutable* and fired at us from within the range of a pistol.
>
> In less than half an hour our ship had been hit by so many shots that she was little more than a pile of debris. In this state, the *Téméraire* hailed us and told us not to prolong such useless resistance. I ordered a few soldiers near me to answer this call by firing their muskets, which they did with great alacrity. At the same moment, the mainmast of the *Redoutable* fell on board the English ship. The two topmasts of the *Téméraire* then fell on us. Our whole poop was stoved in, helm, rudder and stem post all shattered to splinters, all the stern frame, and the decks shot through. All our guns were either smashed or dismounted by the broadsides of the *Victory* and *Téméraire*.
>
> An 18-pounder cannon of the second battery, and a 32-pounder carronade on the forecastle had burst, killing and wounding a great many men. [...] Everywhere the decks were covered with dead men, lying beneath

---

55. Jean Tulard, *Bibliographie critique des mémoires sur le consulat et l'empire* (Paris, 1971), p. 79; R. Monaque and John Welsh, 'Was Nelson killed by Robert Guillemard?', in: *The Mariner's Mirror*, 88 (2002), pp. 469–74.

the debris. Out of a crew of 632 men, we had 522 wounded, including most of the officers. Of the remainder, a large number were employed in the storerooms and magazines, meaning that the batteries and upper decks were practically abandoned, bare of men, and we were unable to offer any further resistance. No one who has not seen the state of the *Redoutable* could ever form an idea of her condition. Nothing on board was not damaged by shot.

In the middle of this awful carnage, brave men who had not yet been killed and the wounded lying on the orlop screamed 'Long live the Emperor! We are not taken yet! Is the Captain still alive?' The canvas at the stern caught fire but we fortunately managed to extinguish it. The ship *Victory* was not fighting any more; she was only trying to get clear of the *Redoutable*, but we were under the cross-fire of the *Téméraire*, with whom we were still engaged, and of the other ship, still firing her guns at our stern. Unable to return fire, and seeing none of our ships, which were all very far away and unable to rescue us, I did not wait to surrender. The leaks were serious enough to sink the ship. When I became certain of this, I ordered the fighting colours taken down. The flag, however, came down by itself when the mast fell.

The ship which had been firing into our stern then left us, but the *Téméraire* continued firing at us and only stopped when it became necessary for her crew to extinguish a fire which had broken out on board their ship. It was then half-past two in the afternoon.

Soon after, the *Victory*, the *Redoutable* and the *Téméraire*, all tangled together since their masts had fallen across from one ship to the other, drifted at the mercy of the wind and were thrown against the ship *Fougueux*, abandoned without having lowered her flag after fighting against the enemy. She was without masts and unrigged, but was boarded by men from the *Téméraire*. She was in no shape to put up serious resistance. Her brave Captain Baudouin,[56] who was in charge, tried his best but was killed in the attempt and his second-in-command was wounded almost at the same moment. A few men of the *Téméraire* jumped on board and took the ship.

The enemy did not try to take the *Redoutable*, in which the leaks were now so significant that I feared the ship would go down before we could get the wounded off. I told this to the men of the *Téméraire*, warning them that unless they took steps at once to send men on board with gear

---

56. Louis Alexis Baudoin was born on 2 December 1766. He served in the French navy from the age of eleven and became a lieutenant during the French Revolution. He was given command of the *Fougueux* but was killed during the battle of Trafalgar.

for the pumps and to give us immediate help, I would have to set fire to the ship, which would spread to the *Téméraire* and the *Victory*.

Two officers and a few sailors from the *Téméraire* immediately came on board to take possession of the ship. At the same time one of the English sailors entered the lower deck through a port, whereupon one of our wounded sailors grabbed a musket and bayonet and attacked him. He said 'I must kill one more of them!' He bayoneted the sailor through the thigh and pushed him between the two vessels. Despite this incident, we were able to convince the English boarding party to remain on board. They wanted to return to the *Téméraire*.

The situation was equally critical on board the *Bucentaure*. Julien Houssart described the damage inflicted by the British, and even interacted with Admiral Villeneuve when the ship was surrendered:

At two-thirty the great mast and the spanker collapsed. [...] At three the foresail fell down. Without sails or ropes, without men on the decks, our guns of 24 [calibre] dismounted, half of the crew out of action, the starboard side covered with the remains of the sails, abandoned by all ships, without any other near us, having not even a canoe to leave by, the admiral ordered us to surrender. The eagle was thrown overboard and at half past three the ship *Bucentaure* surrendered to the enemy. (When the ship was surrendered, the admiral went down to his cabin and I followed him. Entering his room, I saw that he was moving towards the table, on which were his pistols. I ran in front of him, took them and threw them overboard! The admiral then told me quietly: 'You mistake me for someone with little courage!' I begged for his forgiveness for this action, triggered by the fear of seeing him commit suicide in a gesture of despair. Then I threw his documents overboard after having removed a single letter from the minister, the one telling the Admiral to 'be audacious and not hesitate to attack the enemy everywhere, since his Majesty the Emperor was not bothered by the loss of a few ships, as long as they were lost with honour'.)[57]

Rochay,[58] a soldier of the 6th regiment of line infantry who was captured at the battle of Trafalgar and later died in captivity in an English prison, witnessed the carnage and described it in his diary:

57. Houssart, 'Copie du rapport de combat de Trafalgar', pp.291–8.
58. Not much is known of Rochay. He served in the 6th regiment of line infantry and was captured at Trafalgar. He was sent to the prisoner-of-war camp at Norman Cross, where he died. His diary was sent to his family.

I will not attempt to describe such horrible carnage. I would use point-less expressions which would only describe a hundredth of the truth. The atrocious sight of these cadavers is for ever in front of your eyes, the pathetic screams of those unfortunate who suffered wounds, who beg you to take what is left of their lives, all these bloody pictures would move even the coldest hearts. Humanity is assaulted at its most sensitive place.[59]

Captain Jean Lucas was also taken by the British:

At around three the ships attacking our rear-guard fired several shots at our group. A few cannonballs hit the *Redoutable*, and one of the officers of the *Téméraire* lost his thigh and died almost instantly.

At around half-past three the *Victory* separated herself from the *Redoutable*, but she was in such poor shape that she was in no condition to fight. It was not until seven in the evening that we were able to sepa-rate the *Redoutable* and the *Téméraire*, which still remained attached to the *Fougueux*. Then the ship *Swiftsure* came to drag us apart, and despite using two pumps we were unable to keep the water down. The few Frenchmen who were still able to work helped the English to pump, stopped several leaks, blocked up the port holes and boarded in the poop of the ship, which was ready to cave in. Indeed, no toil was too hard for them. In the middle of this I noticed some of my brave fellows, partic-ularly the young midshipmen, of whom several were wounded, picking up arms which they hid on the lower deck, with the intention, as they said, of retaking the *Redoutable*.

Never were so many traits of valour, intrepidity and courage displayed on board a ship and never did the history of our navy show anything like that.

The next day the commander of the *Swiftsure* sent for me, for Lieu-tenant Dupotet, my second-in-command, and for Midshipman Ducrest, and we were brought on board.

At noon, the *Redoutable* lost her foremast, the only one left. At five in the evening the water continued to gain on the pumps. The prizemaster asked for help. All the boats of the *Swiftsure* were lowered to save people. It was very windy and the sea ran high, which made the evacuation of the wounded difficult. These unfortunate fellows, realising that the ship was about to sink, crawled to the quarter-deck. We managed to save a few but the poop of the ship collapsed at seven in the evening and the *Redoutable*

59. Rochay, 'Du Piémont aux Antilles et à Trafalgar: souvenirs d'un fantassin', in: *Carnet de la Sabretache: revue militaire rétrospective*, 417 (1958), pp. 497–511.

went down with most of those unfortunates, who were worthy of a better fate.

At dawn the next day the commander of the *Swiftsure*, seeing men in the water clinging to pieces of wood, sent boats for them. They rescued about fifty, almost all of them wounded.

Now the remainder of the unfortunate crew of the *Redoutable*, 169 men in all, found themselves together on board the English ship. Seventy of them were badly wounded and sixty-four had less serious wounds. All the wounded were sent to Cadiz, and in the end only thirty-five men were taken to England as prisoners of war.

The battle resulted in the loss of the *Redoutable*, whom the enemy was unable to use, and three-quarters of her crew. However, she alone engaged for the whole fight the three-deckers *Victory* and *Téméraire*, and paralysed the vigilance of Admiral Nelson, who, himself involved in the battle, could only free himself by excessive daring.

Nelson, the hero of the English navy, died under the blows of the *Redoutable*, and more than three hundred men, including several officers of distinction, were put out of action on board two enemy ships. The *Victory* lost her mizzen topmast in the action and her main topgallant mast, and in general all her yards were badly damaged, as was her wheel. The *Téméraire* lost two of her topmasts and two lower yards, and her helm and rudder were destroyed by the guns of our upper deck. Both ships had to return to England to undergo substantial repairs.

Anyone who has not seen the valour of the brave officers who led our men to fight the enemy will have trouble imagining their burning courage and intrepid audacity. Everywhere they were leading the crews, on the decks, armed with sabres and pistols, others with muskets and throwing grenades. In these circumstances, sea and land officers as well as seamen and soldiers were competing to be the bravest.

The praises that I owe to these brave men are above words and I would need a list of all these warriors to distinguish the most deserving.[60]

The French and the Spanish lost more than half of their fleet during the battle of Trafalgar. The surviving ships returned to Cadiz, where they remained trapped until 1808. French soldiers serving in Europe only heard of the battle months later. François-Joseph Jacquin[61] of the 37th half-brigade wrote the following in his diary on 25 February 1806:

---

60. Parès, *La bataille de Trafalgar*, pp. 9–23.
61. François-Joseph Jacquin, born in Villers in 1778, was conscripted in 1796. He served as a grenadier in the 37th half-brigade and later joined the Gendarmerie. He continued working in the Gendarmerie after the Napoleonic Wars.

25 February: [...] We heard that the division left Brest and met the English fleet off the Spanish coast; a terrible fight was engaged at Trafalgar. The English were favoured by the winds and we lost almost all our ships, some were thrown on the coastline, other sunk. Some men perished and others were captured by the English.[62]

As this chapter has demonstrated, the French navy lacked inspiring leadership and talented naval commanders. French sailors fought bravely during the battle of the Nile and at Trafalgar, and in various other small encounters, but failed to make a difference. Trafalgar finished what the battle of the Nile had started. The French lost the ability to control the oceans or to invade Britain. The defeat of 1805 was a serious setback but it did not affect the War of the Third Coalition. Indeed, Napoleon Bonaparte won a decisive victory against the Austrians and the Russians at Austerlitz on 2 December 1805.[63] Nelson's audacity and sacrifice had dealt with the enemy navy, but it should be remembered that the British had still to solve the problem of the French army on the continent.

62. François-Joseph Jacquin, *Carnet de route d'un grognard de la révolution et de l'empire* (Paris, 1960), p. 54.
63. Edward Ingram, 'Illusions of victory: The Nile, Copenhagen, and Trafalgar revisited', in: *Military Affairs*, 48 (1984), pp. 140–3.

*Chapter 3*

# The Struggle for Europe

## The French Expeditions to Ireland in 1796 and 1798

French attempts to assist rebel republican groups in Ireland from December 1796 to 1798 have been largely overshadowed by more important campaigns. They were, however, fascinating episodes of the struggle between the British and French during the Revolutionary Wars. These attempts were closely linked to both the American and the French Revolutions, which inspired groups of Irish nationalists to embrace the cause of republicanism as a form of opposition to British rule and the discriminatory laws against the Catholic population. At first non-violent, the Society of United Irishmen turned to armed revolt in 1793 and called on the French Republic for help. This coalition, which sought to create an independent Republic of Ireland, met with various French personalities during the following years. The French were interested in assisting the pro-independence Irish, if only to force Great Britain to divert troops and supplies, but had first to resolve more pressing military matters on the continent. Having crushed her domestic troubles and strengthened her European position in 1795, France made the Irish expedition a reality in 1796. Ireland's rebellious nature had the potential to put the British in a difficult position; it was also a potential rear-base from which the French could launch an invasion of Britain. General Hoche, who had fought the royalists in Vendée, was appointed commander of the expedition and given command of around 14,000 veterans. The organisational phase was, however, more difficult than expected. The French navy proved unable to dispatch the necessary ships in time, while practice voyages failed. After much delay, the fleet finally left France for Ireland in the winter of 1796. They reached Bantry Bay, in County Cork, at the end of December but bad weather made any landing impossible and forced the French fleet to turn back. Twelve ships were either destroyed by the winds or captured by the British, and some 2,000 soldiers and sailors died.[1] This catastrophic outcome did not discourage Irish republicans. Wolfe Tone, the energetic Irish leader, continued to travel to Europe to gather support for the republican cause. In May 1798

1. Grace Neville, 'Up close and personal: The French in Bantry Bay (1796) in the Bantry Estate Papers', in: *Proceedings of the Harvard Celtic Colloquium*, 26/27 (2006/2007), pp. 132–45.

most of the counties around Dublin rebelled and clashed with the British army and loyalists. During the following months both sides committed atrocities against civilians and prisoners. On 22 August that year a French expeditionary corps landed at Kilcummin to assist the Irish republicans. The commander of the French fleet, André Daniel Savary,[2] described in his diary the moment the French troops disembarked:

5 *fructidor* [22 August 1798]

[...] I wanted to disembark all the troops under the protection of all the boats and frigates, but intelligence given by the Irish to General Humbert and I said that there would be no resistance. As a result, the landing was protected only by our frigates, which were close to the shore.

General Humbert asked me to disembark our grenadiers. We did so.

At 2.45 we began to disembark our troops. The frigates *La Franchise* and *La Médée* began later.

By 7.30 all troops were disembarked.

[...] Afraid that the army of General Humbert might not have enough food, I removed from the frigates the following:

Twelve thousand biscuits in bags provided by the frigate, eighteen barrels of flour and six great barrels of eau-de-vie;

120 muskets that were not needed on board the frigate;

Two pikes of 88;

Around eight men who wanted to be attached to the army, a navy officer, a surgeon and around 12 or 15 deserters detained on the frigate.

[...] As soon as our grenadiers were disembarked, General Humbert made them move towards the town of Killala, one L[eague] from there. 100 English soldiers were in garrison there. Our vanguard, made up of seven grenadiers and an officer, energetically charged at the garrison, who, seeing our grenadier corps, promptly fled. We killed four of them and captured 30 prisoners who were hidden in the attic of Killala's bishop (what soldiers they are!).

[...] Irish people have welcomed us favourably; we reciprocated and this persuaded a great number to join our army and they provided beautiful horses for our officers and all our *chasseurs à cheval*. ...[3]

General Jean Humbert and his 1,099 soldiers were quickly joined by thousands of rebels, who were given blue French uniforms. Humbert was counting

2. André Daniel Savary, born in 1743, served first in the French royal navy and then during the Revolution. He rose to the rank of Counter-Admiral and died on 22 November 1808.
3. Daniel Savary, 'Quelques documents sur l'expédition du Général Humbert en Irlande', in: *Carnet de la Sabretache, revue militaire rétrospective* (Paris, 1899), pp. 399–401.

on the support of other expeditionary forces from France but they failed to materialise. One of them, commanded by General Jean Hardy, was delayed by bad weather and by the Royal Navy for a week. The unusual Franco-Irish army immediately moved towards Castlebar, the capital of County Mayo. On 23 August Daniel Savary was about to leave with his fleet when he wrote the following entry:

6 *fructidor* [23 August 1798]

At 3 o'clock I raised the French flag and I saluted it with a salvo. I did not think that I had to fool the Irish with the English flag, which had proved so useful. General Humbert only lacks money and muskets. If he had enough of both, he would foster revolution in Ireland in ten days; he might do so anyway if he can (as I hope) meet with the 20,000 Irish who are 15 leagues from Killala.

At six in the evening, I was told by a letter from General Humbert that at 3 in the morning the next day there would be a significant battle between his little army and maybe 400 to 500 English. He asked me to delay my departure until tomorrow evening. I could have done so if I had not been threatened by the weather. [...] I have therefore been forced to bid them Farewell and wished them the success that their dedication deserves.[4]

General Humbert's letter concerned a minor encounter between the French and the British at Ballina. While the French were assembling local support, Lord Cornwallis, the Lord Lieutenant of Ireland, was busy requesting reinforcements and gathering as many men as he could find. He managed to send 6,000 soldiers and militiamen, as well as artillery, to Castlebar. On 27 August 1798 Humbert reached the capital of the county and decided to attack the British, in spite of being ordered to avoid any confrontation with superior forces. Although outnumbered and under heavy artillery fire, the French launched a fierce bayonet charge and routed the British units. Waves of panicked soldiers and militiamen left behind valuable equipment as they fled as far as Athlone.[5] This brilliant victory encouraged Humbert to proclaim the Republic of Connaught. It was also a major triumph for French propaganda at home and in Egypt. The expedition to Ireland was supposed to prove that French soldiers were willing to help people struggling against tyranny. Humbert, however, was not in an easy position. The French commander

---

4. Savary, 'Quelques documents sur l'expédition du Général Humbert', pp. 401–2.
5. Patrick Hogan, '1798 remembered: casualties sustained by government forces during the Humbert episode, August–September, 1798: a re-appraisal', in: *Journal of the Galway Archaeological and Historical Society*, 50 (1998), pp. 1–9.

received alarming reports of vast numbers of troops approaching Castlebar
and ordered a retreat. Having attempted to link up with the rebel armies, he
was finally intercepted by the troops led by Cornwallis on 8 September 1798.
The large British army of some 26,000 men had no difficulty crushing the
Franco-Irish forces. General Humbert and his men were captured but were
soon released and sent back to France in exchange for British prisoners.
Following the expedition's failure, the Directory abandoned plans to launch
further operations to Ireland. Humbert, furious, wrote the following letter to
change their mind:

> Strasburg, 23 *nivôse* year 7 [12 January 1799] of the French Republic
>
> Citizen Director,
> It is said that the government wants to renounce all maritime expeditions
> for the time being. [...] However, the political and military situation of
> the British Islands is more favourable to us than ever and it is absolutely
> impossible to encounter such favourable circumstances in the future.
> The English government, noticing how close to changing everything its
> subjects are, will be forced to make things better for the people and
> mostly the Irish, who will soon fall back in apathy and will not maintain
> the hatred that they have for their lords; defeated people are harder to
> rally, especially when they are without character: it is therefore essential
> to avoid giving them time to fall asleep.
>
> It is easy these days to land on most parts of the British Islands; but as
> limited as the military genius of the English can be, it is getting better
> every day. They take advantage of the rest we grant them to fortify all
> harbours of the three kingdoms, which will make it very hard for us to
> win in the future. ...[6]

Despite his vigour and his enthusiasm for the republican cause, General
Humbert failed to influence the Directory. French forces were already
stretched, while French ships were incapable of competing with the Royal
Navy. The Irish question would continue to haunt the British for a long time
but large numbers of French troops would never again set foot on the island.

## Planning the Invasion of Britain

By January 1801 the French Republic and Great Britain had been at war for
more than seven years, despite various attempts to bring hostilities to an end.
As early as 1796 the French Directory had entered negotiations but had
finally renounced them, convinced that a revolution in Britain was imminent.
In December 1799 Bonaparte, who had just become First Consul, had

---

6. Savary, 'Quelques documents sur l'expédition du Général Humbert', p. 404.

approached the British but had been turned down.[7] The Prime Minister of Great Britain, William Pitt the Younger, was a major obstacle to a European peace. He had no faith in Bonaparte and favoured a military solution. However, removing the impetuous Corsican First Consul by force was not an easy task. At the beginning of 1801 the French were not far from being totally defeated in Egypt, but they had also won resounding victories at Marengo and Hohenlinden months before. The diplomatic map changed drastically in February 1801. On 9 February the French and the Austrians signed a treaty at Lunéville. France now controlled the Italian republics and the Netherlands and was about to invade Portugal. On 16 February William Pitt resigned over the matter of Irish Catholic emancipation and was replaced by Henry Addington. On 21 March the new government's foreign secretary, Lord Hawkesbury, openly expressed his wish to discuss peace conditions with the French. Negotiations between the two countries followed but it soon became clear that a diplomatic solution would take time. In April Bonaparte gathered men and ships in and around Boulogne to invade southern England. As John Grainger argues, this may have been a bluff to intimidate the British and influence the ongoing negotiations.[8] But Bonaparte's gamble was taken seriously; the Royal Navy was forced to send ships to protect the English Channel and observe what was happening in Boulogne. The threat of an invasion became more imminent after the failure of the first peace negotiations in June 1801. British ships in the English Channel were further reinforced by a fleet returning from the Baltic. By August 1801 the French position in Egypt was clearly compromised and the British had regained confidence in a possible military victory. On 4 August Nelson and his fleet decided to attack the invasion fleet gathered at Boulogne-sur-Mer. This raid caused only minor damage to the French navy, and the British admiral decided to launch a second attack on 15–16 August. François Hamy,[9] a French civilian living in Boulogne-sur-Mer, witnessed both the British naval assaults, which he described in a letter to his family:

> I forgot in my last letter to tell you about the bombardment that we endured. The truth is that this bombardment lasted for a whole day. The English were 1,800 *toises* from the entrance of the harbour. [...] Enemy fire was extremely intense and bombs fell on our fleet; the rain from these infernal machines was continuous around our ships. [...] However, not even one hit was fatal and we suffered no dead or even a single wound.

7. John Grainger, *The Amiens truce: Britain and Bonaparte 1801–1803* (Woodbridge, 2004), p. 1.
8. Grainger, *The Amiens truce*, pp. 32–4.
9. François Hamy was a notary in the city of Boulogne. He died on 28 September 1818.

Two of these ships as well as a gunboat were sunk; the ships because of the commotion of the bombardment and the gunship by a bomb that went through the *Sainte-Barbe* [the room where gunpowder was stored]. It was fortunate that she did not explode or she would have blown up parts of the fleet.

The gunship was beached a few feet away, the ships stayed where they were; the men used canoes to reach the land and those ships were brought back to the harbour the next day, where they were repaired.

While a miracle preserved us from losing anybody, despite such a display of deadly weapons and destruction, it was not the same for the English. They lost several engineer officers and most of their bombing ships, due to the violent tremor to which they were exposed. However, no ship sank near the coastline, and it is only thanks to reports that came in a few days later that we heard of the losses and the disasters inflicted on the enemy.

On the night of 15 August (27 *thermidor*), Nelson, ashamed by the lack of success of his first attempt, tried to capture the whole fleet by sending two to three hundred barges and canoes, with two thousand men, at least, including sailors who had gone through Dover the day before, and line infantry. They took a patrol boat with five men by surprise, but the alarm was heard and we took measures to welcome the English. We used nets to prevent boarding, we cut in small pieces those who dared climb on board, and we fired grapeshot at the crews of the barges. One of our gunships sank seven barges in four shots. The English screamed awfully and begged in their language: *sorry*, but our fierceness would have killed a whole division if those who had survived had not left.

The bridges of our ships where the enemy had attacked were covered with chopped hands and fingers, and the next day the sea was filled with mutilated cadavers. Enemy losses in killed and drowned numbered more than four hundred and at least two hundred men were wounded. We lost seven brave men who were buried solemnly. We had twenty wounded.

Since then, we are still blockaded but the enemy does not dare try anything else. We noticed that even the *Meduse*[10] and her charlatan [Nelson] carried elsewhere the bragging English admiral. Nelson, on top of everything, won in front of our walls, the title of Count of Boulogne, as you have learned from the newspapers. You can count, Sir, on the exactitude of my account.[11]

---

10. HMS *Medusa* was used by Lord Nelson during the raid.
11. Ernest Deseille, *L'année boulonnaise: éphémérides historiques intéressant le pays boulonnais* (Boulogne-sur-Mer, 1886), pp. 418–20.

Hamy's letter is filled with inaccuracies. Nelson lost only four men and two gunboats during the first attack. The British did suffer more serious losses on 15–16 August, but nowhere near the 600 killed and wounded described by the Frenchman. It is estimated that about 170 British sailors and soldiers died or suffered injuries during the raid. On the other hand, Hamy correctly assessed the number of French casualties. The British operation was a failure and a good opportunity for French propaganda to trumpet a victory against Lord Nelson. However, the raid allowed the British to assess the French flotilla and they concluded that the threat of invasion was not realistic.

The situation on the diplomatic front changed again in September 1801. After months of difficulties, negotiations were resumed and it soon became clear that an agreement was now possible. On 30 September 1801 both parties approved a preliminary truce.[12] This agreement did not put an end to negotiations but it stopped further military violence. The prospective treaty was discussed for another six months before being officially signed at Amiens on 25 March 1802. For the first time since 1793 France and Britain were not at war. Upper-class British tourists immediately took the opportunity to visit Paris and see for themselves how the capital had been affected by the Revolution. Others travelled to the warm city of Nice, where a curious episode happened. On 9 November 1802 French officials were celebrating the anniversary of the coup of 18 *Brumaire* at a banquet with several British officers, including General Charles Morgan. Having drunk more than a few bottles of wine, guests offered toasts to different personalities. A report to the interior minister explained what happened next:

> [...] After having drunk to the English nation, a few English soldiers asked the Prefect if we could dedicate a toast to the King of England. The Prefect, after a few negative answers, but desiring to please foreigners of all nations invited to the celebration of 18 Brumaire, agreed. Toasting Spain, England and other allied nations was done without making any distinction between people and governments or the governed, because they are all at one with the French nation.
>
> [...] The English General Morgans [sic] then asked, through an interpreter, permission to drink to the health of 'Napoleon Bonaparte, the greatest and most extraordinary man.'[13]

This seemingly ideal situation did not last long. By January 1803 Britain was once more growing weary of France's hegemony over the European

---

12. Grainger, *The Amiens truce*, p. 46.
13. Quoted in A. Demougeot, 'Les Anglais à Nice pendant la paix d'Amiens 1802–1803', in: *Recherches Régionales*, 1 (1963), p. 34.

continent. On 14 February Charles Whitworth, the British ambassador to France, refused to evacuate Malta. A few days later Bonaparte and Whitworth met. For two hours the First Consul tried to convince the British ambassador of his good intentions and dismissed his fears over the fate of Switzerland and Piedmont as *'bagatelles'* (trifling matters).[14] The situation continued to deteriorate in the following months. At the end of March 1803 Tsar Alexander even began mobilising his troops. Despite a last-minute attempt at negotiation, Britain declared war on France on 18 May 1803. The following month Bonaparte travelled to Boulogne-sur-Mer and its environs to inspect the ramparts, the beach and all the sites that might host an invasion force headed towards Britain. The task was immense. The First Consul needed a large army and a vast number of landing ships. The camp of Boulogne, also known officially as the camp of Saint-Omer, grew significantly between 1803 and 1805. It was home to fewer than 70,000 men at the end of 1803, but this figure had reached 170,000 men by the summer of 1805. Jean-Jacques Bellavoine,[15] a soldier in the 55th regiment of line infantry, served in the camp for a year and a half. His diary recorded numerous interesting details. Here is how he described the force of invasion and the plan of conquest of Britain:

> I want to describe the army in which I serve. It is said that from Dunkirk to Etaples, on the coastline, 100,000 men are based. It is said that we will embark the whole army at the same time. We wait for the rest of the fleet to embark. The Admiral who will command the army told the First Consul that he wants to bring the army as a whole to England without having to endure a single cannon shot, but perhaps this is said to make us brave, so everybody is strong while serving. But let us see if peace might not arrive first for the French.[16]

French soldiers were eager to invade Britain but were also alarmed by the enemy's supremacy over the sea. Bellavoine witnessed the power of the Royal Navy on more than one occasion:

> On the 20th [13 October 1803], the English rallied at sea; so many ships, but they all disappeared in an hour and a half. We had no idea what had happened, considering how fast they disappeared. We did not have to wait long to see them reappear, furiously, with at least 25 to 30 ships.

14. Grainger, *The Amiens truce*, pp. 159–60.
15. Jean-Jacques Bellavoine was born in Gapennes on 16 November 1776. He was conscripted in the 55th regiment of line infantry on 26 March 1803. He served until 1814, was wounded four times and ultimately became a sous-lieutenant in 1813. He died on 19 March 1862.
16. Fernand Beaucour, 'Notes et souvenirs de J.-J. Bellavoine, soldat du camp de Boulogne', in: *Revue du Nord*, 50 (1968), p. 442.

They came to chase us along the coast that we occupy. They approach within cannon range, fire a salvo, and immediately draw off. There is no way to take them by surprise because we have no ships at sea. As soon as our ships go one league to sea, suddenly, ten English ships pursue the unfortunate vessels.[17]

Rumours were rife. The French saw spies everywhere and were weary of British agents:

Details of how a French spy gives news to the English by signal. This is how they act against the government: these citizens, in the middle of the night, use different methods to communicate with the English. They are arrested and brought to Boulogne to be questioned but, usually, wolves do not eat each other. These things should have been discovered but on the contrary, spies were brought in for questioning and released. No arrest was ever made.[18]

News of the Cadoudal plot against Bonaparte did not help. Soldiers were made aware in January 1804 that a group of conspirators had intended to capture the First Consul:

28 January 1804: [...] Georges Cadoudal came from England and had landed in France with 34 accomplices and travelled to Paris alone, where Georges alone had a meeting with Pichegru, a general, and Moreaux to conspire. They wanted to give their accomplices uniforms of the Consular Guard and hide to jump on the First Consul's escort, take Bonaparte and bring him back to England.

24 February 1804: all corps of the division were gathered to celebrate a mass and sing a Te Deum to thank God for discovering the English plot to murder the First Consul.[19]

In these difficult conditions, several soldiers tried to desert. However, discipline was tough and the men were harshly punished. Bellavoine remembered how one deserter was treated:

On 16 *Frimaire* [8 December 1803], at the changing of the guard, the 2nd Battalion was to stand ready to hear the judgment of a young man who had deserted on the 9th and was arrested at noon. He was sentenced to seven years' hard labour and his hair was cut as a punishment for desertion. This seems horrific to us soldiers.[20]

---

17. Beaucour, 'Notes et souvenirs de J.-J. Bellavoine', p. 438.
18. Beaucour, 'Notes et souvenirs de J.-J. Bellavoine', p. 438.
19. François, *Journal du capitaine François*, p. 465.
20. Beaucour, 'Notes et souvenirs de J.-J. Bellavoine', p. 438.

Training was an important aspect of life in the camp of Boulogne. In November 1803 Bonaparte visited the camp and asked to see how prepared his soldiers were. Bellavoine was one of the men who had to demonstrate their endurance to the First Consul:

> On 12 *Brumaire* [4 November 1803], 80 barges were out just in front of Boulogne. The First Consul arrived at the same date at around four in the afternoon and he was not expected. Our ships stayed until Bonaparte had inspected them.
>
> The next day, 13 [*Brumaire*], we were ordered to fire 25 shots from each ship. This was indeed done by our brave soldiers on board each ship but we were soon forced to change our ammunition. Instead of firing blank shots for the Consul's arrival, we had to load cannonballs to defend ourselves against the English, who had come to make some noise. They had seven or eight ships to attack our barges, all 80 of them, lined up in front of Boulogne. The English fired first at the vanguard of the line and the next volley at the line and followed it along to the tail. You should have seen that. There were fire and flames on both sides; they started firing at 11 in the morning and kept it up until two in the afternoon. However, there were no losses on our side, except for one soldier, on board a barge, who had both legs cut off, but it was his own fault.
>
> [...] On 16 *Brumaire*, the First Consul inspected us with his generals and then, afterwards, ordered us to show how we fired. The next day, 17, he wanted to test our 'tiredness' [endurance]; he ordered us to take our backpacks, at exactly 10 in the morning, after the meal, and brought us a league and a half from the camp to exercise as usual. We were in a place covered with mountains and dunes; we had to fire 30 to 40 shots each; we stayed until eight in the evening; we walked and shot for 10 hours in a row and the First Consul asked what time it was; someone answered that it was 8 o'clock; (the First Consul) answered: we need to bring the troops back to the camp and, tomorrow, 18, they will receive a double ration of brandy, he said to the General in Chief; indeed, we received this ration from the brave Consul.[21]

Bellavoine's encounter with Bonaparte was not unusual. The First Consul travelled on several occasions to the camp of Boulogne to improve his image. Such a formidable concentration of men in a relatively small space gave him the perfect opportunity to do so.[22] One of the most famous examples of state

---

21. Beaucour, 'Notes et souvenirs de J.-J. Bellavoine', p. 440.
22. Michael Hughes, *Forging Napoleon's Grande Armée: motivation, military culture, and masculinity in the French Army, 1800–1808* (New York, 2012), p. 21.

propaganda was the first distribution of Legion of Honour awards to soldiers of the Army of England on 16 August 1804. Pierre Bertrand, a civilian doctor living in Boulogne, witnessed this impressive ceremony:

> All troops gathered half a mile from Boulogne. [...] Here, there was a natural amphitheatre, the most favourable place to gather in such a small space the army and the greatest number of spectators. At the centre of this amphitheatre was a platform on which was placed a throne. [...] There was no other decoration than the flags taken to the enemy.
>
> [...] Napoleon was seated on the throne with his brother Joseph behind him, and, at the back, officers of the crown. On a lower platform were the ministers, the colonel Generals, the senators; lower again, the aide-de-camps, and at the foot of the throne, on benches, were the advisers of the state and generals, civilian administrators and the corps of music of the army, more than 2,000 drums, and on both sides, all the headquarters of the camp. This line was 150 *toises* long and was the centre around which the army was gathered. In front of the throne were 60 regiments in twenty columns, formed up like rays directed at the centre. [...] At the front of each column were the warriors who were waiting for the Legion of Honour. Behind, flags and division generals ... When the sign was given, drums played the charge and the whole army moved. The columns went forward with admirable order and advanced halfway to the throne. [...] Another signal stopped this impenetrable masse. The great chancellor said something and the emperor swore the oath of the order, repeated by the knights [of the Legion of Honour], followed spontaneously by the whole army.[23]

Training the soldiers was only one part of the plan to invade Britain. The French military also needed men who knew the country and were able to communicate in English. The First Consul published a decree to recruit interpreters for the Army of England in the *Journal militaire*, the official army newspaper, on 5 October 1803:

I. There is to be created a company of scout-interpreters to be used by the Army of England.

II. This company will be composed of 1 captain, 2 lieutenants, 1 sergeant-chief [*Maréchal des Logis*], 4 sergeants, 1 *fourier*, 8 corporals, 96 scouts, 2 drummers. Total: 117.

[...] To be admitted, it is necessary to be no more than thirty-five years old, to be fit, to know how to speak and write in English, to have lived in

---

23. Pierre Bertrand, *Précis de l'histoire physique civile et politique de la ville de Boulogne-sur-Mer, depuis les Morins jusqu'en 1814* (Boulogne-sur-Mer, 1815), pp. 375–80.

England, to know the country and to possess certificates of good conduct. Irishmen living in France and young people from districts not belonging to the army will be admitted if they fulfil the criteria mentioned above.[24]

Napoleon, who had been Emperor since 18 May 1804, was confident in the ability of his army to capture Britain. In that year he even had a prototype medal struck to commemorate the forthcoming invasion. Only one example survives, and it shows an interesting design, depicting Hercules crushing in his arms an animal representing Britain.[25] However, the Royal Navy proved too strong for the French fleet and prevented the French from crossing the Channel. Nonetheless, on several occasions French soldiers believed that the big day had arrived. Jean-Auguste Oyon,[26] a soldier serving in the 4th Dragoons, was convinced one night that he was about to sail to England:

Two months ago, I was happy; this nice and friendly society made me forget my lack of success as a soldier. Suddenly, an order took me away from these pleasures: we need to go to England; we must cross the Channel or 'go under'. To do so, my dragoons have to step on the ground; their horses and boots replaced by backpacks and gaiters.

I leave Amiens and arrive in Calais, my shoulders irritated by my pack, my face burned by the strong sun, and my feet torn by the difficult march. Before I can rest, I have to replace my sabre and my musket with a shovel and a pick, unfold my tent, and dig a bed in the sand. My body is broken, my hands wounded, but the camp is ready. I will finally lie on the ground that I watered with so much sweat.

[...] Men from each regiment are asked to work on the transport ships in the port, while waiting for the full boarding of the poor devils who are about to invade England. I was sent aboard [ship] number 69. [...] On the last day, I was lying in my hammock when, at around midnight, my ear heard a scream and warned me of something extraordinary. In a

24. Anonymous, *Bulletin de la société académique de l'arrondissement de Boulogne-sur-Mer: tome sixième* (Boulogne-sur-Mer, 1903), pp. 597–8.
25. Ironically, the only original medal still existing today can be found in the European galleries of the British Museum. H. Grueber, 'The "descente en Angleterre" medal of Napoleon I', in: *Royal Numismatic Society*, 7(1907), pp. 434–9.
26. Jean-Auguste Oyon was born in Laon on 27 September 1783. In 1792 his six brothers left for the French army and four died on the battlefield. He joined the French army in 1802 in the 4th Dragoons and spent some time in the camp of Boulogne before fighting at Austerlitz. He served with distinction during the following years and was wounded in 1808. His injuries brought him home the same year. He later became Mayor of Laon and died on 15 September 1852.

minute, all troops are ready; sailors are manning ropes, ships are about to leave. The invasion is about to begin! The port bell is joining the sailors' noise and I hear the rumble of the drums being carried in the dunes.

Soon, we will have to go through the English ships or be sunk by them ... They are so big! ... Ours are so small! Ah! English bandits, if we do not sink in front of you, you will pay for these emotions! ...

I was deep in my thoughts when I was interrupted by an officer carrying orders. His voice was certainly going to order us to sail to Dover! ... Eh! No, not at all! ... The officer ordered us to disembark; we came back to the camp. There, he disappeared and was replaced by our regiments, ready and waiting for us, and the last word: March![27]

The invasion of Britain, however, would never happen. Soldiers and officers were starting to betray signs of boredom and discipline became problematic. Even generals were causing trouble, as seen in this letter written by Mayor Nicolas Souquet-Marteau on 20 *ventôse* year XII (11 March 1804):

Citizen Sub-Prefect,
I need to denounce the rather indelicate behaviour of citizen Loison, divisional general, in my home. Soon after having arrived, a family from Liège came here under his protection. The father was so vile that he gave his daughter, aged 18 years old, to the general. She lives openly with the general in my home. Is it not, Citizen Sub-Prefect, a vexation for me to be forced to have to accommodate this and to know that my house is used in this manner? Is it not the epitome of carelessness to introduce this girl into the house of an honest citizen, who is the administrator of the commune? Should not we send the contemptible father of this shameful family back to the city, instead of his being protected by a commander who should be a model of good habits? You can imagine, Citizen Sub-Prefect, how much my ladies suffer from this behaviour. Put yourself in my position and I have no doubt that you would do your best to force the general to expel this girl from my house.[28]

A year later the French soldiers were still waiting to invade Britain. Toussaint Walthéry,[29] a rather uneducated man who served in the 13th Dragoons, wrote the following letter to his brother Nicolas:

---

27. Jean-Auguste Oyon, 'Campagnes et souvenirs militaires de Jean-Auguste Oyon', in: *Carnets de la Sabretache: revue militaire rétrospective* (1913), pp. 101–9.
28. Jacques Chochois and M. Poultier, *Napoléon, le camp de Boulogne, et ... la Légion d'Honneur* (Boulogne-sur-Mer, 2003), p. 203.
29. Toussaint Walthéry, born in Embourg (now Belgium) on 5 October 1780, was the son of Toussaint Walthéry and Marie-Jeanne Delsemme. He was conscripted during the year X

From the barracks of St Pierre Calais [France], 21 *Thermidor* year 13 [9 August 1805]

My dear brother

This is the second letter and I do not understand why you are not answering me. If I have displeased you, please be friendly enough to say so in a letter. The lack of news is making me anxious. Answer me as soon as you can because we are about to invade England. I am poor, my brother. At the camp, we do not have enough supplies. Bread costs nine *sous* for a pound. Everything else is lacking and a beer costs ten *sous* a bottle.

My dear brother, I am in such misery and I suffer a lot. It is perhaps my last letter because I can see my grave in front of my eyes. We are at the camp, sleeping on the floor and always cold. We carry our weapons from morning to evening and we often fight. All of that is very hard, my dear brother. I kiss you ten thousand times and I am your brother for life. [. . .][30]

The plan to invade Britain was abandoned in the summer of 1805 when Austria, Russia, Naples and Sweden joined the British in their war against France. The Army of England was reorganised to form the *Grande Armée*, a formidable war machine comprising around 180,000 men. The experience they had accumulated at the camp of Boulogne did not go to waste. After a brilliant campaign, Napoleon crushed the Third Coalition at the battle of Austerlitz and forced his continental enemies to sign the Treaty of Pressburg on 26 December 1805.

## The War in Italy

The victory at Austerlitz left the British once again in a difficult position. Their most powerful continental allies had suffered a crushing blow, leaving Napoleon the supreme power in Europe. On 27 December 1805 the French Emperor turned his attention to the Kingdom of Naples, a minor member of the Third Coalition. King Ferdinand IV of Naples had already fought against the French republic in 1793. After a short-lived peace treaty in 1796, Naples had once more gone to war against the French in 1798. However, the Neapolitan forces were easily crushed, and Ferdinand himself was forced to flee to Sicily; his reign was replaced by the Parthenopean Republic on

---

of the Republic but, on his way to the military depot, tried to flee to avoid military duty. He was eventually caught and sent on 5 *vendémiaire* year XII (28 September 1803) to the 13th Dragoon regiment (light cavalry). He survived the Napoleonic Wars and was sent home on 7 July 1814.

30. AEL: FFP 1044. Toussaint Walthéry to his brother, 9 August 1805.

21 January 1799. In June of the same year Ferdinand, helped by the British, entered the Bay of Naples and reinstated the monarchy. Napoleon was determined to punish this upstart king, and was equally eager to control this part of Italy in pursuit of his vast geopolitical project and deprive the British of an important commercial partner.[31] In February 1806 Joseph Bonaparte, the nominal commander of the French army, and André Massena began the invasion of the Kingdom of Naples. The French swiftly took the capital city and moved towards the two places still in enemy hands: the fortress city of Gaeta and the southern region of Calabria. The French crushed the Neapolitan army at the battle of Campo Tenese on 9 March 1806 and Joseph Bonaparte was made King of Naples by imperial decree on 30 March 1806. However, the French did not manage to pacify the country. In Calabria the army of General Reynier[32] seized most supplies but failed to compensate the population. At the end of March 1806 unhappy peasants began what would later become known as the Calabrian insurrection of 1806–1807.[33]

It is largely forgotten that the British played a significant role during the siege of Gaeta and the following troubles in Calabria. General John Stuart and Admiral Sidney Smith had a British army and the power of the Royal Navy to assist Ferdinand IV from Sicily. The British ships made a fundamental difference to the campaign: they protected Sicily from a French invasion, allowed the British to land in Calabria and resupplied the besieged city of Gaeta. As Joseph Bonaparte said to his brother: '8,000 men on English ships are worth 50,000 because in eight days they can be in eight different places.'[34] The Royal Navy was a significant cause of frustration for the French. General Reynier wrote to Joseph Bonaparte on 21 March 1806 to explain the situation:

> [...] While the Neapolitans were retreating and embarking, the English were busy removing all coastal batteries and every item from castles and public buildings around Reggio, Scylla, etc. When our troops approached, they burned whatever they had been unable to take. The population is hostile to them.

---

31. Nicolas Cadet, 'Violences de guerre et transmission de la mémoire des conflits à travers l'exemple de la campagne de Calabre de 1806–1807', in: *Annales historiques de la Révolution française*, 348 (2007), pp. 147–63.
32. General Jean Reynier (1771–1814), encountered in the first chapter during the Egyptian expedition.
33. Finley Milton, 'Prelude to Spain: The Calabrian insurrection, 1806–1807', in: *Military Affairs*, 40 (1976), pp. 84–7.
34. Joseph Bonaparte, *Mémoires et correspondance politique et militaire du roi Joseph. Tome 2* (Paris, 1854), p. 358.

[...] The English even took all the fishermen's boats. This greatly upsets our soldiers, who, looking at Messina and the strait, are frustrated to be stranded on this side of the shore. They even make bets to see who would be able to swim across and reach the other side. They sometimes forget how tired they are; they are afflicted and all say that they would prefer a winter campaign in Germany to this little campaign in Calabria. They cannot even bear the thought of going back home by the road they took on their way in ...[35]

The siege of Gaeta did not make things easier for the French army. Joseph Bonaparte was forced to divert his men to the fortified city, leaving Reynier with only 9,240 troops. On 12 April the new King of Naples asked his brother for help, telling him that 'the English have for the whole of Sicily seven to eight thousand men but they have several ships and four frigates'.[36] The next month an English fleet led by Sir Sidney Smith captured the island of Capri. Once again, Joseph Bonaparte sent a letter to his brother to explain the situation:

15 May 1806
Sir,
Sidney-Smith moved, with five ships of 74 guns, three frigates and eighteen rowboats equipped with cannon, in front of Capri. He took the city after trying for three days. He was able to disembark in various places that were not defended and came ashore with two thousand men, mostly sailors. Our detachment of 250 men fought well but, having lost their commander and being turned, and without any hope of being rescued, since the island was surrounded by enemy troops, they capitulated. They were transported to the continent with their weapons and belongings. Sidney-Smith took good care of them, offered dinner to the officers, and left two hundred men on the island, which we will take as soon as the weather takes enemy ships away. It seems that the enemy wants to take other islands; these ones have fortified castles. I sent 1,200 men and General Merlin to Ischia; this island is inhabited by 25,000 souls.
    I continue to fortify the coast. [...] We are experiencing setbacks, losses, but we will prevail; I do not disregard anything ...[37]

On 1 July 1806 Major General Stuart landed with 5,200 British soldiers in the Gulf of Sant'Eufemia (Calabria). The British commander had planned a simple but effective campaign, betting on the unpopularity of the French

35. Bonaparte, *Mémoires et correspondance politique*, pp. 157–8.
36. Bonaparte, *Mémoires et correspondance politique*, p. 181.
37. Bonaparte, *Mémoires et correspondance politique*, pp. 233–4.

army. He was perfectly aware that Reynier lacked the manpower to thwart a full-blown revolt and correctly guessed that a British landing in Calabria would fuel the insurrection. General Reynier marched south to meet the British army but managed to assemble only 5,400 men, including nearly 1,000 inexperienced Polish conscripts. On the morning of 4 July the armies met at San Pietro di Maida. The French commander made significant strategic mistakes and handed the victory at Maida to Major General Stuart. Sous Lieutenant Antoine Boussard d'Hauteroche[38] fought in the battle on the French side:

> The French general occupied the high ground of Maida. On 4 [July] he made the mistake of attacking the English with only a single battery of light artillery. They [the British] had hidden several batteries and, once uncovered, they brought chaos into the French ranks and forced us to retreat.[39]

Charles Griois,[40] an artillery officer, was also at the battle of Maida. He was not far from General Reynier when the infantry began to march towards the British:

> Our confidence was such that once we were within only half the range of musket fire from the enemy Colonel Huard, of the 42nd, asked General Reynier if it was not about time to order our men to load their weapons. The general smiled and answered: 'Indeed, unless you want to wait for the English to give the order.' This movement was executed and the charge was ordered on the whole line. The English moved at the same time. [...] The two armies were fifty *toises* from each other while walking and we had barely fired when the whole English line stopped and fired at us. [...] This salvo was so dense that our lines opened up everywhere. A few men, lightly wounded, left their ranks to retreat and caused even more chaos. This retreating movement spread to the 1st light [infantry regiment], and then to the 4th line [infantry regiment]. Soon, everybody followed and only quantities of dead and wounded men, including most of our superior officers, remained behind.

---

38. Antoine Boussard d'Hauteroche was born around 1788. He joined the French army in 1806 and served as a sous-lieutenant in the 21st regiment of line infantry. He later became a major and was awarded the Legion of Honour.
39. Boussard d'Hauteroche, *La vie militaire en Italie sous le Premier Empire*, p. 223.
40. Charles Pierre Lubin Griois was born in Besançon on 21 December 1772. He graduated from the artillery school in 1791 and became a sous-lieutenant. He fought in various campaigns, including in Italy and Russia, and rose to the rank of general under Louis XVIII. He died in Paris on 28 November 1839.

[...] Histories of war might never have seen a battle decided so quickly. Our defeat was complete in fifteen minutes and we had one thousand five hundred men killed or badly wounded.[41]

Paul-Louis Courier,[42] a French artillery officer, described the battle and the behaviour of British soldiers under fire. He also reported what happened after the battle at Maida:

Letter to Sir de Sainte-Croix
Mileto [Calabria], 12 October 1806
Sir,
Since my last letter and your courteous answer, many things of importance have happened here. I am not sure they will be mentioned in your country. Nonetheless, you should not trust these newspapers, Sir, but what I am about to tell you.

[...] The English fought us well and cheaply because I think they did not lose more than fifty men. It was on the fourth of July. We lost a third of our people (about 2,000 men) during the battle of Martini [Maida], including our artillery, baggage, supplies, money and administration, in one word everything that can be lost. The whole of Calabria rose and turned against us with the weapons that we had so carelessly given away. We retreated for thirty days on a sun-baked beach, through flocks of ferocious hillmen, well-armed, good shooters, and the amount of suffering was unimaginable. We lived by the sword, fighting with our muskets for a few puddles of muddy water, seeing our injured and ill men being slaughtered a hundred feet from us, as well as all those who were too tired or too weak to keep up with us. We lacked ammunition and it was easy to predict that we would all be killed by the peasants when we had nothing left with which to push them back ... Finally, there was not a wood or a ravine that I did not cross, often alone.

One day, five horses and four out of the seven men who were following me were killed by hillmen. We have lost, and are still losing, quantities of officers and small detachments. Another time, I went on a boat to avoid such an encounter and forced the owner to leave the shore despite the bad weather. I was carried up the sea and was happy to disembark on the

41. Charles Griois, *Mémoires du general Griois 1792–1822* (Paris, 1909), pp. 310–12.
42. Paul-Louis Courier was born in Paris on 4 January 1772. He fought for the young French Republic from 1792 and was sent to Italy in 1798. He became an artillery officer in the 1st regiment of horse artillery in 1803 and received the Legion of Honour the next year. Courier served in Italy until the end of 1808, left the army the next year and moved to Switzerland. He became a distinguished Hellenist but was murdered by his own servants on 10 April 1825.

coast of Otranto [on the east coast of the Salento peninsula], sixty miles from the place where I was headed. Another time, when I was once again on a boat, I was fired at by an English frigate; she fired a few shots at me. My sailors jumped into the water and reached the coast but I was incapable of doing the same. I was alone, like Ulysses – a good comparison because I was approaching the strait of Charybdis near the little city of Scylla [the strait of Messina, between Sicily and Calabria], where I do not know which God let me land peacefully. [...] The English fight well, even on the ground. Even though they outnumbered us, there is no debate that their calmness and firmness won against our carelessness. They walked towards us, we ran towards them; we charged them without firing. They waited for us to come close and their first volleys shot down entire rows. We were soon routed. They did not pursue us. I did not manage to find out why. Their conduct after the battle was extremely generous. They took more care of our wounded than we did, and they did much to protect us from the peasants' fury. I saw a letter from Sir Stuart[43] to an officer that he was forced to leave behind in a village, his wounds being too serious to allow him to be transported, and there was nothing more honest. We never had such attention for wounded Austrians in Castel [Castelfranco Veneto, Italy], despite counting among their ranks a French general, the Prince of Rohan.[44] This is what I thought after this battle. Most of our officers found their belongings where they had left them. Missing objects had been stolen by our own servants and Neapolitan troops. The English took only the papers. This is not our method. They paid exactly for what they took. In contrast, we took food and money from the locals ... Imagine how much they like us. There is a village in Calabria where young men cannot marry if they have not killed a Frenchman.[45]

The British not only supported the peasant insurrection but also tried to encourage black soldiers serving with the French, who had enrolled during the Saint-Domingue expedition, to desert. To do so, they left stacks of leaflets wherever they disembarked. These texts also threatened Neapolitans working for the French. So unusual were those leaflets that one of them was sent to the French Emperor:

---

43. General Sir John Stuart (1759–1815), a veteran of the American Revolutionary War, led the British troops during the battle of Maida.
44. At the battle of Castelfranco Veneto on 24 November 1805 the Austrians under General-major Prince Louis Victor de Rohan-Guéméné were defeated by the French army.
45. Paul-Louis Courier, *Lettres écrites de France et d'Italie* (Paris, ND), pp. 121–4.

To the soldiers of the black corps

Fraternal greeting.

The French have treated you like dogs and they only brought you here to be slaughtered. Save yourself, there is still time. Leave the French, your tyrants, before they remove your freedom. Remember your unfortunate countrymen, slaughtered in the West Indies.

Remember the brave General Toussaint Louverture, brought to France for treason and left to die in prison for having served for several years.

Come to Gaiete, you will receive plenty to drink and eat without having to do anything for it. When peace comes, you will be free to go home, see your brothers and your friends, and enjoy with your families the government of your great Emperor Dessalines, who managed to triumph and cut into pieces all the French in Hayti [Haiti]; he is the friend of the king of Naples and the English, and the sworn enemy of Bonaparte.

After having given this notice to those poor men taken by force and made to fight against a king who has never hurt them or attempted anything against their country, we must warn those treacherous and perverse Neapolitans who, forgetting the goodness of their legitimate king, fight against loyal troops. If they do not surrender, or abandon the wrong side that they have embraced to follow the right cause, there will be no pity and those captured will hang in repentance for their crimes and to satisfy public vengeance.[46]

As Major General Stuart expected, the British victory at Maida inflamed the whole region of Calabria. The insurrection quickly spread north, threatening the capital city of Naples. Peasants and bandits adopted guerrilla tactics and harassed enemy troops in a form of warfare that would be seen again in the Peninsular War. However, the British commander did not pursue his advantage. Instead of pressing General Reynier and his men, Major General Stuart stayed in Maida for days before turning south. The British wanted to prevent the invasion of Sicily but had no intention of moving in the direction of Naples. Stuart was probably right to be cautious. The capitulation of Gaeta on 18 July 1806 allowed Marshal Masséna to march south with an army 15,000 men strong. The British, realising how dangerous their position would soon become, evacuated Calabria altogether in August and retreated to

---

46. Bonaparte, *Mémoires et correspondance politique*, pp. 272–3. Napoleon later blamed his brother for using black troops during the siege of Gaeta. See the letter of Napoleon written on 13 June 1806 in: Bonaparte, *Mémoires et correspondence politique*, p. 294.

Sicily. Masséna and Reynier joined forces on 11 August to reconquer the region. Paul-Louis Courier took part in this operation, which he described in a letter to a friend:

To M***, artillery officer, Naples
Mileto, 16 October 1806

[...] After having destroyed, without much reason, the pretty town of Corigliano [Calabria], we walked towards Cassano [Cassano all'Ionio, Calabria]. [...] The Swiss battalion, quite dirty like the rest of us, was walking at the front and was commanded by Muller, Cavel having been killed at Sainte-Euphémie [eastern France]. The people of Cassano, seeing troops in red uniforms, mistook us for English soldiers. This happened a lot. They come out, approach us, kiss us and congratulate us for having corrected those French rascals, those thieves, those excommunicated. They talked to us without flattery. They told us about French stupidity and said things that we did not deserve. Everybody cursed the soldiers of *maestro Peppe* [King Joseph], everybody bragged about killing one [French soldier]. Using gestures, they said: *I stabbed six; I shot ten.* One told us that he had killed Verdier; another said he had killed me. It was really bizarre. Portier, a lieutenant, I do not know if you are acquainted with him, saw his own pistols that he had lent me in the hands of one of them. It had been stolen when I was robbed. He jumped on them and said: *To whom do those pistols belong?* The other, you know how they talk, said: *Sir, they belong to you.* He did not suspect how correct he was. *But from whom did you take them? – From a French officer that I killed.* It looks like they thought Verdier and I dead and had completely forgotten about us.

You can see how they dealt with their business. They told us all their secrets and only recognised us when we opened fire on them at short range. We killed many of them. We captured fifty-two, and in the evening we executed them in Cassano's main square.

[...] Our adventure in Marcellinara [Calabria] was of the same spirit. We were mistaken for English soldiers and, as such, welcomed into the city. Once there, the crowd surrounded us. A man who had hosted Reynier recognised him and tried to flee. Reynier ordered him stopped; we killed him. The troop fired at once; the main square was filled with dead people in less than two minutes. We found there six gunners of our regiment in a cell, half-dead of starvation and entirely naked. They had been kept to be burned the next day ...[47]

47. Courier, *Lettres écrites de France et d'Italie*, pp. 124–6.

Irregular fighters were no match for French soldiers in set-piece battles but guerrilla warfare was a serious problem. Taking refuge in mountain shelters and remote locations, partisans harassed French troops and disrupted communications. As always in such circumstances, atrocities were committed on both sides. In November 1806 Joseph Bonaparte wrote to his brother Lucien Bonaparte to complain about the guerrillas and the role played by the British:

Naples, 24 November 1806

[...] We are still fighting a *chouan* war.[48] The English have again sent a few thousand bandits, who will be soon destroyed, but who increasingly exhaust my men and bring harm to the people of this country; they pillage, steal, kill and run ...[49]

The brutality was so extreme that rumours of cannibalism surfaced. French prisoners were regularly executed, as this letter by Colonel Lebrun shows:

My lord, I am in Cosenza and I do not know for how long.

On the 25th of this month, a convoy of fourteen mules, a few bakers and employees, escorted by eight soldiers, was attacked in the village of Soveria, near Scigliano. Ten men were killed, including five soldiers.

Yesterday, 26, a detachment of two hundred men, including twenty-five *chasseurs* of the 9th, was attacked and routed after having lost thirty men, including an officer, near the same place. This detachment retreated up to here and this is what the officers told me:

The cavalry was in the vanguard in the defile when hidden peasants were spotted. The infantry commander was just warned when those bandits started firing at the column. They fired back and killed a few but the Polish, about sixty of them, who were at the end of the column, fled. The rest, not strong enough and about to be turned, were forced to flee too, leaving on the battlefield thirty dead and wounded, who were killed by the bandits.

Considering their position, their movements and the orders that were heard, we must assume that they were led by officers. French was heard. Witnesses say that there were at least seven to eight hundred men ...[50]

At the end of December 1806 the insurrection was still raging in Calabria. Marshal Masséna was recalled by Joseph for other duties but General Reynier was left behind to pacify the region. The French commander turned his

---

48. A reference to the *Chouannerie*, the French royalist revolt during the Revolutionary Wars.
49. Jacques Rambaud, *Lettres inédites ou éparses de Joseph Bonaparte à Naples (1806–1808)* (Paris, 1911), p. 108.
50. Bonaparte, *Mémoires et correspondance politique*, pp. 160–1.

attention to the most significant enemy stronghold: the city of Amantea. After months under siege, the castle was finally surrendered by its defenders in February 1807. The fall of Amantea marked the end of the insurrection. Bandits and irregular troops sporadically attacked French soldiers afterwards but General Reynier, using local soldiers, was able to secure the region.

If the British failed to protect the south of Italy, they managed to save Sicily. The island served as a home for Ferdinand IV and became a major source of frustration for the French. When Joachim Murat was given the crown of Naples in 1808, he tried on several occasions to invade Sicily but repeatedly failed. The flamboyant new King of Naples was more successful in retaking the island of Capri, which had been lost to the British in May 1806. Interestingly, the island was defended by Lieutenant Colonel Hudson Lowe, the future governor of Saint Helena during Napoleon's final exile. The recapture of Capri was described by a French officer, Jean-Baptiste Duret de Tavel,[51] who took part in the attack in October 1808:

The island of Capri [...] is a rock located near the Gulf of Naples. The English used it to intercept all sea communications and to send their ships close to the capital. Twice under the reign of Joseph we tried to recapture this little Gibraltar (as the English name it). This task was of the greatest difficulty and Murat just managed to do it by one of those audacious raids that define his luck and great valour ... Our soldiers arrived at the bottom of the island in broad daylight on small boats and only managed to progress by climbing peaks of 80 to 150 feet under heavy fire. Guns of 12 and 14 were also brought up after extraordinary efforts. These guns were carried to the highest peak of the island, 700 *toises* high, to assault the main fort. Divisional General Lamarque,[52] commander of this beautiful expedition, was determined to succeed or perish in the attempt, and ordered all the small boats to be removed as soon as our 1,500 men were disembarked. A few days later an English squadron circled the island and our troops became both besiegers and besieged. Soon, the lack of supplies and ammunition put the French in a critical situation, almost forcing them to surrender. But luckily a strong wind drove away the English and our ships managed to resupply our troops. Finally, after 13 days of hard work, the English were driven out of all the forts and were forced to evacuate the island.[53]

---

51. Jean-Baptiste Duret de Tavel was born in Villeneuve-les-Avignon on 7 September 1770. He fought during the Napoleonic Wars and rose to the rank of lieutenant colonel. He died in 1861.
52. Jean Maximilien Lamarque, born in 1770, was a general who served during the Revolutionary Wars and in various Napoleonic campaigns. He died in 1832.
53. Duret de Tavel, *Séjour d'un officier français en Calabre* (Paris, 1820), p. 184.

The campaign in Calabria taught valuable lessons to both sides. The British witnessed the power of guerrilla warfare and demonstrated, once again, that the Royal Navy could probe and weaken remote parts of the Napoleonic empire. The British also learned the value of carefully planned landings, such as the one performed by Stuart, and of prudent retreats. Wellington would later hold dear these principles. The French saw that irregular troops supported by foreign resources and troops were capable of disrupting a whole country. General Reynier, very much like his predecessors who fought French royalists during the Revolutionary Wars, answered the challenges posed by the guerrillas with brutality. Combining violence against civilian populations with a judicious use of local troops, he successfully managed to tame the south of Italy. Calabria, however, was just a prelude. Soon, both the French and the British would meet in a deadly campaign on a much bigger scale in the Iberian Peninsula.

*Chapter 4*

# Portugal and Spain

## The First Invasion of Portugal

After the collapse of the Amiens Treaty in 1803 France was again at war with Britain. As we saw in the previous chapter, Napoleon came to realise that a military invasion of Britain was unrealistic as long as France remained unable to match the Royal Navy. The power of Britain at sea was a constant problem, but one that sometimes brought rather amusing stories. A Prussian officer named von Brandt[1] was with the Emperor in Biarritz at the end of 1807. Fearing the Royal Navy, the Imperial Guard followed Napoleon into the water when the Emperor decided to swim:

> The Emperor swam in the sea near this beach. I was told that every time he went to the sea with an aquatic escort to prevent any English surprise. While Napoleon was swimming, a squadron of cavalry of the guard was going as far as possible in the sea.[2]

At the end of 1806 the French Emperor decided to use another method to weaken and eventually defeat his most persistent enemy: economic warfare. Britain relied heavily on European trade and traded with several European states. The concept of economic warfare was not new; the young French Republic had already banned commerce with Britain in 1793.[3] However, Napoleon's plan was more ambitious. On 21 November 1806 he issued a decree to start the so-called Continental System (or *Blocus continental* in French). All European countries were to stop trading with Britain and all commercial ships headed for the continent had to be inspected first in a French port. Not all the European nations were willing to follow the Continental System. Portugal, a traditional ally of Britain, relied heavily on trade and would have been ruined by the blockade. Unsurprisingly, the Portuguese chose to defy Napoleon. In July 1807 France signed the Peace of

---

1. General von Brandt served in a Polish regiment of the French army from 1808 to 1813. He later served in the Prussian army.
2. Alfred-Auguste Ernouf, *Souvenirs d'un officier polonais, Scènes de la vie militaire en Espagne et en Russie* (Paris, 1877), p. 11.
3. Jean Tulard, *Dictionnaire Napoléon* (Paris, 1999), pp. 231–52.

Tilsit with Russia and Prussia, ending the Fourth Coalition. With peace in the east, Napoleon was now free to take care of Portugal. On 2 August 1807 the 1st Corps of the Gironde Army was created by Imperial decree. Jean-Andoche Junot,[4] a veteran of the Revolutionary Wars, led the invasion of Portugal. Nobody realised then that this new war would drag on for years and claim the lives of thousands of soldiers and civilians. To reach Portugal, the French army needed to cross Spain. This country had been allied with France since 1795 and had even fought with the French at the battle of Trafalgar. With the blessing of the Spanish government, General Junot crossed the border on 17 September 1807. His army reached Salamanca and entered Portugal without encountering much resistance. On 30 November the French took Lisbon without a fight. The day before, the regent Jean VI of Portugal had left the country for Brazil, taking with him some 15,000 high-ranking officials. Safely in America, he declared war on France.

At first, the occupation of Portugal was relatively peaceful. Two French soldiers writing to their families described the beginning of the campaign. Nicolas-Joseph Dejardin,[5] of the 58th line infantry regiment, described this dangerous and exciting country to his father:

Peniche [in the Estremadura Province] Portugal this 18 April 1808

My very dear father

I am pleased to let you know that I am still well, thank God, and I hope that you are well too. This is the third time that I have written but I have yet to receive a reply. I am in a far-away country and have had a hard time on the road. We went through Spain before reaching Portugal. We saw no peasants and their houses were empty. They had all fled and left everything behind. We were left without food and were forced to cross many rivers during the worst season. We slept in the countryside and in the woods and were forced to band together to find food near the camp. Misery and peasants killed many of us on the roads. Once in Lisbon, we received supplies but we did not stay for long and were given once again only half of what we were due. We go for days without bread. I will also tell you that this country is very warm and it is as hot as in August back home. During Christmas and New Year we went swimming in the sea

---

4. Jean-Andoche Junot, born on 24 September 1771, volunteered during the Revolutionary Wars. He became Bonaparte's secretary during the siege of Toulon. He was made a general in Egypt and later fought at Austerlitz. Wounded several times and mentally unstable, he died in 1813.
5. Nicolas-Joseph Dejardin, born in Jupille (Liège) on 2 February 1787, was conscripted into the 58th line infantry regiment on 7 February 1808. He deserted on 30 April 1814.

and we found oranges and figs. Laurel is as common as spikes and olive trees and vines are very common as well.[6]

François-Joseph Bourguignon[7] wrote a similar letter to his parents. Ships of the Royal Navy were his first sight of the British during the campaign:

Written in Faros [the southernmost city of Portugal], 14 May 1808

My very dear father and mother
I write these words to give you news and at the same time to hear from you. I wrote on 14 December but have not heard a word. Perhaps you have not received my letter but I hope that this one will reach you and that you will write as soon as possible because time is passing by slowly. I will tell you, father, that we have been miserable. I was sick, with a fever, and was sent to a hospital in Toulouse where I remained for six weeks but, thank God, I am now well. We ran across Spain and Portugal. Towards the end of the campaign we endured much misery and had to sleep outside. Sometimes we walked for two days without seeing a house and we are in a country covered with mountains and forests. In this country everything is expensive, except fish. Bread is really expensive and we receive a bottle of wine per day. Nothing new for the moment. We are close to the sea. We see the English at sea on a daily basis ...[8]

The French soldiers were not given the opportunity to rest for long. On 1 February 1808 the Regency Council of Portugal and the Portuguese army were disbanded to prevent more agitation. In June of the same year the Portuguese population, inspired by anti-French incidents in Spain, rebelled against the occupiers. But Portugal alone did not have the means to resist Napoleon and his army. The newly formed rebel Junta sent a delegation to London to beg for assistance. A British expeditionary corps, initially destined for Coruna, was redirected to Portugal after having heard of the Spanish defeat at the battle of Medina del Rioseco on 14 July 1808. In August a 5,000-strong British force led by Sir Arthur Wellesley and Sir John Moore landed at Mondego Bay.[9] The British also brought weapons and money to support the Portuguese rebellion. With the landing completed, Wellesley headed for Leiria and from there moved on towards Lisbon. A first battle was fought near the village of Roliça on 17 August 1808, when Wellesley

---

6. AEL FFP: 1042. Nicolas-Joseph Dejardin to his father, 18 April 1808.
7. François-Joseph Bourguignon, born in Landenne (Liège) on 1 September 1786, was conscripted into the 26th line infantry regiment. He died of fever at Navalmoral (Spain) on 31 August 1811.
8. AEL FFP: 1042. François-Joseph Bourgignon to his parents, 14 May 1808.
9. Antoine d'Arjuzon, *Wellington* (Paris, 1999), p. 103.

encountered General Henri Delaborde,[10] a veteran of the Revolutionary Wars. The French, largely outnumbered, lost the battle of Roliça but managed to retreat in good order. Delaborde's courageous stand was considered a moral victory by the French, who conveniently forgot that Wellesley had no cavalry unit to pursue the retreating army. The British success inspired the Portuguese population. In several places Portuguese men gathered and screamed at the occupiers, 'Down with the French! Death to the French!'[11] Four days later Wellesley, now reinforced and supported by 2,000 Portuguese soldiers, fought against Junot at the battle of Vimeiro. The French attempted to engage Wellesley's left flank but the British commander managed to redeploy his army. Junot sent dense columns towards the enemy to engage in hand-to-hand combat but this exposed his men to devastating suppressive fire. Panic followed and infantrymen from Charlot's brigade ran away. The retreating men obliged the French artillery to hold its fire, as Captain Jacques-Louis Hulot[12] explained:

> Soon, an English column moved towards our battery. I was loading canister shots when a group of retreating soldiers hid the enemy, who was much closer than the rest of the French army. [...] We tried to halt the retreat. I backed up to occupy and guard the access to a neighbouring village, where I brought my guns. We were disorganised more than once by streams of retreating men. However, none of my men, except the wounded, thought of abandoning us or leaving the battery. If we had been supported by even a single infantry battalion, we would have held the village and would have saved enough time for our regiments and divisions to rally.[13]

Junot ordered his grenadiers to move forwards to rescue the situation. The village of Vimeiro was taken by the French but was soon recaptured by the British. Colonel Taylor, leading the 20th Light Dragoons, charged some of the routed French infantry units but was too enthusiastic and when the British regiment was counter-charged by French horsemen, Colonel Taylor and

---

10. Henri Delaborde was born on 21 December 1764. He served as a private soldier before 1789. During the Revolutionary Wars, he was made a general. He served during the Peninsular War and in Russia. He retired after the Hundred Days and died on 3 February 1833.
11. C. Jeannin, *Le Général Travot, pacificateur de la Vendée* (Paris, 1862), p. 20.
12. Jacques-Louis Hulot, born on 22 April 1773, joined the Revolutionary army and fought at the battle of Valmy on 20 September 1792. He became an artillery officer in 1794 and was promoted to the rank of captain in 1803. He fought at the battle of Austerlitz and in Spain. He died on 3 May 1843.
13. Jacques-Louis Hulot, *Souvenirs militaires du baron Hulot, général d'artillerie, 1773–1843* (Paris, 1886), p. 235.

several of his men were killed during the action. In the end, however, British volleys, discipline and numerical superiority led to Wellesley's victory. Junot was forced to negotiate a surrender but was blessed by the timely arrival of Generals Harry Burrard and Hew Dalrymple. Dalrymple, a veteran of the Revolutionary Wars, had been appointed commander of the expedition by London and, as a result, superseded Wellesley. Dalrymple and Burrard had no desire to chase the French or cut off their retreat. Ignoring Wellesley's protests, both sides signed the Convention of Cintra on 30 August 1808. Dalrymple even agreed to transport the French army, including its equipment and stolen Portuguese goods, to Rochefort aboard Royal Navy ships. In other words, the British saved 21,000 French soldiers from captivity. This embarrassing convention, unsurprisingly denounced in London, led to an official inquiry. Wellesley, Burrard and Dalrymple were all cleared, but only the future Duke of Wellington returned to active duty.

Despite this major setback, Napoleon had no intention of leaving Portugal alone. A new expedition was promptly organised. Lambert Berlandeux,[14] a soldier serving in the 9th Dragoons, was among the French who departed for this second Portuguese campaign. He wrote a letter to his parents:

Niort [western France], 17 December 1808

My dear father and mother,

I hope that you are in good health. I am still well, thank God, but your silence surprises me. This is the third letter written without receiving an answer. I do not know if you are negligent or if my letters are failing to arrive.

I will tell you that I am full of vermin and I was forced to borrow 15 francs from my friends to buy shirts and pants. I need 24 francs and would ask you to send money to repay my debts. The rest will be used during the Portuguese campaign. Answer very quickly and send money very quickly as we are about to leave [...][15]

## The War Spreads to Spain

As mentioned before, Spain and France had been allies since 1795 and had fought together at the battle of Trafalgar. However, the ruling class of Spain was divided between Francophile elements and those who feared and disliked Napoleon. The country was also facing internal conflicts. For example, Manuel Godoy, the Prime Minister of Spain, was a favourite of King

---

14. Lambert Berlandeux, born in Liège on 9 March 1787, was conscripted into the 9th dragoons on 7 March 1807. He survived the Napoleonic Wars and went home in 1813.
15. AEL FFP: 1045. Lambert Berlandeux to his parents, 17 December 1808.

Charles IV but was at odds with the heir to the Spanish throne. Such an unstable situation was an invitation for Napoleon to intervene. Using the invasion of Portugal as a pretext, the French Emperor sent troops to Spain.[16] The
presence of French armies was resented by the Spanish. Captain François,
already encountered in the previous chapters, wrote in his diary on 13 January
1808:

> We noticed that the presence of French soldiers displeased them [the
> Spanish] greatly. They even told us so but, despite not liking us, [they]
> treated us quite well, if we except a few assassins.[17]

In March 1808 Charles IV and his son Ferdinand were brought to France to
settle the conflict between them. In fact, the French Emperor detained
Charles and forced him to abdicate. Captain François, still in Spain, realised
that the situation was deteriorating as the French became increasingly un-
popular. On 17 March he wrote:

> Officers of the division's regiments told us that soldiers from the rear
> columns had been murdered, that a group of men had been attacked and
> that we should expect a general uprising in Spain.[18]

Hubert-Joseph Remouchamps,[19] serving in the 105th line infantry regiment,
also complained about Spain and the Spanish people in a letter to his parents:

> Madré [Madrid], 31 March 1808
> My dear father and mother,
> I write this letter to enquire about your health. I am quite well, thank
> God. I hope that the present letter will find you in good health as well.
> Many regards to my family and friends and to those who think about me.
> This country is really bad and those who venture too far away from the
> camp are murdered by the Spanish. [...] My dear father, I ask you to send
> money and it will make me very happy. I need it badly. Since 1 February,
> when we arrived in Spain, we have not been paid. The money that you
> sent me, I did not receive.[20]

At the beginning of May 1808 Marshal Joachim Murat, commanding the
French troops in Spain, sent the youngest son of Charles IV to France. This

---

16. Tulard, *Dictionnaire Napoléon*, pp. 737–9.
17. François, *Journal du capitaine François*, p. 549.
18. François, *Journal du capitaine François*, p. 550.
19. Hubert-Joseph Remouchamps, born in Nandrin on 26 June 1787, was conscripted into the
    105th line infantry regiment on 18 July 1807. He was sent to the 6th foot artillery regiment
    on 6 June 1813.
20. AEL FFP: 1043. Hubert-Joseph Remouchamps to his parents, 31 March 1808.

act, perceived as another French act of provocation, triggered a rebellion in Madrid. Known as the *Dos de Mayo* (the second of May), this day saw citizens rise against the French and kill about 150 of their soldiers. Charles François fought for his life in the streets of Madrid on 2 May:

> In the street, stones, roof tiles, bricks, tables, etc., were thrown at us from the houses. They also fired at us from the windows, the basements, etc. Some said that this revolt cost us 500 men, killed or wounded. I believe that this figure is inferior to the truth. My company lost seven men. Most of those killed or wounded were hit by stones or bricks in the streets. On the Spanish side, it is not possible to know how many people have been killed, shot or wounded but we talked about 5,000 men, more or less.[21]

Murat sent reinforcements to crush the rebels, but also ordered the execution of hundreds of people the next day. The French soldiers were convinced that the rebellion had been inspired by British spies, a suspicion fuelled by Murat's proclamation to the city of Madrid and to the army:

> 3 May 1808
>
> Brave Spaniards! Soldiers!
> The population of Madrid has rebelled and committed murder.
>   I know that many good Spaniards have complained about the lack of order. I am far from mistaking them with those miserable individuals who only seek profit and pillage. However, French blood has been spilt. It begs for revenge. As a result, I ordered the following:
> One: Divisional General Grouchy, commander of the army, will gather a military commission tonight.
> Two: Those arrested with a weapon will be shot.
> [...]
> Seven: Those who write, distribute or sell printed leaflets or manuscripts calling for sedition will be seen as agents of England and shot.[22]

Britain was once again seen as a disruptive shadow working against peace on the continent. The French, however, underestimated the threat posed by the Spanish population. Instead of dying down, the uprisings spread to the rest of the country. Independent rebellions rose both in the south and in the north, forcing the French to dispatch troops. Gaining the upper hand after weeks of fighting, the French crowned Napoleon's brother Joseph in Madrid on 25 July 1808. But what should have been a French triumph was in fact the beginning of a painful retreat. Just days before Joseph seized the crown of Spain, a

---

21. François, *Journal du capitaine François*, p. 561.
22. François, *Journal du capitaine François*, pp. 561–2.

French army suffered a humiliating defeat in the south of the country. Indeed, General Pierre Dupont had surrendered nearly 22,000 men to a Spanish army led by General Castanos at the battle of Bailen. His men were sent to prison-hulks in the Bay of Cadiz and from there to the island of Cabrera, where many died of starvation. For the first time in years Napoleon's men had been defeated on the battlefield. This crushing blow forced the French to evacuate Madrid on 1 August 1808. Worse, the battles of Bailen and Vimeiro, noted in the previous section, inspired the enemies of France in Austria, Prussia and elsewhere in Europe. This French defeat was largely responsible for the creation of the Fifth Coalition. The French soldiers themselves were shocked by this setback. Hubert-Joseph Dantinne,[23] who died just days after writing the following letter, explained the situation to his parents:

> Miranda, 29 August 1808
>
> [...] We had to retreat from the city because, as you know, all the farmers of Spain have rebelled and fought against us. We chased them up to Valencia but we had to retreat and ended twenty leagues from the French border. We are here for the moment but do not know if we are going back to France or are headed towards Madrid.[24]

The first phase of the Peninsular War was over but the French were determined to fight back. Napoleon knew how dangerous the situation was and how badly it reflected on his prestige. At the end of 1808 he came to Spain in person with 200,000 experienced soldiers drawn from the Armies of Italy and Germany. On 6 November 1808 he reached Vitoria, and the balance began to tip in his favour once more.[25] A soldier named Sérignat wrote about the chaos in the country and diplomacy in general. His letter shows that French soldiers understood very little about the international situation:

> My very dear father,
>
> [...] They told me that on 2 May there was a revolution between the bourgeois and the soldiers, and the troops were not in great numbers. They were forced to flee and they killed those who were at the hospital. [...] I heard that the Emperor of Germany was thinking about peace, but it is not decided yet since our Emperor wants him to be only King of

---

23. Hubert-Joseph Dantinne was born in Ville-en-Hesbaye. He served in the 115th line infantry regiment and died of disease in Spain at the end of August 1808.
24. Emile Fairon and Henry Heuse, *Lettres de grognards* (Liège, 1936), p. 169. A very similar letter, written by a friend of Dantinne, was published in our previous book *Fighting for Napoleon*. One man probably wrote both letters at the same time, a common practice in the French army.
25. Tulard, *Dictionnaire Napoléon*, pp. 739–49.

Bohemia and Hungary. Prince Murat has replaced King Joseph, who is now King of Spain, and is going to Naples and Prince Murat will be King of Austria and Beauharnais, who was Vice-Roy of Italy, is now King. The Emperor gave him the crown to take the Spanish one and he wants to whip the Spanish with iron sticks, meaning bayonets, because they do not want to recognise his brother as King. He wants to treat them harshly ...[26]

On 4 December 1808 Madrid was recaptured by the French Emperor. So far, the French and the British had fought only on Portuguese territory. A bulletin aimed at the French army in Spain said that the Emperor was impatient to crush the British:

4th Bulletin
Burgos, 15 November 1808

[...] We walked another six leagues but no Englishmen, only promises.

It seems that one of their divisions landed at the Coruna and another entered Badajoz at the beginning of the month. The day we find them will be a day of celebration for the French army. May they stain this continent with their blood, this continent that they destroy with their intrigues, their monopoly and their incurable selfishness!

May they send 80,000 or even 100,000 men instead of 20,000 men so English mothers can learn how painful war is and so their government stops playing with the blood and the lives of the continent's people.

The Machiavellian English spread absurd lies and use the vilest tricks to confuse the Spanish nation.[27]

In the next bulletin, published after the French successes at Burgos and Espinosa, the writer even accused irregular fighters of being equipped by the British:

Terror is in the soul of the Spanish soldier. He throws away his red coat, his English musket, and tries to disguise himself as a peasant.[28]

Sir John Moore, who had been in Portugal with 30,000 men since October, now moved from Lisbon towards Salamanca to threaten the rear of the French army but cautiously left for Galicia when he heard that Napoleon was manoeuvring to face him. For the British, a long and difficult retreat through a hostile environment now began. The French Emperor, unable to confront

---

26. Croyet, *Paroles de grognards*, pp. 268–9.
27. *Quatrième Bulletin de l'armée d'Espagne*, November 1808.
28. *Cinquième Bulletin de l'armée d'Espagne*, November 1808.

Moore, returned to Valladolid. From there, he left the country with some of his troops to lead the war in Austria. He would never come back to Spain, a country that he disliked. Napoleon's intervention in Spain had reassured the French, many of whom had been destabilised by the defeat at Bailen. In a letter to his brother, Commander Alexandre Coudreux clearly expressed his confidence in the future of Spain, realising nonetheless that a lot of work was still needed to pacify the country:

> 21 December 1808: Regarding Spain, I heard that things worked for us. It seems nonetheless that our soldiers still have a lot to do. Up to now, it does not seem that the English want to try their luck against us.[29]

After the Emperor's departure, his brother King Joseph became the nominal commander in Spain. Not trusting Joseph's military abilities, the French Emperor regularly sent him written instructions. Marshal Soult was ordered to pursue and destroy Sir John Moore's army. Moore and his men were disorganised, dangerously scattered and still fifty miles from Corunna, where they were to board ships of the Royal Navy. Antoine Jomini,[30] a Swiss colonel in the French army, saw the trail left by the retreating British army:

> I will not say much about this pursuit, which offered nothing but the pitiful picture of a few destroyed villages filled with dying or drunk men. Forced to steal to live, soldiers had become looters, finding almost exclusively wine and turning to debauchery. The road was filled with starved horses which, in this rocky landscape, had not found any food. Their owners, unable to drag them and unwilling to abandon them to the French, had killed them.[31]

The British were nonetheless dangerous. On 3 January 1809 Auguste Colbert, one of the most talented French generals in Spain, was killed in action. Antoine Jomini explained:

> The English passed Ponteferrada but had lost many horses and men. Tailed by Soult and stuck on difficult roads near Doncos, they left behind a rear-guard at Villafranca. Two battalions of Scottish soldiers

---

29. Alexandre Coudreux, *Lettres du commandant Coudreux à son frère, 1804–1815* (Paris, 1908), p. 141.
30. Antoine-Henri Jomini was born in Payerne (Switzerland) on 6 March 1779. Serving under the orders of Ney at the beginning of 1809, he became famous for his books about the art of war. Jomini rose to the rank of general but later fought against Napoleon. He died on 24 March 1869.
31. Antoine Jomini, *Guerre d'Espagne: extrait des souvenirs inédits du général Jomini* (Paris, 1892), p. 52.

Napoleon Bonaparte during the siege of Toulon.

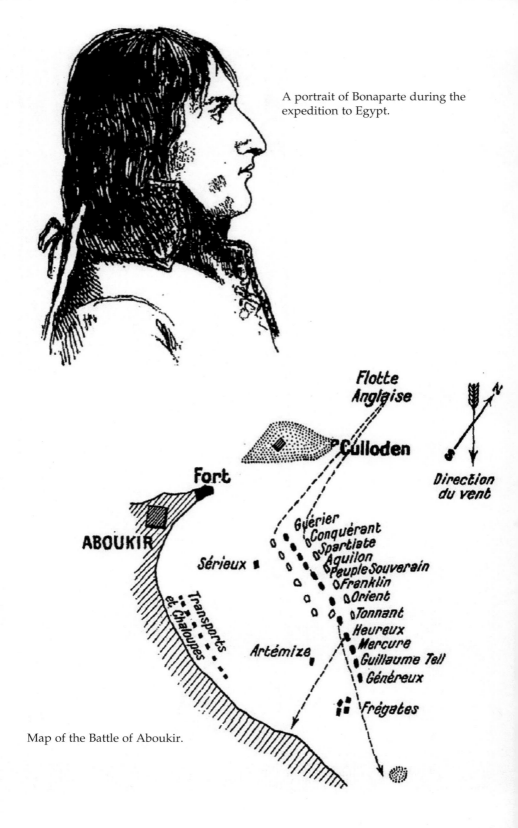

A portrait of Bonaparte during the expedition to Egypt.

Flotte Anglaise

Culloden

Direction du vent

N

Fort

ABOUKIR

Sérieux

Transports et Chaloupes

Artémize

Guérier
Conquérant
Spartiate
Aguilon
Peuple Souverain
Franklin
Orient
Tonnant
Heureux
Mercure
Guillaume Tell
Généreux
Frégates

Map of the Battle of Aboukir.

General Menou.

e British at the Battle of Talavera.

Joseph Bonaparte as King of Naples.

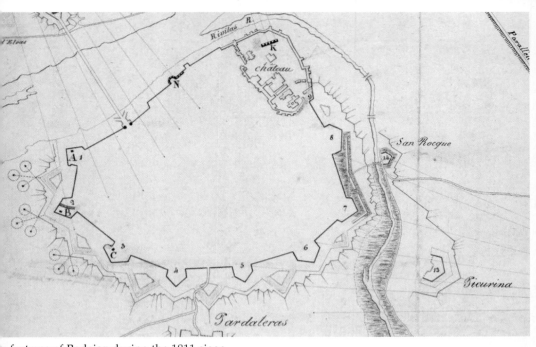

e fortress of Badajoz during the 1811 siege.

poleon on the island of Elba.

Quatre-Bras in 1816.

Napoleon at the Battle of Waterloo.

(*Right*) Assassination attempt on Wellington by a French veteran in 1818.

(*Below, left*) Cantillon, one of the men tried for the assassination attempt on Wellington.

(*Below, right*) Marinet, a co-conspirator in the assassination attempt.

CANTILLON

MARINET

Anonymous (after David) the French painter refusing to paint Wellington

were very advantageously positioned in nearby vineyards and gardens. Colbert's brigade was at the front of Soult's column. Either too brave, as it has been said, or motivated by other purposes, he went ahead to recognise or engage this infantry, so well-positioned. He was fatally hit in the head and the young Latour and Maubourg,[32] his aides-de-camp, were badly wounded.[33]

In fact, General Colbert was killed not by Scottish soldiers but by a sharpshooter of the 95th Rifles. Thomas Plunket, from Newtown (Ireland), shot Colbert in the head at the impressive range of 600 metres. On 6 January 1809 the British engaged in a skirmish at Lugo but managed to slip away. Moore finally reached Corunna on 11 January 1809, only to find that the Royal Navy had been delayed. Fortunately, supplies, including muskets, cartridges and food, were waiting for the British. Parts of the French army began to arrive the following day and prepared for the assault. On 14 January British transport ships finally reached Corunna but Moore was dangerously threatened by the enemy and faced annihilation. The French attacked the heights of the city on 15 January before launching a final assault the next day. The British fought while embarking. This episode, known as the battle of Corunna, saved the British army but cost Sir John Moore his life. Very badly wounded by a cannon shot during the battle, he died a few hours later. Dieudonné Rigau,[34] a cavalry colonel, fought at the battle of Corunna on 16 January 1809 and witnessed the departure of the British army:

The battle of Corunna took place on 16 November.[35] The English position was formidable. The French, led by Soult, attacked at two in the afternoon. The battle was difficult and lasted until the night. The commander of the British army, General Moor, died on the battlefield with 5,000 of his men;[36] General Baird[37] lost an arm, and command was given to General Hope, who used the night to sneak away with the remnants of his army in Corunna. To accelerate the surrender of the city, Marshal Soult ordered a battery to be placed on a hill overlooking the city. At

32. In fact, he was probably talking about one man, Alfred Latour-Maubourg, who died the following day.
33. Jomini, *Guerre d'Espagne*, p. 51.
34. Dieudonné Rigau, born in Maastricht in 1789, joined the 25th Dragoon regiment in 1805. He served in Germany, Spain, Portugal, Russia and finally as a colonel during the battle of Waterloo. He survived the Napoleonic Wars and died in Neuilly on 23 March 1848.
35. Rigau was obviously mistaken about the date.
36. In fact, about 1,000 men were lost, either killed, wounded or captured.
37. General David Baird, born on 6 December 1757, was indeed wounded at the battle of Corunna.

dawn, it fired at the quays, where English soldiers were sitting, waiting their turn to embark. This artillery fire must have made their life difficult. All the shots were successful and it is easy to imagine the desperation, the screams of the wounded, the noise of confusion and chaos brought by this imposing and sad show. The English army left the port and the French army captured the city.[38]

Both sides regarded the battle of Corunna as a victory. The British managed to contain the French army long enough to embark, while the French saw Moore's death and the enemy's departure as a success. An interesting episode, illustrating the lack of hostility between enemy officers, happened at the end of the battle of Corunna. This anecdote was told by Lieutenant Octave Levavasseur,[39] Marshal Ney's aide-de-camp:

> We soon entered Corunna. One day, the Marquise of Belesta told me that during the boarding of General Moore's army, she welcomed and hid two English officers. She asked me to help them if possible. I promised to do my best and asked to see her protégés. These officers came, one night, to her place and I saw them but did not try to talk. Soon after, an English ship came close to the port to negotiate. Ney sent me to welcome her. This ship belonged to a French officer who had lost a leg in Lisbon. I ran back to the Marshal to explain the situation and he gave me instructions. When I returned to the port, I visited the Marquise of Belesta and ordered the two English officers to follow me. They boarded the ship with me. They were the sons of two Members of Parliament.[40]

## Invading Portugal Again

Having temporarily dealt with the British in Spain, Soult turned his attention towards Portugal. Leaving Ney in charge of Galicia, Soult launched an offensive with 40,000 men and on 6 March 1809 he crushed General La Romana before winning another brilliant victory against the Portuguese at the battle of Porto on 29 March. This success allowed the French to secure large stocks

---

38. Dieudonné Rigau, *Souvenirs des guerres de l'empire: réflexions, pensées, maximes, anecdotes, lettres diverses, testament philosophique; suivis d'une notice sur le général Rigau* (Paris, 1846), pp. 33–4.
39. Octave Levavasseur, born in Breteuil on 20 September 1781, fought as a lieutenant in the artillery from 28 November 1803. He was transferred to Ney's headquarters in 1807 and went the next year to Spain. At the end of 1809 he returned to civilian life but asked to return to the army in 1813. He was promoted to captain and battalion chief in 1814. He followed Ney and in 1815 he fought at Waterloo. Levavasseur continued to serve in the French army after the fall of Napoleon and died on 14 March 1866.
40. Octave Levavasseur, *Souvenirs du général Levavasseur* (Paris, 1908), pp. 167–8.

of food and ammunition, as well as a key region of the country. As before, however, Portuguese civilians proved difficult to control. For example, General Jardon was going through a village on 25 March 1809 when he was attacked by an old man. His secretary explained the circumstances of his death:

> General Jardon moved with his vanguard near a little village called San Justo, where a wooden bridge was defended by 700 to 800 Portuguese soldiers. [...] The General sent a few men but the non-commissioned officer was not fast enough. He left his horse, took his rifle and deployed with them. Suddenly, he saw a seventy-year-old man who had already shot at us from the right bank. He rushed towards the man and broke his weapon. Encouraged to be kind and tolerant by Marshal [Soult], Jardon told him that the French were here not to wage war against the people but against regular soldiers. However, the old man, who lived nearby, grabbed another weapon and took the life of the man who had just saved him with such kindness. The general was shot in the eye. He told a grenadier named Fagard (from Verviers) to ask Colonel Méjean to lead the brigade. Fifteen minutes after, he died. [...] Soldiers of the regiment, so sad to have lost this man, were crying with anger. They were so furious at this miserable man that they massacred him without pity and tore his body into little pieces.[41]

Fortunately for the Allies, General Wellesley returned to Portugal on 22 April 1809. At Lisbon he met Cradock and his men. Wellesley had brought reinforcements with him but was also given Portuguese troops to attack Marshal Soult. Wellesley was even appointed General in Chief of the Portuguese army by the Portuguese regent on 25 April 1809.[42] Until 1814 Portuguese soldiers were to fight alongside the British in the Spanish peninsula and in the southwest of France. The British commander headed north with the intention of capturing Porto, and on 10–11 May 1809 his forces met Soult's at the minor battle of Grijo. The next day the British found a way to cross the river east of Porto and take the French by surprise. By the time the French realised the enemy was on the other bank, it was too late. Helped by the people of Porto, the British captured the city and forced the French to flee. Soult and his army retreated northwards. Wellesley tried to manoeuvre to trap them but failed to block the escape route. Trailed by his enemies, Soult left the country through

---

41. Jean-Louis Guérette, *Un général de vingt-six ans, Henri Jardon 1768–1809* (Verviers, 1988), pp. 60–1.

42. In fact, Sir William Beresford was made General of the Portuguese army but he was outranked by Wellesley. Tulard, *Dictionnaire Napoléon*, p. 225.

the mountains. The French soldiers, who had expected to hold Porto, were angered by the defeat. Joseph de Naylies[43] wrote the following after what became known as the battle of Porto:

The surprise of Porto by the English is a grave mistake that can be blamed on Marshal Soult, but he put it right. Without his skills, we would have faced a new Baylen[44] or Cintra or we would have been the victims of the Portuguese fury.[45]

Others even accused Soult of conspiring against Napoleon. Levavasseur, Ney's aide-de-camp, wrote the following:

We entered Lugo on 30 May [1809] and found the city filled with the remnants of Soult's army. He had been attacked by surprise by the English and had fled in the greatest disorder via Orenza, leaving behind all his war equipment. Officers and soldiers returning from Portugal were terrorised and scandalised. Marshal Ney, entering his accommodation, was surrounded by Soult's generals.[46] They told him that a few officers serving the Duke of Dalmatia had been travelling from Porto harbour to English ships, that letters were exchanged between the Marshal and the commander of the British forces, that the French army was pleased to see these negotiations which seemed to announce peace between France and Portugal, that the Duke of Dalmatia, with the agreement of Lisbon and the English, had taken the title of King of northern Lusitania and the name of Nicolas I, and that public proclamations, signed by him, were put on the walls of Porto. They also said that one day, on 11 May, Marshal Soult, who was eating, was warned that English troops were disembarking. He did not care much about this news. He was warned again that the landing was going on and only then did he send an aide-de-camp to see what was happening. Soon, shooting was heard in the streets of Porto and the city rose. Abandoned soldiers had no choice but to flee. Avoiding deadly paths and roads, they crossed the border with difficulty and reached Orenza in these awful circumstances, from where they had gone on to Lugo. A few leaders of this routed army accused Soult of trying to proclaim himself an independent Prince and ignore the Emperor's orders. They wanted to arrest this Marshal. But

---

43. Joseph de Naylies was born in Toulouse on 16 November 1786. He fought from 1799 to 1813 and became a captain in the 2nd regiment of *éclaireurs* of the Guard.
44. The battle of Bailen on 16–19 July 1808 was a Spanish victory.
45. Joseph de Naylies, *Mémoires sur la guerre d'Espagne: pendant les années 1808, 1809, 1810, et 1811* (Paris, 1817), p. 135.
46. Marbot accused Generals Delaborde, Mermet, Thomières, Merle, Loison and Foy.

Soult sent his aide-de-camp Brun de Villeret[47] to Napoleon and rumours about this story suddenly stopped. The next day Soult, with the rest of his army, went in the direction of Madrid via Salamanca. It is possible to think that the Emperor had told Soult, when he had entered Portugal, that if he managed to conquer this Kingdom, he would be named Vice-King and that the Marshal was misled by the English and the Portuguese, with whom he believed himself to be on good terms.[48]

The failed Portuguese expedition, combined with Ney's defeat at the battle of Puente Sanpayo against a Spanish army, forced the French to evacuate the whole of Galicia. This setback did not entirely demoralise the French. Guillaume Logist,[49] a Dutch-speaking soldier serving in the Imperial army, wrote the following letter to his parents:

Salamanca, 24 July 1809

[...] After having been through Portugal and Spain, we fought hard against the English and the peasants. We were lucky in all of this and we made them run in their own country, across the mountains.[50]

## Wellington in Spain

Authorised by the British government in June 1809 to pursue the French in Spain, Sir Arthur Wellesley crossed the border to join forces with General Cuesta. Both armies walked for days until they finally reached the town of Talavera de la Reina, 120 kilometres south-west of Madrid, on 27 July 1809. There, the combined British and Spanish armies, some 53,000 strong, fought a battle against 46,000 French under the orders of Marshal Victor. On 27 July the French launched a surprise attack on British troops in an attempt to capture the high ground. Initially routed, the British launched a counter-attack and succeeded in holding the hills. If the British did well under pressure, their allies performed poorly. Firing from too far away at French dragoons, more than 2,000 Spanish soldiers panicked at the sound of their own weapons and ran away. The next day, at dawn, the French attacked again on the left in another attempt to capture the hills. This renewed assault was once again defeated by the British but was followed in the afternoon by an artillery duel and more French attempts to take the high ground. More than 7,000 French

---

47. Louis Brun de Villeret, born on 3 February 1773, was a French general. He died on 11 February 1845.
48. Levavasseur, *Souvenirs*, pp. 167–8.
49. Guillaume Logist was born in Elixem on 4 April 1786. He served in the 26th line infantry regiment. In his letter, he apologised for writing in French to his parents, having been unable to find a friend who could write the letter for him in Dutch.
50. Fairon and Heuse, *Lettres de grognards*, p. 173.

soldiers were either killed or wounded but the British lost an equal number of men.[51] Alexandre-Auguste de Vanssay[52] fought at the battle of Talavera:

On 26 July [1809], we were ordered to push forward and cross the river; we exchanged a few shots with the British cavalry. Only two of their squadrons moved in front of their lines and charged our light brigades. The colonels of those regiments spotted them and moved their squadrons into narrow columns. Most of the English, unable to control their horses, went through the gaps; the lines closed and more than one hundred horsemen were taken by surprise and without giving or receiving a blow. Nightfall stopped these skirmishes. Forward lines were established on both sides. [...] The sun was not even on the horizon when cannon began firing. Brave cohorts of French and Englishmen were getting ready for a vigorous assault; the main action moved towards the centre, which was held by a German division from the Rhine Confederation. Many of its artillery pieces had been dismantled and, after heavy bombardment, disorganisation struck. Scottish soldiers renewed their assault and penetrated through the middle of this division, already crushed by the enemy artillery's fire. Soldiers bringing supplies and officers' assistants were fleeing the battlefield, alarming all the troops they encountered. The right flank, where we were, moved forward and reorganised, forcing the enemy to retreat to their initial position. [...] We were crushed by English grapeshot and explosive bombs. They fired hollow cannonballs filled with round shots, which wounded several of our horses. My horse's inner leg was torn by this instrument of destruction. Luckily, it was a horse borrowed from the troop and its wounds were not serious enough to dispatch it. A shell blew up on my right, only four feet from me. [...] Our position was critical and was made worse by the landscape. Trenches and hills covered with vineyards were exposed to artillery fire. Our own batteries were silent, either because they were out of range or because they were aimed elsewhere. This resulted in a disastrous day. The English, fortified on the high ground, were not afraid of our assaults.[53]

---

51. Digby Smith, *The Greenhill Napoleonic Wars data book* (London, 1998), pp. 326–7.
52. Auguste-Alexandre de Vanssay, born on 30 December 1784, joined the 5th regiment of dragoons and fought in Austria in 1805. He served during the following years and was captured at the battle of Eylau. Freed after the peace of Tilsit, he followed his regiment to Spain. He was promoted to the rank of sous-lieutenant but was demobilised after having sustained heavy wounds in 1811. Vanssay survived the Napoleonic Wars and was eventually awarded the Legion of Honour in 1846. He died in 1869.
53. Auguste-Alexandre de Vanssay, *Fragments de mémoires inédits écrits en 1817 sous le titre de « Souvenirs militaires d'un officier de dragon »: pendant les campagnes de la Grande armée des années 1804 à 1811, armée d'Espagne* (Mortagne, 1864), pp. 8–12.

Joseph de Naylies, who also fought at the battle of Talavera, had only harsh words for his commanding officers:

> The French attacked with extraordinary courage, they displayed prodigious valour, but there was no coordination, no liaison between operations. They wanted a regiment to take a position defended by plenty of artillery and held by several divisions. We lost many people in successive attacks, so badly combined that they had no result. Our losses were more considerable than the enemy's, and the French army crossed again the Alberche [river].[54]

The question of who actually won the battle of Talavera is a matter of disagreement between French and British historians. The French failed to destroy the British and had to retire from the battlefield. On the other hand, the British were forced to retreat to avoid being cut off by Soult, who was approaching with his army. Even at the time, French soldiers were divided on Talavera. Lieutenant Maurice de Maltzen[55] wrote the following letter to his mother:

> Burgos, 28 August 1809
>
> [...] Everything we have read in the newspaper about the English defeat at Talavera is exaggerated. We fought well. We took enemy artillery pieces and captured a few thousand of their injured men, who bother us greatly, but we did not beat them. All we can guess is that they are going to leave us alone for a while. It is all we ask for as we are defending everywhere in Spain.[56]

A few weeks after the battle of Talavera, he wrote again to his mother to summarise the French predicament in Spain:

> Dear mother,
>
> The last communiqués would lead us to believe that after the last battle of Talavera, near Portugal, we would be able to reach Ciudad-Rodrigo and start our operations. But according to the officers who fought at the

---

54. Naylies, *Mémoires sur la guerre d'Espagne*, pp. 162–3.
55. Maurice de Maltzen entered the *Ecole polytechnique* in 1804 and was promoted lieutenant in 1809 while serving in Spain. He became a captain the next year and was awarded the Legion of Honour. He died of his wounds during the siege of Salamanca on 29 August 1810.
56. Maurice de Maltzen, *Correspondance inédite du baron de Maltzen* (Braine-le-Comte, 1880), p. 23. In fact, Napoleon saw the battle of Talavera as a defeat. He wrote on 25 August 1809: 'If you look at the English General Wellesley's battle report, you will see that we lost twenty cannon and three flags. [...] Tell the King [Joseph] that I was saddened to hear that he told the soldiers we had won. The fact is that I lost the battle of Talavera.' Bonaparte, *Correspondance générale: Tome 9* (Paris, 2013), p. 1076.

battle, we did not chase the English from their positions, despite four attacks on fortified points. The result is that we had eight thousand killed or wounded and we are not strong enough to attack the enemy in his positions or to manoeuvre without taking the risk of being divided.

Therefore, we stay here, dear mother, before the Emperor comes to revive the army with his presence and to lead one hundred thousand men. We will be very happy if we can keep the country where we are established now. There was a second battle. Some say that Marshal Soult crossed the Tagus to prevent the English and the Portuguese from retreating to Lisbon, but do they not have Andalusia? And if they wanted to, who would prevent them from coming here in Old Castile, to move towards Santander or to go up to the Asturias by Jaccora? Madrid revolted for a few days when the enemy was a two-day walk from the capital. We charged the people and all the French took refuge in the Retiro [a district south-east of the city centre]. The King was very unhappy at this and at the bad spirit of his capital.

The soldiers are reduced to drinking water, one reason why more of them are ill in the hospital every day. To avoid such a fate, we prefer to pay 4 *sols* for a bottle and be a bit thirsty. Wine is as necessary in this country as bread. They say that peace is not about to happen. I believe nonetheless that the Emperor Francis II will accept all the conditions that we want to impose on him ...[57]

Not everybody was as honest as Maltzen. Lieutenant Levavasseur wrote the following:

This retreat continued through Lugo to Salamanca, from where we hurried towards Plasencia to manoeuvre behind the English army. The enemy was already on the move towards Madrid and we were supposed to cut his path. King Joseph, who had left Madrid on 23 July, fought in the field of Talaveyra [sic] on 28, this famous battle where Wellington was defeated. Unfortunately, Ney arrived too late and our artillery was only able to fire at the tail of a column fleeing for Badajoz.[58]

The British were no better off. Unable to trust the Spanish, who had abandoned wounded soldiers in French hands and had failed to resupply the British army, Wellesley decided to retreat to Portugal. This decision was criticised by some in Britain but his leadership at Talavera and his cautious attitude, appreciated by most, was rewarded with the peerage of Viscount

---

57. Bourachot, *Les hommes de Napoléon*.
58. Levavasseur, *Souvenirs*, p. 169.

Wellington. Wellesley's departure was taken as a positive sign by the French. Alexandre Coudreux wrote to his brother:

> 28 September 1809: We heard from the newspapers that the English have disappeared. These people are not a match for us; they will never win anything against us.[59]

During the second half of 1809 the French faced various Spanish armies and recorded several successes but they also suffered some serious defeats. As in the previous year, many soldiers were once again hoping that the Emperor would come to solve the situation, as this letter by Hubert-Joseph Aubot[60] shows:

> Madridejos, 8 December 1809
>
> [...]. I am well despite having to walk all the time around the country. I am also on guard duty and have to endure the miseries of a soldier at war. We have fought against the English and the Spanish on different occasions but I have always been lucky. We are stationed a few leagues from the enemy and are waiting for the Emperor to come with reinforcements to this country to march on Andalusia. This will bring the war to an end. Other than that, there is a lot of food and the wine is abundant. It eases our pain ...[61]

Early in 1810 the end of the war with Austria allowed Napoleon to reinforce his brother. On 20 January 1810 Joseph Bonaparte launched an offensive, without Napoleon's agreement. His men forced the Central Junta to leave Seville for Cadiz. Despite this success, Joseph soon heard that his brother had divided Spain into small military governments under his own authority. This decision led to a higher degree of independence for French generals but also resulted in a lack of coordination between the French armies. Another problem also became increasingly difficult to handle: guerrilla fighters. In battle, regular Spanish armies were usually defeated by better trained French troops, but irregular warfare proved highly effective in tying down French soldiers and destroying their morale. Initially disorganised and independent from each other, the guerrilla groups were later reformed in more traditional armies. The French often suspected the British of being behind the guerrilla groups and irregular troops. For example, in a letter to his wife

---

59. Coudreux, *Lettres du commandant Coudreux*, p. 165.
60. Hubert-Joseph Aubot, born in Stembert on 28 May 1787, was conscripted into the 9th dragoons on 24 February 1809. In 1812 he was serving with the 26th dragoons.
61. Fairon and Heuse, *Lettres de grognards*, p. 179.

Jean-Jacques Ballard[62] wrote about the Royal Navy disembarking armies of Spanish men:

Vittoria, 9 May 1810

My dear friend,
I arrived yesterday in the evening and I leave in the morning for Miranda. The insurgents have not bothered us in Biscay but they saluted us for six hours outside Pamplona, where they are far more barbaric and numerous. The country I have still to travel to reach Valladolid is said to be quite safe when you go with such a strong escort as ours.

We have been told that the English have landed at Bilbao with three thousand men and the insurgents have forty thousand Spanish led by Castanos[63] and the little marquess of La Romana,[64] the nephew of the general. This happened eight leagues from us, and we are not so confident about the road.[65]

## The Third Invasion of Portugal

Despite twice failing to hold Portugal, the French were still determined to conquer the country and prevent the British from using it as a rear-base for their operations in the Spanish peninsula. In July 1810 Marshal Massena invaded Portugal with 65,000 men. Lieutenant Pierre-François Guingret[66] was more than sceptical:

They conceived the strange notion of removing our beautiful and formidable army of Spain, so useful there, to invade Portugal. Spain, already desperate, discouraged by multiple failures, was looking for peace. Already, the Spanish were openly cursing the English, who encouraged war and had left them at our mercy as soon as our armies had arrived. [...] We reached Viseu [in the centre of northern Portugal] on 19 September. The 8th Army Corps, under the command of the Duke of

---

62. Jean-Jacques Ballard, born in Autun on 15 September 1776, was a military doctor in the French army. He died on 7 October 1841.
63. Francisco-Javier Castanos, Duke of Bailen, was a Spanish general who won the battle of Bailen.
64. La Romana Pedro Cero y Sureda was a Spanish general who served under Wellington.
65. Jacques Resal and P. Allorant, *Un médecin dans le sillage de la Grande Armée: correspondance entre Jean Jacques Ballard et son épouse Ursule demeurée en France (1805–1812)* (Paris, 2013), p. 205.
66. Pierre-François Guingret was born in Valogne on 24 March 1784. He joined the 6th regiment of artillery in 1803, studied at the polytechnic school in 1804 and served as a sous-lieutenant in the 69th regiment of line infantry. He fought in Spain, Portugal and the south of France and during the short campaign of 1815. He served in the army during the Restoration and saw action in Spain, Guadeloupe and Algeria. He died in Paris in January 1845.

Abrantès [Junot], had preceded us by a few hours. His vanguard fired at the rear-guard of the English–Portuguese army. [...] From the moment we left Almeida, we barely saw a Portuguese. Excited by the English and determined to follow their government's orders, all fled as we arrived, taking or destroying everything that could be useful or necessary to the subsistence of the French army. The English predicted that our soldiers would lack everything and would be forced to leave the ranks to explore the countryside and maraud. They knew that the lack of discipline would trigger excesses and inevitably turn the people against us. Indeed, a few soldiers behaved in such an abominable way with women and children that they took the countryside by surprise. The troops, however, lacked supplies and we were forced to tolerate this type of behaviour in our companies. [...] The people had also left Viseu. We found only a few elderly ladies who were too old to flee and people who wanted to take advantage of the chaos to pillage opulent houses. All the evil-doing was blamed on our army.[67]

In fact, Wellington had been expecting and preparing for a French offensive since the autumn of 1809. When the French launched their invasion, the Anglo-Portuguese army adopted a scorched-earth policy, as described above by Pierre-François Guingret, and moved to a defensive position. Wellington chose the ridge of Bussaco, one of the strongest defensive points on the French route. The French, used to following aggressive military doctrines, did not understand Wellington's defensive strategy. Guingret commented:

Proud and confident as usual, many soldiers said that the English army was rushing in its retreat to have time to embark.[68]

This view was widespread in the French army. Poumiès de la Siboutie,[69] studying medicine in Paris during the Peninsular Wars, met officers who had served in Spain. These officers explained to him what they thought of Wellington:

In general, English people, no matter what rank they held, behaved as expected: rogue and pretentious. Wellington was the best example. He only spoke of France, of our army, of Napoleon, with disdain. However,

---

67. Pierre-François Guingret, *Relation historique de la campagne de Portugal, sous le maréchal Masséna, prince d'Essling, contenant les opérations militaires qui se rapportent à l'expédition de Masséna et les divers faits de l'armée de Portugal, jusqu'à la fin de la guerre d'Espagne* (Paris, 1817), pp. 35 and 45.

68. Guingret, *Relation historique de la campagne*, p. 45.

69. Poumiès de la Siboutie was born in Périgord on 8 June 1789. He studied medicine during the Napoleonic Wars and later pursued a distinguished career. He died in 1863.

we must be fair to everybody, even to the enemy, and we must acknowledge that he had great military skills. During the Spanish war, our
officers were the first to admit his abilities. He only fought when everything was on his side. When he was not in a favourable position, he was
not afraid to retreat. He was, before all, keen to save his soldiers' blood.
He never exposed them [to danger] without reason, which is very different from bad generals who always attack. During the retreat from
Miranda, he left behind only one broken cart. His soldiers were always
correctly fed, dressed and taken care of, while his enemies did not even
have the bare minimum. Is that a reason to compare Wellington to
Napoleon, to put him at the top as the English always do? No, he does
not even come close to him.[70]

On 27 September 1810 the Anglo-Portuguese army fought the French at
Bussaco. The British soldiers took up positions on the reverse slope of the
ridge, unseen and protected from the French guns. Massena, believing that
he outnumbered Wellington, sent Reynier's Corps straight at the middle of
the British line. Once at the top of the ridge, the French realised how precarious their position was. Under heavy fire, they were forced to retreat. Ney
launched an assault north of Reynier's position but this too faced heavy fire.
Sergeant Nicolas Marcel[71] was at the battle of Bussaco:

The next day, we took our weapons and, without having eaten, walked
towards the enemy as happy as someone who has just had the best meal.
Massena told his soldiers the following: 'Do not fire, use your bayonets!'
He was obeyed and we attacked fiercely. Our brigade had to climb steep
rocks and go through almost impenetrable thorny plants covering the
mountain. We were under English fire and the enemy was comfortably
sitting on top. Our two regiments walked at the same rate and a competition soon started between men of the 69th and those of the light 6th
to arrive first. We arrived close to masses of enemy and stopped under
heavy rolling fire. Despite our losses, my light infantrymen, excited,
screamed at the English: 'Hey! *Goddem*,[72] we will make you eat breakfast
with a fork!' But, unbelievably, we suddenly realised that the battle was
lost. On the right of Simon's division of the eight Corps was arriving a

---

70. Poumiès de la Siboutie, *Souvenirs d'un médecin de Paris* (Paris, 1910), p. 171.
71. Nicolas Marcel was born in Riceys on 14 March 1786. He was conscripted into the 69th line
infantry regiment on 23 October 1806 and became a sergeant in May 1807. By 1813 he was
a captain and fought at the battle of Friedland; he was sent to Spain in 1809. He was
awarded the Legion of Honour in 1820 and died on 20 September 1845.
72. A nickname for the British commonly used by French soldiers. Spoken by a French speaker,
*Goddem* sounds like God Damn.

column of English, four times our number, supported by heavy artillery fire. It was our turn to be crushed. We fought back, firing everything we had, and the English did not get far. Sergeant Roussel, of the fusiliers of the battalion, was alone, badly wounded, surrounded by Scottish soldiers who wanted to capture him. He knocked out two of them with his musket and made the others run. On our left, General Reynier managed to capture the top of the mountain three times but was chased off by the same column that had defeated us. The English, free to move around, used this column to left and right to push back our attempts. This fatal battle cost the Army of Portugal 10,000 men.[73] The 69th lost 60 men killed and 500 wounded, including 26 officers. Despite that, the General in Chief presented this deadly day as a simple skirmish aimed at keeping the English busy while we were turning our army to the right. I am ashamed to say that vile admirers presented this as one of Massena's best battles.[74]

Charles-Rémy Beaujot[75] also fought at the battle of Bussaco:

Wellington hid most of his men behind a mountain [the reverse slope of the Bussaco ridge]. His position appeared impregnable because it made our cavalry and artillery useless. However, Massena believed in his strength and knew how much his soldiers wanted to fight the English–Portuguese army. They had chased it for days and were resolved to take the high ground of Al-Cobra. The attack was planned for the next day. [...] French soldiers, 50,000 infantrymen and 1,000 horses,[76] had to fight against 60,000 infantrymen and 3,000 horses[77] positioned on what appeared to be a stronghold.

Finally, the day came and the attack began. [...] The enemy, positioned behind high entrenchments, was occupying the high ground and seemed impregnable. Moreover, they had many more men than our whole army of Portugal and were supported by formidable artillery,

---

73. In fact, 4,500 killed or wounded. The British lost about 1,250 men.

74. Nicolas Marcel, *Campagnes du capitaine Marcel, du 69e de ligne, en Espagne et en Portugal (1808–1814)* (Paris, 1913), p. 117.

75. Charles-Rémy Beaujot, born in Liège on 13 February 1784, was conscripted into the 26th line infantry regiment on 9 February 1809. He was promoted to the rank of sergeant in 1807 and to sergeant-major in 1809. He was sent home in 1814 and later served in the Belgian army and in the Gendarmerie. He died on 1 November 1855.

76. These figures are not far from the truth. The French had 45,774 men on the battlefield. Smith, *Napoleonic Wars data book*, pp. 346–7.

77. As usual, the enemy figures are exaggerated by the French soldiers. The British–Portuguese army had about 35,000 men. Smith, *Napoleonic Wars data book*, p. 347.

which bombarded us without pity. You will easily understand how brave we had to be to fight the enemy, especially since we had to climb half a league on the steepest side of the mountain.

The enemy, who was confident in his strength, fought hard. Despite the fact that their artillery was pouring death into our ranks, we managed to reach the top of Al-Cobra, although not without suffering considerable losses. There, we took several cannon left by their teams and we screamed 'Long live France! Long live the Emperor!' During the action, I was shot in the left thigh but this light wound did not prevent me from fighting, did not lower my enthusiasm.

Like many others, I was already convinced that the day was won. Joy was filling my heart when something bad happened! English–Portuguese forces, until then hidden, poured on us with surprise and fury. The shock was frightening. However, we fought bravely against these fresh troops, despite being exhausted by the previous assault. The ranks were so close that we fought in confusion. Most of my brave brothers-in-arms were already out of action when a bullet, fired from 10 to 12 feet away, broke my left leg.

We lost all hope of winning and our defeat was total. We tried nonetheless to retake the position that we had abandoned and which was covered with French bodies. New columns were sent onto the battlefield after our bloody failure. [...] I cannot describe the awful situation I was in. I was drenched in my own blood, in severe pain, extremely thirsty, exposed to the sun. I could see only wounded men and cadavers around me. I could hear only screams, pathetic shouts mixed with the loud hurrahs of the winners! In the afternoon the shooting stopped on both sides and during the evening the commanders negotiated. The French, the English and the Portuguese all took this opportunity to help the wounded. [...] A sergeant of the 66th line infantry regiment came close to me. I asked him to bring a few men to transport me to an ambulance. He agreed and moved to another part of the battlefield. But the soldiers that he sent, instead of obeying the sergeant, robbed the dead officers and only came to me once this task was done.

[...] The next day I heard of our regiment's losses. Of more than 2,000 men, only 500 were alive, including many wounded. Our Colonel Barrer,[78] the leader of the fifth battalion Carbon, nine captains and two

---

78. Jean Barère, born on 9 February 1761, was a lawyer before joining the army in 1793. He was made a lieutenant colonel a month later. He fought in Spain and in Italy, and was made colonel of the 26th line infantry regiment on 28 March 1808. He was killed at the battle of Bussaco.

*adjudants Majors* were killed. M. Guillemin, commander of the fourth battalion, was badly wounded. The captain commanding the sixth battalion had to temporarily lead the regiment.[79]

The French lost the battle but managed to outflank the British during the night. The next morning, judging his position compromised, Wellington retreated towards the defensive lines used to protect Lisbon, known as the Lines of Torres Vedras. Massena followed but his men soon began to suffer starvation and disease. It must be remembered that the French army usually brought little or no food supply and was supposed to live off the land. After the unsuccessful battle of Sobral on 13–14 October 1810, Massena was forced to accept that the British defences were too strong to break and he elected instead to wait for reinforcement. This decision proved costly and unsuccessful. Harassed by the British and suffering from hunger, the French army left Portugal for Salamanca in March 1811.

## War on the Border

The failed third campaign in Portugal left the British free to strike the enemy in Spain. In March 1811 Wellington ordered General William Beresford[80] to besiege the fortress of Badajoz, close to the Portuguese border. Soult, who had captured Badajoz in January 1811, was busy in Andalusia and had left 11,000 soldiers, as well as Marshal Edouard Mortier, to defend the place. The 35,000-strong Anglo-Portuguese army faced several problems on the way: flooding, a shortage of rations and the need to bring artillery pieces from another fortress delayed Beresford considerably. This respite gave Mortier's men the opportunity to prepare for the enemy. The British were finally able to begin the siege of Badajoz on 4 May 1811. Marshal Soult, still busy in Andalusia but determined to hold this strategic town, gathered all the men he could spare and marched towards Badajoz. On 16 May 1811 he reached the village of Albuera, where he met the Anglo-Portuguese army. Once again, the British deceived the French by positioning men out of sight behind hills. Soult, who had underestimated the number of enemy soldiers, tried to turn the British but Beresford was quick to redeploy his line. Joseph de Naylies, encountered earlier in this chapter, fought at the battle of Albuera:

> [...] Most of the French infantry, commanded by General Girard, crossed the river above the bridge, and formed a column to attack the hill. The shout 'Forward!' was heard from everywhere and our infantry

---

79. Charles Beaujot, *Relation de captivité* (Paris, 2001), pp. 11–12.
80. General William Beresford, born on 2 October 1768, fought during the Egyptian Campaign, the Anglo-Spanish War and the Peninsular War. He died on 8 January 1854.

charged the enemy lines. They were met by terrifying fire, so intense and so well-directed that our columns were cleared in a few moments. Many senior officers and generals fell dead. Our soldiers wavered for a while, and a few said out loud what they thought about this attack. Disorder and disorganisation followed this lack of subordination. The English general realised it and took his chance. A few battalions were thrown against our infantry, which had broken their order of battle. The attack was repulsed and they [the French infantry] retreated to the river to reform, protected by the artillery. This fruitless attack cost us many people.[81]

Both sides lost many men at Albuera, without managing to claim victory. More than 12,000 soldiers were killed or wounded on 16 May 1811. The next day Soult and Beresford formed up again for battle but the French held just long enough to evacuate their wounded. In fact, the French army was not fit enough to fight another day. Worse, Soult soon heard that the British were expecting reinforcements. On 17 May 1811 the French wisely abandoned one of the bloodiest battlefields of the campaign. Soult had failed to lift the siege of Badajoz but he had given the garrison enough time to prepare. Wellington joined up with Beresford in June 1811 but Soult and Marshal Marmont forced the British to lift the siege in that same month. François-Joseph Zickel,[82] serving in the 10th chasseurs, fought at Albuera and in the struggle for Badajoz:

> A few miles from Baza [Granada, Spain]
> 24 August 1811
>
> [...] I was inactive for a while and hoped to tell you about new successes but nothing happened until now. Six months after the Spanish retreat, the English reorganised and reinforced their army and they came forward to take Badajoz and forced us to give up our forward bases, something we did methodically, despite having against us 25,500 soldiers who did not manage to prevent us from taking positions wherever we wanted to. We retreated to Grenada, sixteen miles from Baza, arriving only a month later, taking every day many men and horses from the enemy without a single loss on our side. We gathered near this city with around 4,000 men. I need to underline, my dear father, that most of our army

81. Naylies, *Mémoires sur la guerre d'Espagne*, pp. 288–9.
82. François-Joseph Zickel was born in Oberbronn on 18 January 1779. In 1791, at the age of twelve, he began serving as a grenadier in the *garde citoyenne* of Colmar! He joined the 10th chasseurs in 1798 and went on to serve in the Napoleonic army. He eventually became an officer and earned the Legion of Honour. He survived the Napoleonic Wars and died on 30 January 1842.

corps had left for Badajoz, where Marshal Soult defeated the English and freed this place.

After this city was resupplied and the English were kept at bay by the Marshal Marmont's army corps, the Duke of Dalmatia joined us with 8,000 men on the eighth of this month. We left Grenada and arrived at Guadix [province of Granada] (our regiment was at the front) where we met the whole Spanish cavalry: we did not hesitate to charge their rearguard, despite being ten times fewer, and forced them to retreat to a reinforced position four miles from there. We captured a few men and had a few wounded. [...]

We were not strong enough to conquer and hold this kingdom and the one of Grenada and, still fearing a new English attempt on Badajoz, we moved to Lorka [Lorca], 16 miles from here and 14 from Murcia, to resupply and take our old positions, the forward posts of Baza [province of Granada], so we could either help Marshal Marmont or be helped by him. [...][83]

Gérard Huppertz,[84] a French soldier from Verviers, was also there:

Porto Reale, 1 August 1811

[...] I will tell you that, during the months of April and May, we had three bloody battles against the English and the Portuguese between Rodrigo and Almeda, on the Portuguese border. From there, we were ordered to help Badagosse [Badajoz], where we stayed for twelve days. After our soldiers got out, we were ordered to join our regiment at the siege of Cadiz. So, we crossed the whole of Andalusia and many mountains. There are lots of bandits in Spain and they try to slit the throats of the French and stop convoys and the post. You need up to six or seven men to escort the post from one place to another. We met our regiment at Port Royal, two leagues from Cadiz by sea, on 18 July. Every day, we see our enemy.[85]

It must remembered that if the British were fighting on land, the Royal Navy was also helping the Spanish from the sea. British ships frequently engaged with French soldiers. Angebault,[86] who had served in the 20th chasseurs since 1810, fought in Catalonia in 1811. His description of an incident involving

---

83. François-Joseph Zickel, 'Lettres et souvenirs d'un officier de cavalerie légère', in: *Carnet de la Sabretache: revue militaire rétrospective* (1907), pp. 767–9.

84. Gérard Huppertz was born in Verviers. He served in the 63rd line infantry regiment.

85. Fairon and Heuse, *Lettres de grognards*, p. 195.

86. Angebault was a medical student when he joined the 20th chasseurs in 1810. He fought in Spain and survived the Napoleonic Wars.

British frigates demonstrates the ability of the Royal Navy to harass French troops and barracks:

> On the third day, we patrolled the seaside. We had two infantry battalions and two small cannon carried by donkeys. The road did not go far into the mountain and we were forced to walk next to the sea. After a while, we suddenly saw a [British] war brig nearby. The ship fired a shot to warn two frigates, of which we could see the masts far away. We galloped and, after a while, took a path on the right to take refuge in the mountain. [...] Despite being hidden in a ditch from English artillery, curiosity encouraged us to climb a rock looking at the sea. The brig saw us and fired a shot at us. We heard the cannonball whistle but, believing that we were out of range, we did not move. They quickly fired a second shot. Judging by the noise and the smoke, we guessed that it was a bigger calibre; indeed, a cannonball of size 24 crashed with much noise in front of us and crushed the foot of *maréchal des logis chef* Oswald. Luckily, it landed in the sand and did not bounce. Then came another cannonball which whistled far above our heads and landed behind us. [...] Before the city of Caneille [Canyelles, Catalonia], the mountain opens onto a beach leading to the city. It was there that the two frigates were waiting for us. We suddenly saw them, their ports open. Pinel, our trumpeter, who was riding a sturdy horse, walked a few steps and suddenly shouted 'Colonel, they are firing their cannon.' At the same time, a volley struck like thunder. We thought that they were aiming at us but suddenly realised that they were firing at an infantry column on the left. [...] Several cannonballs fell in the middle of our ranks but did not hurt anybody. I remember that *maréchal des logis* Gilbert, who had stayed behind for whatever reason, came out of the mountain on the right of the beach and rushed towards the city under the frigates' fire. He had the best horse of the squadron. The whole squadron, watching him from a distance, applauded the *maréchal des logis* for arriving safe and sound.[87]

During the rest of the year 1811 the French recorded a few successes against the Spanish but guerrillas continued to be a source of concern. Most French armies had to be used to protect supply lines instead of being engaged in conventional battles. Despite its numerical superiority, the Imperial Army was therefore unable to crush the Spanish and the Anglo-Portuguese or to pacify the country. On 28 October 1811 the French suffered one of the most severe defeats of the entire Peninsular War at the battle of Arroyo dos Molinos. Major General Rowland Hill managed to trap and annihilate General

---

87. Angebault, *Mémoires sur les campagnes d'Espagne* (Paris, 1997), pp. 622–7.

Jean-Baptiste Girard's Corps. Jean-Michel Richers[88] fought in the battle of Arroyo dos Molinos. He was visibly impressed by the British:

> 2 February 1812
>
> [...] We have fought twice since I joined the regiment. In the first battle, there were fifteen thousand English, a Spanish division and a Portuguese division. Our army had two infantry regiments and three regiments of cavalry, in total five thousand men. We had to retreat fast and, after a fight lasting at least three hours, only 350 men of the 40th and 34th regiments came back. [...] There is no doubt that the war must end soon because the English are too strong.[89]

Like Jean-Michel Richers, cavalry captain Pierre Ballue de la Haye-Descartes fought the British at the battle of Arroyo dos Molinos. Writing his memoirs while in captivity, he saluted the enemy's bravery and explained how he had been captured. During the battle, a British soldier used his lance to knock him from his horse. Falling to the ground, he was quickly surrounded by an officer and six soldiers, who pointed their muskets at him and ordered him to surrender. Ballue broke his sword against a rock, threw it away and gave himself to the British.[90] Like Ballue, many French soldiers did not voice any hostility when talking about the British. Lieutenant Jean-Baptiste Barrès[91] even mentioned the existence of truces and trading sessions between the two armies:

> Our general, Comte Régnier, sent his aide-de-camp Captain Brossard, who was fluent in English, into the forward English lines once or twice a day to take letters, and collect answers and English newspapers. He [Brossard] took me with him, as well as the bugler, and the three of us went to the barricades in the middle of the road. Once there, I would order the bugler to play while an English officer handed over newspapers and letters. The captain was doing the same. We talked, drank rum, ate excellent sea biscuits brought by the English and parted as good friends. We agreed that we would not attack without warning and that guards on duty would not shoot at each other. There was therefore a temporary sense of safety and a tacit truce.[92]

---

88. Jean-Michel Richers, born in Meyrode on 7 April 1788, was conscripted in 1808 into the 40th line infantry regiment.

89. AEL: FFP 1042. Jean-Michel Richers to his parents, 2 February 1812.

90. Pierre Ballue, 'Mémoires du capitaine Ballue', in: *Société Archéologique de Touraine* (1963), pp. 351–65.

91. Jean-Baptiste Barrès was born in Blesle on 25 July 1784. He served as an officer in the Imperial Guard and described his war in a diary. His grandson, the famous politician and writer Maurice Barrès, published this diary in 1923. Jean-Baptiste died in January 1849.

92. Jean-Baptiste Barrès, *Souvenirs d'un officier de la Grande Armée* (Paris, 1923), p. 139.

On 7 January 1812 Wellington began a new offensive, and secured frontier towns and strongholds close to the Portuguese border. Having captured the fortress of Ciudad Rodrigo on 19 January, the British began the siege of Badajoz on 16 March 1812. The town was held by fewer than 5,000 men but the French were about to make the British and the Portuguese pay dearly for its capture. The British worked slowly to destroy the defences but the French made several raids to kill the working parties. On 6 April 1812 the British launched a surprise assault in the evening to capture the city. Quickly spotting the enemy movement, the French fired deadly volleys at the attacking troops. General Picton himself was wounded while climbing a ladder. The British eventually captured the castle and the town but lost more than 4,500 men during the night. Moreover, discipline disintegrated and Wellington's men committed various atrocities against the population and the garrison of Badajoz. This bloody success, however, allowed the British to move towards Salamanca, where, on 22 July 1812, Wellington's men fought against the army of Marshal Marmont. Captain Marcel, already encountered in this chapter, was at Salamanca:

> Forward posts started shooting in the morning. [...] The fire became more and more violent on both sides and the English sent regiments to take the village of Arapilès[93] on our left. They were pushed back by the 8th division, which fought heroically and captured 1,800 prisoners. A lieutenant of the 118th, Guillemard, ex-sergeant of the 69th, chopped off the arm of an enemy flag-bearer with one blow and captured the English flag.
>
> Until about six in the evening everything went well, and our divisions were winning everywhere, but we were unable to push further because we lacked cavalry units. This arm is always necessary for victory, especially in open country, when enemy infantry units are shaken. Around that time our General in Chief was observing the English army when, it has been said, Wellington spotted the Marshal among a group of officers of the General Staff and had his artillery fire in their direction. A hollow cannonball exploded near Marmont, sending up shrapnel that broke his arm and penetrated the Duke of Ragusa's right side. He gave orders for General Clauzel,[94] who was the oldest and was next in the chain of command, to take over. But by an unbelievable twist of fate, he had also been wounded. We tried to find General Bonnet,[95] who was supposed to

---

93. The battle of Salamanca is known as the *bataille d'Arapilès* in French.
94. General Bertrand Clausel was indeed wounded at the battle of Salamanca but survived. He died on 21 April 1842.
95. General Jean Bonnet was also wounded during the battle. He also survived and died in 1857.

replace Clauzel, but he was also wounded. Therefore, the army was left without command for nearly two hours. Confusion and anarchy replaced order and tranquillity. [...] So far, my division had not seen action. We soon moved and went left, but were ordered to go to the rear and cover the retreat of the third division. [...] Soon, Defrance, from Riceys [like Marcel], warned me that the English had just sent squadrons to turn us. I went to check the situation and tried to position a few soldiers and the reserve section, but the noise was such that they did not hear me. The cavalry, which I believed to be further away, was upon us. Several artillerymen were killed. An Englishman charged me; I was expecting him to be brave enough to capture me, seeing that I had no other weapon than a sabre. On the contrary, he tried to hit me with the tip of his sword, which I fortunately managed to avoid. Since he was not going to spare me, I was determined to fight back. I hit his thigh but fell to the ground. I would have won this duel had he been alone, but suddenly I felt a blow on the back of the head and my shako fell off at the same as I received another blow on the left side that split my head. Losing a great deal of blood, I passed out and stayed where I was for a few minutes. But soon, I woke up and heard another battalion firing in our direction. This fire scared off the enemy cavalry, which left as fast as possible ...[96]

As always, Marcel was exaggerating. The French were not winning when Marmont was struck but were in fact wavering. Combined Anglo-Portuguese infantry assaults and a superb charge by Major General John Le Marchant, leading the 3rd and 4th Dragoons and the 5th Dragoon Guards, had already dealt a severe blow to the left wing of the French army. Marmont, Bonnet and Clauzel were all wounded, leaving the army leaderless for around an hour. Unsurprisingly, Wellington's army won the day.[97] Salamanca had grave consequences for the French presence in Spain. Madrid was lost in August 1812 and Andalusia was evacuated. Wellington pushed on towards Burgos but, threatened by King Joseph's army, failed to take the city. Once again, the British commander retreated towards Portugal to protect his troops. The French recaptured Madrid but were in a tricky situation. Having lost his army

96. Marcel, *Campagnes du capitaine Marcel*, pp. 166–9.
97. Wellington's strategy at Salamanca was described by Major General Sir Neil Campbell: 'Lord Wellington, I should suppose, is confident that he can ultimately gain his object by teasing and wearing them out, and does not therefore wish to lose men, even while gaining some advantage by it, and inflicting greater loss on the enemy. For we might certainly have thrashed them at Salamanca, when they remained two and a half days before us; they in a flat, we on a hill, and scarce a stone or tree to interrupt us.' Neil Campbell, *Napoleon at Fontainebleau and Elba, being a Journal of occurrences in 1814–1815* (London, 1869), p. 35.

in Russia, Napoleon recalled 20,000 men from Spain to fight the Austrians and the Prussians. The remaining French troops in Spain were scattered between Bilbao and Valencia.

Wellington used the winter of 1812 to reorganise his army before launching another offensive from northern Portugal in May 1813. The French, unable to match the 120,000-strong Anglo-Portuguese–Spanish army, were forced to retreat. In the south-east Lieutenant General John Murray[98] led another army. Supported by Spanish troops, he defeated Marshal Suchet at the battle of Castalla on 13 April 1813. Murray, however, managed the capture of Tarragona poorly and issued such confusing orders that he was relieved of his command on 18 June 1813. Meanwhile, Wellington managed to outflank the French and met King Joseph at the battle of Vitoria on 21 June 1813. François-Joseph Zickel, already met in this chapter, explained the battle of Vitoria to his brother in the following letter:

> To Sir Zickel, employee at the prefecture of the Haut-Rhin department, Colmar
> Saint-Maixent, 19 August 1813
>
> [...] They have made a big deal of our retreat! We faced a few minor setbacks from Madrid to Vittoria. The English have made sure not to attack us with their full strength during our retreat because they were convinced that we would exterminate them if we turned back. This is why they let us go, quietly, until after Vittoria, where our army took position and stayed for three days. Then, the English attacked us from all sides, having turned us with three divisions. Retreat was ordered and we left in good order, from one position to another, making the English pay dearly.
>
> But, unfortunately, most generals lost their heads, saying that there was no good ground for our cavalry, that there was nobody, no cavalry, no infantry, to back up our artillery pouring death from all sides. This gave the victory to the English, who were all drunk as only the English can be (as the proverb says!). Without that, it would have been like the battle of Fleurus!
>
> We lost all our artillery pieces, our luggage and our treasures, because we had to retreat to the hills where no cart could follow. We lost more than six thousand men and the English lost twice that number! Our cavalry did not fight and lost nothing but a few horses, because we did

---

98. General John Murray, born in 1768, served in India and during the Peninsular War. He was court-martialled after the Tarragona incident but was cleared of all charges. He died on 15 October 1827.

not have horseshoes, which we had to leave behind. Without that, the cavalry would not have lost thirty horses in this battle.

We left from there to the border of France, where the English tried to take our lines but French courage always pushed them back with heavy losses. There, they were ashamed to be unable to defeat an army of no more than fifty or sixty thousand men with more than one hundred and eighty thousand men! [...][99]

The battle of Vitoria was followed by chaos. Instead of pursuing the French, exhausted British soldiers plundered the French wagons and treasures. The French were able to retreat across the border and soon assembled in the Pyrenees. The war in Spain was now over. Year after year, the French had failed to secure the country and had lost valuable commanders, men and resources in the Peninsula. French soldiers experienced frustration in the country. Hating the climate and fearing guerrilla warfare, they also learned to respect the British. If many officers disliked Wellington's tactics, rankers saw in the British soldiers steady and disciplined men. The Peninsular War was also a symbol. Foreign nations were inspired by the spirit of resistance and the first French defeats on the battleground. The war, however, was far from over. The French were retreating but still had talented commanders and brave men. As the next chapter will demonstrate, the Allies had a long way to go before bringing Napoleon to his knees. Wellington and his Anglo-Portuguese army was about to fight more costly battles, this time on French territory.

---

99. Zickel, 'Lettres et souvenirs d'un officier de cavalerie légère', pp. 770–2.

*Chapter 5*

# The Invasion of France, the Hundred Days and Occupation

## The First Invasion of France

By 1813 the French Empire was in a difficult position. Having suffered enormous losses in Russia the year before, Napoleon fought costly battles at Lützen, Bautzen and Dresden between May and August 1813. In Spain the French armies faced a never-ending cycle of violence against guerrilla fighters and Anglo-Spanish armies. It became increasingly clear that the battle for France was looming on the horizon. Becoming more and more daring, the British launched audacious operations on the French coast, such as the raid described by Jean Jacques Cambacérès in a letter to the French Emperor:

26 August 1813

During the night of 17 to 18 [August], 800 English landed simultaneously on five different points between La Ciotat and Marseille. Despite our batteries' fire, they burned a house in the village of Cassis and took a despatch boat as well as twenty merchant ships.[1]

These operations were soon followed by a full-scale invasion of France led by the Duke of Wellington. On 7 October 1813 British, Spanish and Portuguese soldiers crossed the Bidasoa river separating the north of Spain and the south-west of France. The next day Captain Nicolas Marcel,[2] whom we encountered in the previous chapter, and who was one of the few soldiers who fought the campaign in the south-west and left a written testimony, was among a group of Frenchmen who made a surprise attack against the rear of the British army:

Our division was ordered to attack the rear of the enemy and capture the supplies in a valley two leagues from there. We left our backpacks and marched fast. My company was at the forefront. The Spanish battalions

---

1. Jean Jacques Régis de Cambacérès, *Lettres inédites à Napoléon, 1802–1814. Tome Ier: janvier 1802–juillet 1807* (Paris, 1973), p. 1032.
2. See page 98.

left by the English in the rear to guard the baggage wagons and the path leading to them were quickly pushed back and our regiment captured the wagons. We had taken almost everything when the enemy soldiers, who were advancing towards Orogne, heard the shooting in their rear and sent two divisions to cut off our retreat. We were forced to leave, but my skirmishers took many horses and cases belonging to English officers. Some found five to six thousands francs.[3]

Interestingly, Captain Marcel experienced a civilised encounter between French and British soldiers the same day:

During the evening the English came and, as we were preparing ourselves to fight, their officers shouted in French that we should hold our fire, that they did not want to attack now or during the night. They placed their sentinels in front of ours and so close that these men could talk. I must add that neither the English nor the French showed any hostility, a common feature when not in battle. Soldiers of both nations rather hated the Spanish and the Portuguese.[4]

East of the Rhine, members of the Sixth Coalition met and defeated Napoleon at the battle of Leipzig on 16–19 October 1813. This decisive Allied victory forced the French Emperor to retreat and fight for his survival. German, Austrian and Russian armies crossed the Rhine and entered France just a few weeks later. Despite being attacked from all sides, Napoleon was not going to give up without a fight. Reluctant to be too far from the capital, he led the armies against the northern invasion in what was to become one of his most brilliant campaigns. Lack of manpower prevented him from delivering a fatal blow, but he severely damaged his enemies' confidence. In the south-west, meanwhile, some of his most trusted generals were tasked with resisting the invaders there. On 9 December 1813 the French and the British fought the battle of the Nive near the city of Bayonne. Soult had formed a defensive line and was hoping to halt Wellington's advance. Captain Marcel was in a ditch fighting Scottish soldiers:

The Scottish came and I left my position. A bagpiper fired his rifle so close that the flame burned my collar and the shot grazed my right ear. Skirmisher Pensot was more skilled than this *sans-culotte* [a derogatory term from the French Revolution used here as a humorous term for kilt-wearing soldiers] and brought him down with a shot. As I was only separated from this Scotsman by the trunk of a tree, I ran and put my sword

3. Marcel, *Campagnes du capitaine Marcel*, p. 218.
4. Marcel, *Campagnes du capitaine Marcel*, pp. 220–1.

through his body as I was not quite sure that he was dead and I feared another attack.[5]

The French lost the battle but the British were unable to carry on the invasion of France owing to bad weather. British operations in the south-west of the country resumed in the middle of February. Wellington moved towards Bayonne, leaving Hope in charge of the siege, before pushing further towards Soult's army. The two armies met again at Orthez on 27 February 1814. Here, some 36,000 French soldiers, including Captain Marcel, fought 43,000 British:

> [...] I had 20 men put out of action in a moment, the commander of the second battalion was killed, General Maucune[6] dangerously wounded. We had lost so many officers that a battalion leader led the brigade and a captain the regiment. [...] By half past three in the afternoon nothing was decided. The enemy was moving forwards and backwards. Several corps were trying to manoeuvre and we were in danger of being charged. [...] At four we were ordered to go backwards. I was in the rear-guard and positioned my skirmishers. A few moments later English hussars showed up with light artillery but they were so frightened by our fire that they left, leaving their artillery to fire at us unsupported. A few soldiers of the 39th [line infantry regiment], thinking that we were about to be charged, abandoned their weapons and equipment to flee. I was so infuriated that I ordered my skirmishers to fire at these cowards.[7]

Captain Marcel, always a braggart, forgot to mention in his book that the battle of Orthez was won by the British. His position compromised, Soult was forced to retreat with his army. Other Frenchmen felt overwhelmed by the enemy's strength. Guillaume Peyrusse wrote the following entry in his diary two weeks after the battle of Orthez:

> 15 and 16 March [1814]: [...] Marshal Soult lost the battle of Orthez; we have just heard the news. He cannot stop Wellington any more; he retreats to Toulouse. The enemy is coming from everywhere. His Majesty, in this campaign, as in Saxony, uses much energy to fight the enemy. The armies he is leading show such dedication that no danger, no tiredness, can undermine them.[8]

5. Marcel, *Campagnes du capitaine Marcel*, pp. 227–8.
6. Antoine Louis Popon de Maucune, born on 21 February 1772, was a sub-lieutenant in 1786. He was made general on 10 March 1807. He died on 18 February 1824.
7. Marcel, *Campagnes du capitaine Marcel*, pp. 245–6.
8. Guillaume Peyrusse, *1809–1815, memorial et archives de M. le baron Peyrusse, trésorier général de la couronne pendant les cent-jours* (Carcassonne, 1869), p. 211.

Still unable to stop Wellington, Soult retreated north towards Toulouse. The British captured Bordeaux without a fight on 12 March. Meanwhile, Wellington advanced towards Toulouse, hoping to deal once and for all with Soult's army. This city was not an easy place to take. The Garonne river was a natural barrier and Wellington required engineers to get his army across it. Canals and redoubts were also well-defended obstacles. Although demoralised by recent defeats and bad news from the north, the French soldiers were unaware that Napoleon had already lost and agreed to abdicate. After days of planning, the fighting at Toulouse began on 10 April. The British attacked from three sides but soon ran into difficulties. An anonymous French officer, who left behind a diary, witnessed the British assaults against his redoubt:

> Wellington probably gave them three rum rations: the more grapeshots open their ranks, the more they run at our positions screaming ferociously. With fire in their bellies, the fittest climb our palisades above the earthen obstacles. They might be able to climb this ultimate obstacle, using a dead angle to escape our bullets. Despite the bullets whistling over their heads, our veterans face them on top of the rampart and, completely exposed, fire down at the attackers. The last Scots, still running, cannot escape. Our soldiers do not have time to reload their muskets and throw big rocks torn from the road. This stoning, combined with our fire, puts an end to this valiant assault and many dead and wounded men, two hundreds perhaps, lie close to our position. An English major is among them ...[9]

The same officer witnessed a brave charge by a few British soldiers led by a courageous officer:

> [...] The enemy launches a third assault, this time using a whole division. It is stopped once more, only a few audacious men reach the parapet and are immediately shot. However, a small detachment of men manages to reach the arch of the first bridge. Protected, they cross the footbridge used by our skirmishers and reach the stairs leading to the redoubt. Encouraged by his achievement, the leading officer puts his hat on top of his sword and climbs to glory with his men, but he is shot. Others kill half of his group and the bayonets of the 65th line infantry regiment push the rest back to the canal ...[10]

---

9. Felix Napo, *Pâques rouges: Toulouse, la bataille oubliée de l'Empire* (2003), p. 60.
10. Napo, *Pâques rouges*, pp. 60–1.

Congreve rockets were used against French troops:

> [...] The bombardment was coming from the other side of the Garonne river, and suddenly became stronger with strange explosions. We saw long tubes propelled by fire. They ended their trajectory by burning their targets. One fell on a building that we were occupying on the left side of the port. The building burned immediately. [...] These Congreve rockets, as they are called, would be particularly dangerous if their aim was equal to the fear they cause. But many land anywhere, when they do not land on their expeditors. According to our best artillerymen, their reliability is not satisfactory enough for them to be used in large numbers.[11]

Toulouse was held by the French until the following evening. Soult ordered a retreat but his troops did not go far as an armistice was signed with the British a few days later. While Wellington was busy fighting the French at the battle of Toulouse, General John Hope was conducting the siege of Bayonne with his corps and 10,000 Spanish troops. Despite having been in front of the city since the end of February, Hope had made little progress. There is little doubt that his conduct of the siege left much to be desired. On 14 April 1814 General Thouvenot, who commanded the French garrison in Bayonne, organised a sortie at three in the morning. This daring move led to a fierce encounter that saw the capture of John Hope himself and the death of Major General Andrew Hay. Hundreds of soldiers on both sides were also killed or wounded. Commander Jean Stanislas Vivien[12] was in charge when John Hope was taken by French soldiers:

> [...] This cavalry was made up of Lieutenant General Sir Hope,[13] commander in chief of the siege, his two aides-de-camp, including his son, and about twenty dragoons escorting him. The fire of the company, ordered at the right time, brought down almost all of them. The general in chief was hit twice, his son had a broken thigh, nine or ten dragoons were killed and the others were almost all wounded. Then the soldiers fell on their prey and pulled the English from under their horses. One of

---

11. Napo, *Pâques rouges*, p. 61.
12. Jean Stanislas Vivien was born in Orléans on 14 August 1777. He volunteered for the army in 1792 and almost immediately became a sergeant. He became an officer in 1796. He fought at Austerlitz and in many other battles and stayed in the army after 1815. He reached the rank of commander and won both the Legion of Honour and the Order of Saint-Louis. Jean Stanislas Vivien died on 17 December 1850.
13. Sir John Hope (1765–1824) commanded the First Division during the battle of Nivelle and the battle of the Nive. He was captured by the French at the battle of Bayonne.

my men grabbed a hat with white feathers and said 'I have the general's hat!' It was indeed Sir Hope's hat, and he was begging to be left unharmed and brought to the commander. Sergeant Bergeot,[14] who had just pulled him by the shoulders from under his dead horse, brought him to me. He was a tall dry man and was about sixty years old. He had been shot in the right forearm and in the left foot, so I had him carried by two of my engineers, and escorted by my sergeant major to my camp, three hundred feet from there, where my surgeon treated him at the post.[15]

The French were ultimately forced to retreat back into the city and the siege continued. Despite Napoleon's abdication and the armistice of 17 April between Soult and Wellington, General Thouvenot[16] refused to surrender the city of Bayonne. The siege was finally lifted on 27 April when written orders from King Louis XVIII reached Thouvenot. After an armistice, the Treaty of Paris ending the War of the Sixth Coalition was signed on 30 May 1814. King Louis XVIII was brought back from exile, while the Congress of Vienna was called to redraw the map of Europe. Napoleon Bonaparte was exiled on the island of Elba in the Mediterranean. French soldiers, like Captain François-Joseph Zickel[17] of the Old Guard, viewed the transition with scepticism:

Saint-Aignan, near Blois, 9 May 1814

I can finally, my dear brother, write a letter to make you feel better about my fate and appease my dear family, probably very worried about my situation.

[...] We left from Saint-Dizier at the end of March to help Paris, but her fate was already sealed. Arriving in the surroundings of Fontainebleau, we heard that allied troops had already captured the city. I did not know where to write to reach my father, who probably left Versailles when foreign forces entered the capital. Since that time, we have done nothing and have been unable to stay in one place. We only arrived here yesterday night and are waiting for orders or until our fate has been

---

14. Nicolas-Victor Bergeot, born in Rebaix on 12 July 1788, fought in the 82nd regiment of line infantry from 1807. He was transferred to the 71st line infantry regiment on 11 August 1814.
15. Jean Stanislas Vivien, 'Souvenirs de ma vie militaire (1795–1822), in: *Carnet de la Sabretache: revue militaire rétrospective* (1905), pp. 667–8.
16. Pierre Thouvenot (1757–1817) was promoted to the rank of general on 25 November 1813. He defended the city of Bayonne against Wellington and only gave it up when ordered to do so by King Louis XVIII.
17. See page 102.

decided. It might not be so happy: it is assumed that our regiment, of which three-quarters belong to the 300,000 men conscription,[18] will cease to exist and we will be sent to a regiment of line infantry, where we will lose our ranks. [...] I have received the Order of the Reunion[19] and have been proposed for the rank of captain major in the regiment. [...] I was hit by a sabre on the tip of my nose on 20 March [1814] but I am not disfigured because the blow was given with the back of the blade. My nose was dreadfully swollen and bled but healed after fifteen days! But now, there are residues and half of my face is swollen. I hope that this is not serious ...[20]

## The Hundred Days

Napoleon, now in exile on the island of Elba, followed the international situation with interest. The Congress of Vienna began in November 1814, but the participating nations immediately clashed over important issues. Indeed, Napoleon's legacy on the European continent was far from easy to solve. The Russians wanted Poland, while Prussia coveted Saxony and Austria the north of Italy. Lord Castlereagh, the principal diplomat for Britain at the Congress of Vienna, tried to intervene on Austria's behalf, without the agreement of the British Parliament, but this caused further international tensions in the process. In France King Louis XVIII tried his best to restore the legitimacy of the crown but he faced enormous challenges. The nobility of the ancient regime was a thorn in his side. Unable to accept social change and reforms, many nobles, bitter about the Revolutionary period, managed to offend several layers of French society with their unreasonable behaviour. The most serious problem, however, was what to do with the veterans of the *Grande Armée*, hundreds of thousands of men who had lived off occupied territories for years.[21] It was inconceivable to keep them in the ranks for no purpose but putting them out of employment was dangerous. The army was largely devoted to Napoleon and the soldiers unwilling to abandon a life of adventure and prestige. A few officers even plotted to remove Louis XVIII and bring back the exiled French Emperor. Baron Louis Lahure[22] explained:

---

18. On 15 November 1813 the French government mobilised 300,000 men born between 1780 and 1794.
19. The Order of the Reunion (*Ordre de la Réunion*) was established in 1811 and was intended to reward civil servants and soldiers. It was abolished in 1815.
20. Zickel, 'Lettres et souvenirs d'un officier de cavalerie', pp. 775–6.
21. 'Pillage and indiscipline were endemic in the Napoleonic armies,' wrote General Bonnal, *Vie du maréchal Ney* (Paris, 1911), p. 205.
22. Louis Lahure, born on 29 November 1767, fought for France during the Revolution and became a general. He died on 24 October 1853.

There was an attempt to organise an uprising and its execution even began. I witnessed this incident. As I have said before, Count Drouet d'Erlon was leading the 16th military division of Lille. During the first days of March, not knowing that Napoleon had landed, he conspired to trigger a Parisian insurrection. He worked on this project with the Lallemand brothers,[23] two generals commanding troops in the Aisne department, and General Lefebvre-Desnouettes, in charge of the Royal Chasseurs, formerly the chasseurs of the Imperial Guard, in Cambrai. Drouet d'Erlon's plan was to march on Paris and the north with his troops. He was hoping to rally more men on the way and wanted to remove the government once in the capital. He was convinced that the public was eager to welcome the Emperor back.

Without revealing his project, General Drouet d'Erlon, my direct superior, had explored my feelings and intentions on different occasions. During our conversations, I made him understand that soldiers were to do their duty and obey the established government. Nonetheless he launched his coup. I was ordered to move three battalions from Valenciennes to Cambrai and send the 3rd regiment of line infantry, based in Douai, to Soissons. I was also to send the 6th regiment of artillery to Paris. [...] I was told that the Royal Chasseurs had left Cambrai. Indeed, they left the city on 9 [March 1815] in the morning, led by General Lefebvre-Desnouettes and reached La Fère in the evening. They found Artillery General Lallemand and his brother, who thought that they could capture the arsenal easily. But General Aboville refused to let them enter. Realising that it was not wise to fight, they decided to carry on, thinking that they would meet the men promised by Drouot d'Erlon.

They reached Compiègne and the 6th chasseurs. This regiment was in formation in the court when Lefebvre-Desnouettes and the Lallemand brothers arrived. They talked to the soldiers and had almost managed to convince them [to join the uprising] when Lieutenant Colonel Lyons arrived. He reminded his men of their duty and kept them disciplined. At the same time he explained to the three generals how unrealistic their plan was. He made them renounce their attempt to overthrow the government and encouraged them to flee to save their lives. [...] Fleeing was the only way. They left for the countryside but were soon recognised

23. François-Antoine Lallemand, born on 23 June 1774, joined the 1st regiment of *chasseurs à cheval* in 1793. He was made a general in 1811. He was sentenced to death after the Hundred Days but left for the United States of America. He came back to France after 1830 and died on 9 March 1839. His brother, Henri Dominique Lallemand, was born in 1777. He was made a general in 1814. He died in Philadelphia on 15 September 1823.

and arrested the next day or the day after. They were not tried by a military court because the Empire was re-established soon after.[24]

As can be seen, the situation was explosive both on the national and on the international stage. On 26 February 1815 Napoleon escaped from the island of Elba and returned to France. With 1,000 men, mostly veterans of the Guard, he landed at Golfe-Juan on 1 March 1815. Avoiding royalist Provence, he went through the Alps, gathering troops on the road to Paris. The most famous episode of this journey to the capital took place on 14 March, when Marshal Ney turned against Louis XVIII and joined Napoleon with 6,000 men. Five days later the King of France was once again forced to flee the capital. Contrary to the claims of Bonapartist historians, most French civilians were opposed to the return of Napoleon. The lack of freedom (censorship, arbitrary imprisonments, and so on), the pressure of conscription and the never-ending wars had turned the charismatic Emperor into a vilified figure.[25] However, the army was ecstatic, knowing perfectly well that Napoleon's return meant new opportunities and a fresh chance of gaining wealth and fame. Commandant Coudreux, a supporter of the Emperor, witnessed the army's enthusiasm for Napoleon:

> 22 March 1815: The Emperor, on his horse, inspected all the regiments and was welcomed with great enthusiasm by men who had been treated as murderers, mamelukes and bandits by the last government [that of Louis XVIII]. Troops shouted their happiness for four hours and were only interrupted for a few minutes when Napoleon gathered the officers and the non-commissioned officers. He said wonderful and energetic words. He made us forget our problems and encouraged us to face danger! [...] He promised us new eagles and asked us if we were ready to swear fidelity ... All swords and helmets rose. Screams of 'Vive l'Empereur! Vive Napoleon!' were repeated a thousand times and must have been heard in the whole of Paris! All of us, no matter what rank we had, embraced one another and more than 50,000 Parisians, witnessing the scene, applauded this noble and generous demonstration! [...]
>
> We have been ordered to stand ready to free our beautiful northern provinces[26] from the enemy. Our fellow countrymen wait for us and call for help. We will go at once and if 100,000 English try to stop us, they will realise that the French are invincible when traitors are unmasked and

---

24. Louis Lahure, *Souvenirs de ma vie militaire, 1787–1815* (Paris, 1895), pp. 295–6.
25. Bernard Coppens, *Waterloo, les mensonges* (Bruxelles, 2009), pp. 19–21.
26. Meaning Belgium and the Netherlands.

Napoleon is in charge. Farewell. I kiss you and I love you with all my heart.[27]

The Allied nations, still gathered in Vienna, did not waste any time in taking action against Napoleon. On 13 March 1815 he was denounced by the Declaration at the Congress of Vienna as 'an enemy and disturber of the tranquillity of the world' who had 'rendered himself liable to public vengeance'.[28] This time there would be no negotiated peace or diplomatic action. The War of the Seventh Coalition had begun. Austria, Britain, Prussia and Russia, as well as other nations, were now committed to crush once and for all the troublesome Corsican. The disputes of the Congress of Vienna were temporarily forgotten and were replaced by a determination to beat the French. The Prussians and the British were ready to act quickly, but the Russians and the Austrians needed at least until July to gather and move their armies. This delay gave Napoleon a few months to prepare. He had many challenges to overcome. Entire provinces were hostile to him and the risk of local revolts was a matter of concern in the capital. Alexandre Coudreux wrote to his brother:

29 March 1815: Royalists said that 40,000 national guards were armed and ready to defend the throne! I was pretty convinced that these *monseigneurs* were mistaken by at least two zeros but I am not unhappy to hear that everything was quiet on the border of the Loire river. We talk, write and sing with total freedom. Everybody is free to say what he thinks and it seems that police spies have disappeared with the previous government.[29]

But Alexandre Coudreux spoke too soon. The region of Vendée, which had proved troublesome during the French Revolution, rose against Napoleon in May 1815. Loyal to Louis XVIII and opposed to conscription, the region received much-needed weapons and ammunition from Britain. This insurrection was a problem for the Emperor, who was already short of troops. He was forced to dispatch General Lamarque[30] and 10,000 men to pacify the Vendée, although these men were urgently needed for the coming war on the eastern border. Meanwhile, the French army was busy reorganising. Under Louis XVIII there were fewer than 150,000 soldiers still on active

27. Coudreux, *Lettres du commandant Coudreux*, pp. 244–7.
28. Edward Baines, *History of the wars of the French Revolution* (London, 1818), p. 433.
29. Coudreux, *Lettres du commandant Coudreux*, pp. 247–8.
30. Jean Maximilien Lamarque (1770–1832) joined the French army in 1792 and quickly rose to the rank of general. In 1808 he was noticed during the action against Capri. During the Hundred Days he fought against the rebels in the Vendée region.

duty, far too few to face the coalition. A new round of conscription brought back many men but the French army of 1815 was not the feared weapon of the previous campaigns. In total, 200,000 soldiers were found, of which 120,000 would serve in Belgium. However, the organisation was poor, training insufficient and communications lacking. Moreover, many talented officers and non-commissioned officers had died in Spain and in Russia and had been replaced by less qualified men, while many others had preferred to follow Louis XVIII into exile. Even Napoleon looked tired and uninspired, his health having declined steadily since 1813.[31] The atmosphere in Paris was electric. Everybody knew that war was likely but few understood that the odds were not in favour of the French. Alexandre Coudreux described the climate of suspicion and the army's anxiety:

> 8 April 1815: I think that you should be more careful than ever in the management of your commerce. Much will happen in the next three weeks. It is better to stay safe now. We see many English in Paris. Two powerful persons of this nation dined with King Joseph three days ago.
>
> 28 April 1815: It seems sure now that the war is about to begin. There are talks of the Emperor leaving very soon for the army. The first battle will be terrible and will decide the fate of the campaign, or rather the Empire's fate.[32]

Others were far more optimistic. René Bourgeois wrote the following at the beginning of the campaign:

> Everybody was guessing at this campaign's likely result. The enemy armies were not united, were unlikely to regroup. Pursued with vigour, these separate corps could be outflanked and would find it impossible to defend themselves. Wellington is not able. Surprised by an offensive that he was far from expecting, his plan of campaign is worth nothing, since he would lose the initiative and would not be able to fight on his chosen ground. To summarise, unbounded faith in Bonaparte, who has certain and admirable plans; the English will be destroyed or they would have to embark in a hurry; we will soon reach the Rhine, acclaimed universally by the Belgians, who would all gather to celebrate their freedom. Their whole army was only waiting for the moment to join their old comrades in arms.[33]

31. Coppens, *Waterloo, les mensonges*, pp. 34–5.
32. Coudreux, *Lettres du commandant Coudreux*, pp. 250, 257–8.
33. René Bourgeois, *Relation fidèle et détaille de la dernière campagne de Buonaparte, terminée par la bataille de Mont-Saint-Jean dite de Waterloo ou de la Belle-Alliance* (Paris, 1815), pp. 26–7.

But the public was wrong on all accounts. Wellington was a very able commander, and one who was far more cautious about the lives of his men than Napoleon was. He had not only experience but also a precise knowledge of Belgium's geography, which he had explored the year before. Belgium, separated from France and given to the Netherlands after Napoleon's first abdication, had no desire to be brought back into the Napoleonic empire. In fact, thousands of Belgian soldiers and veterans of the *Grande Armée* would play a decisive role at the battle of Waterloo fighting on the Dutch–British side.[34] French soldiers, blinded by Napoleon's charisma, were oblivious to the problems ahead. A Cambridge graduate, John Cam Hobhouse,[35] witnessed the preparations for the campaign, which he described in a letter. The enthusiasm of those gravitating around the Emperor was clear:

> Visiting an aide-de-camp of the Emperor, I found him busy mapping in detail the country on the Belgian frontier, and was asked by him whether a separation of the Prussian and English armies, and a rapid march upon Brussels would not surprise our politicians in England. 'We can beat Blucher first, and then,' added he, smiling, 'we shall try your Wellington. No one doubts the undaunted bravery of English soldiers, but the loss of 20,000 men would make the people of London look a little pale. You are rather sparing of your own blood, though I cannot say that you care about that of your friends.' The general was right, I thought, in the former part of his remark, and as to the latter, I presume he had been lately reading the comparative valuation of flesh and blood made by Lord Castlereagh in the house of commons, on the 24th, when he set down an Englishman at from sixty to seventy pounds sterling, but assured his friends and the public that he had bargained for the continental creature of the same species and requisite pugnacious properties, at eleven pounds two shillings a head, and would sell them to his countrymen at prime cost.[36]

Lieutenant Jacques Martin,[37] a Swiss fighting for the French, served during the Hundred Days. Writing after the battle of Waterloo, he explained to his

34. See Veronica Baker-Smith, *Wellington's hidden heroes: the Dutch and the Belgians at Waterloo* (London, 2015).

35. John Cam Hobhouse, later 1st Baron Broughton, was born on 27 June 1786. He was educated in Cambridge, where he became friends with Lord Byron, and later became a Member of Parliament and Secretary at War. He died on 3 June 1869.

36. John Hobhouse, *The substance of some letters, written by an Englishman resident at Paris during the last reign of the Emperor Napoleon* (Philadelphia, 1816), p. 313.

37. Jacques Martin, born in Geneva on 12 August 1791, joined the French army in 1812 and served as an officer in the 5th corps from 1813. He fought in Germany and in France and

mother his state of mind at the beginning of the campaign and confirmed the unrealistic expectations of the French army. This is one of the very few letters of the campaign to have survived[38] to this day:

Arras, 1 August 1815

My dear mother,

You will be surprised and, I am sure, happy to receive this letter. You probably did not expect it. You probably thought that I was dead, which is understandable considering that I believed it too for a while. But luckily we are now both convinced of the contrary. [. . .] As soon as the raging war inflamed the earth, as soon as positive orders confirmed rumours, when, finally, it was time to fight, we came to desire what we could not avoid any more. You can trust soldiers; everybody was waiting for it. Officers were eager to fight. The certainty of winning was animating them.

We talked only of our future victories, of the glory that we were about to earn, of the promotions awaiting us. Gone the barracks; this vile rest is not made for true soldiers! Leave everything, love, mistress, everything ... to fight! That was what we were writing, what I was writing on 12 June.[39]

While the Allies were assembling their troops, Napoleon was weighing his options. He could wait for his enemies on the French border or take the initiative. An offensive in Belgium was a daring move but it made sense. The Allied armies were disorganised and at risk of being divided. Napoleon intended to crush them separately, as he had done in previous campaigns, in order to impose a peace treaty favourable to the French. The Emperor was also hoping to rally the Belgians to his cause. Meanwhile, in Paris civilians still expected that the situation would be resolved through diplomatic channels. This hope vanished in a matter of days when it became clear that the Allies wanted to remove Napoleon by force. Coudreux wrote:

20 May 1815: The political landscape seems to be better in the last few days! Our outposts fraternise with foreign ones. The French army will become larger than before. They will get scared of us and will try to solve the situation!

---

during the Hundred Days. He went back to Switzerland in 1815, became a pastor and died in 1874.

38. By 1815 the postal service was not working as well as before and many letters were never sent.

39. Jacques Martin, 'Waterloo: lettre d'un officier genevois du 45e', in: *Carnet de la Sabretache: revue militaire rétrospective* (1895), pp. 493–528.

24 May 1815: For the moment, my friend, everything is quiet on the border. We watch each other but nobody knows when the war will start. The army is growing each day. Neighbouring departments display unlimited patriotism and devotion. Free Corps are also growing. If citizens show good faith, our situation will be good, very good, and the Allies will probably not dare to attack us.
10 June 1815: We believe that the war will start soon. Our forces are gathered; our soldiers are animated by the best spirit; the first shock will be terrible and there is little doubt that we have a great advantage. It is really sad that the Vendée gets in the way of border operations.[40]

From March to June the mood in Paris deteriorated rapidly. Many civilians saw spies or foreign agents everywhere and believed in conspiracies inspired either by the British or by the royalists. A similar phenomenon would happen again in France in August 1914, sometimes with deadly consequences for those accused of working for the Germans.[41] Emile Labretonnière, a civilian living in the capital, witnessed one of those incidents:

While such noble dedication was inspiring the army in the defence of our territory, the supporters of those exiled in Ghent [Louis XVIII and his family] were working hard to paralyse it. Leaflets were slipped under doors to announce the arrival of foreign nations and to state how vain it was to resist. But these things were only helping their cause marginally. They had to find a better way to surrender Paris to the enemy.

During the last days of May, near the boulevards by the street Saint-Denis, I saw two gendarmes riding towards us from a distance, escorted by a group of children. When they arrived at the market, we witnessed a pitiful sight. An unfortunate old man, without a hat but with a bloody head, was bound to the tail of one of the horses, and was being dragged along in the gutter. The crowd, shocked, stopped them and asked what this poor man had done to be treated like this. 'What has he done?', answered the brigadier?[42] 'We should have shot him on the spot. Would you believe that this old bugger was arrested at Saint-Chaumont, just when he was sabotaging a battery! And he had lots of nails in his pocket for all the unguarded batteries that he could have found! He is lucky that an officer saved him from the gunners because, otherwise, his fate would have been sealed. We are escorting him to the police Prefecture.'[43]

40. Coudreux, *Lettres du commandant Coudreux*, p. 279.
41. On this matter, see: Jean-Jacques Becker, *Les Français dans la Grande Guerre* (Paris, 1982).
42. A non-commissioned officer in the French Gendarmerie.
43. Emile Labretonnière, *Macédoine. Souvenirs du quartier latin: Paris à la chute de l'Empire et pendant les Cent-Jours* (Paris, 1863), p. 253.

The campaign began when the Army of the North moved towards the Belgian border on 15 June 1815. A few hours earlier, Napoleon had addressed his army in a proclamation commemorating the battles of Marengo and Friedland. The French Emperor used this opportunity to attack the main enemies of the campaign:

> [...] Now, however, leagued together, they strike at the independence and sacred rights of France. They have committed unjust aggressions. Let us march forward and meet them; are we not still the same men? Soldiers: at Jena, these Prussians, now so arrogant, were three to one; at Montmirail six to one. Let those who have been held captive by the English describe the nature of their prison ships, and the sufferings they endured. The Saxons, the Belgians, the Hanoverians, the soldiers of the Confederation of the Rhine, lament that they are obliged to use their arms in the cause of princes who are the enemies of justice and the destroyers of the rights of nations. They well know the coalition to be insatiable. After having swallowed up twelve million Poles, twelve million Italians, one million Saxons and six million Belgians, they now wish to devour the States of the second order among the Germans. Madmen![44]

This proclamation was clearly a monumental piece of hypocrisy, the French having invaded and brutally ruled all their neighbours for years. The French soldiers, entirely devoted to their Emperor, were nonetheless unwilling to criticise him. The advance of the French army into Belgium was spotted by the allied outposts, but Wellington and Blücher decided to wait for more information before moving. Further intelligence convinced the Prussians to move towards Sombreffe in order to protect Charleroi, but also to be able to reinforce Wellington. The same day, 15 June, saw the first action of the campaign. A skirmish occurred at around 3.30 in the morning between Prussian soldiers and the left column of the French army. The rest of the day saw further encounters, which forced the Prussians to concede Charleroi and retreat. Also on the same day Wellington was informed at 18.30 that the Prussians had been attacked. He immediately ordered his army to move. He received another message at 22.00 confirming that the real attack was indeed coming from Charleroi, while Wellington's divisions were headed in the direction of Braine-le-Comte, Ath, Grammont, Audenarde and Enghien. The next day saw two significant battles. In the first the French fought the Prussians. Blücher, having secured a line of communication with Wellington

---

44. Proclamation on the anniversary of the battles of Marengo and Friedland, 14 June 1815. Available at: http://www.napoleon-series.org/research/napoleon/speeches/c_speeches14.html [consulted 8 November 2016].

and the British army on his flank, made a stand near Ligny. Napoleon was in charge of the French army in what would be his last victory. The French captured Fleurus before moving towards Saint-Armand and the Fleurus road. The right wing advanced towards Tongrinne. The main battle began at 14.30, quickly turning into a bloody contest to capture key villages and positions, and only finished when darkness made it impossible to fight on. Lieutenant Martin described this battle in a letter to his mother:

> The morning of 16 [June], the army deployed and moved forward towards Fleurus, where Blücher and the Prussians were waiting for us. The English, the Hanoverians, the Dutch, the Belgians, etc., were on the right, probably to turn us. As a result, troops were positioned to face them. Our corps was among them, and we manoeuvred during the whole day and went forward only at three in the afternoon.
>
> The road was busy with wagons bringing back a huge number of wounded, and we soon saw those who had remained on the battlefield. What a horrible thing to see! I can assure you that you need more courage to walk casually to the enemy when the battlefield is already covered with dead and dying than to assault frontally the most formidable battery. Those were certainly not the first [dead men] that I had seen, but I do not think that it is possible to pass this crowd of happy men, so ready a moment before, and now soaked with blood, piled without order and all this anguish painted on their faces, without feeling your heart race. These same men [the wounded] looked the least affected by their unfortunate fate; they were the ones who took the keenest interest in our success, forgetting their pain to encourage us. Some, raising their pale faces on top of the wagon, told us with a strong voice: 'Go! Comrades: do not be afraid. All is good. A bit more courage and the cowards will run.' I have seen some that were followed closely by death, and who had only a little bit of life left, using it to scream: 'Long live the Emperor! Fuck the Prussians.' Others, waving bloody, mutilated arms, looked still threatening and were only sad because they could not avenge their own demise. What soldiers are these people that neither death nor pain can scare them and who can remain faithful to the nation, until their very last moment! I must also admit that I have never seen soldiers so animated with such enthusiasm as in this campaign. Such courage was not in vain. The Prussians were defeated, chased off from all sides, almost entirely cut off from the rest of the Allied army and forced to retreat all night. The French army slept on the battlefield.[45]

---

45. Martin, 'Waterloo: lettre d'un officier genevois du 45e', pp. 493–528.

The French won the battle of Ligny, killing or wounding 14,000 Prussians. René Bourgeois, like many other French soldiers, was convinced that the enemy army had been annihilated:

> Different versions, almost all contradictory, spread in the army about the battle of Ligny and we never knew the final result. First, it was nothing less than the total destruction of the Prussian army, leaving 25,000 dead on the battlefield and a similar number of prisoners. According to the first reports, Marshal Blücher had been killed …[46]

The same day the British and the Dutch also faced the French. While Blücher was busy with Napoleon, Wellington was attacked at Quatre-Bras by the left wing of the French army, commanded by Marshal Ney. The battle for this key position began at about 14.00 when the French bombarded the enemy. The British line threatened to give way but timely reinforcements gave Wellington the opportunity to fight back. Paul de Bourgoing,[47] an officer of the Guard, recorded an unusual story concerning his brother, a sous lieutenant in the chasseurs du Berry cavalry regiment, at Quatre-Bras:

> That day his regiment was fighting on the front line and facing the Dutch and the Belgians; he fired for a while against a regiment of chasseurs wearing a similar uniform to his. Among the enemy cavaliers, he recognised and called to several of his old Belgian comrades who, eighteen months before, were serving the Emperor with him.
>
> At that moment the French line moved forward and the chasseurs du Berry charged quickly and pressed the opposite cavalry. My brother was at the front of the charge, so enthusiastically led by Colonel de Faudoas,[48] and galloped through the enemy army. After fifteen minutes the young sous lieutenant looked around and realised that he was alone behind a long line of English infantry.
>
> Hoping that his uniform's resemblance to that of the regiment he had just attacked would conceal his true identity, he came back quietly, at walking pace, hoping to reach the French army. All went well at first, but as he passed to the left of a Scottish regiment he was recognised as an enemy cavalier. Shouts to surrender came from all sides. He answered this insolent request by spurring his horse to a full gallop. A whole

46. Bourgeois, *Relation fidèle et détaille de la dernière campagne de Buonaparte*, p. 37.
47. Paul de Bourgoin, born on 19 December 1791, served in the Jeune Garde from 1811. He fought in Russia, Germany and during the campaign of France. He became a diplomat after the Restoration and had a distinguished career. He died on 16 August 1864.
48. Paul Eugène, marquis of Faudoas, was born on 18 May 1788. In 1815 he was leading the 6th regiment of *chasseurs à cheval*. He died in 1844.

platoon fired at him. His horse was killed and both of his feet were hit by musket balls. Soon afterwards, a returning battalion of the black chasseurs from Brunswick went through the field where he had fallen. This column passed to the side of him, and even over him, without hurting him. 'Do not fear, comrade,' said the soldiers in German with friendly compassion. Another laggard, one of the looters without honour that are sometimes found on battlefields, was not as kind. This man, taking a sabre and coming close to the poor wounded man, said that he wanted to kill him. Fortunately, the Scottish soldiers of the 92nd regiment, who had shot him, noticed this cowardly act. These brave soldiers ran to protect and save the prisoner. Among them was one Lieutenant Winchester, whom I name to express my gratitude.[49]

René Bourgeois was also at Quatre-Bras. His testimony, which included the story of General Bourmont's desertion to the Prussian army, revealed the climate of mistrust and disorganisation in the French army in 1815:

> We complained a lot about the cuirassiers' charge [at Quatre-Bras] and its failure was seen as the cause of all our troubles . . . We even saw an act of treason; these rumours spreading in the whole army did weigh on the soldiers. It was said that several generals had betrayed us, including General Bourmont,[50] and they had been court-martialled and shot.[51]

Both the British and the Prussians were forced to retreat following the battles of the day. The Prussians were beaten but not destroyed and were able to leave in good order during the night. In order to finish the task, Napoleon famously sent Grouchy with 33,000 men to pursue the Prussians. Wellington, wary of being trapped at Quatre-Bras, retreated towards a defensive position that he had explored the year before. On 17 June 1815 Lieutenant Jacques Martin witnessed the skilful retreat of the Anglo-Allied army towards Mont-Saint-Jean:

> The seventeenth, in the morning, we attacked a position held by the English and the rest of the enemy army. A violent rain then started and

---

49. Paul de Bourgoing, *Souvenirs militaires du Baron de Bourgoing: sénateur, ambassadeur d'Espagne, ancien pair de France, ministre plénipotentiaire en Russie et en Allemagne . . . 1791–1815* (Paris, 1897), pp. 334–5.
50. Bourgeois, *Relation fidèle et détaillée de la dernière campagne de Buonaparte*, p. 39.
51. Louis Bourmont, born on 2 September 1773, was from a noble family and fled France during the Revolution. In 1807 he came home and served in the French army. He rose to the rank of general but was suspected of being a spy for Louis XVIII. On 15 June 1815 he deserted with his staff to give Napoleon's plans to Blücher. He later served Louis XVIII and died in 1846.

lasted during the rest of the day, something which bothered us a lot because it is not easy when you are soaked for a long time. The Allies occupied a position across the main road to Brussels; it was therefore necessary to chase them but it was going to be difficult. This place was called the farm of Quatre-Bras. We stayed there all morning, looking at each other, and no cannon fired, only skirmishers fired a few shots with their muskets. We were nonetheless waiting for the order to charge the position with our bayonets at any time, a sure way to lose many people but the only solution available to us. We were even surprised to be delayed. Suddenly, we saw columns of men moving on the left side of the enemy. At first, we thought that they belonged to the opposite side but suddenly we realised that they [the British occupying the above-mentioned position] were leaving after having fired a few rounds at the newcomers. This skilful move preserved us from considerable losses. They did not manage to retreat fast enough and our cavalry slashed their rear-guard. We chased them for the rest of the day and the heavy rain was more of a problem for them than for us, because we collected what they had been forced to abandon in the mud. But we must admit that they left little. The night forced us to stop; we were half a mile from Mont-Saint-Jean, near the farm of the Belle-Alliance. [...] We knew that Wellington had most of his army near Brussels but we did not expect a big battle for another few days. [...] We wished them [the British] good night by firing a few rounds until nine and tried to camp, which was not easy. All the army was gathered on this plain [...][52]

Louis Vivant Lagneau,[53] a surgeon of the Imperial Guard, also saw the British retreat. He clearly took this as a good sign:

17 June. Fighting on our left, in the direction of Nivelles, where the English are, on the road to Brussels. We have once again the upper hand. (This is where, for the first time, I saw Scottish soldiers on the battle-field.) Marshal Ney is in charge.[54]

Civilian voices are often forgotten in Napoleonic studies. Pierre-Joseph Tellier,[55] born in Waterloo, was sixteen in 1815. All his life he kept a diary in

52. Martin, 'Waterloo: lettre d'un officier genevois du 45e', pp. 493–528.
53. Louis Vivant Lagneau was born on 8 November 1781. Serving from 1804, he worked as a surgeon for the Old Guard and went to Russia, Italy, Poland, Spain, etc. He received the Legion of Honour in 1808 and later worked as a surgeon until he died in 1867.
54. Louis-Vivant Lagneau, *Journal d'un chirurgien de la Grande Armée (L.-V. Lagneau), 1803– 1815. Avec une introduction de M. Frédéric Masson*, Paris, 1913), p. 298.
55. Pierre-Joseph Tellier, born in Waterloo on 20 October 1799, became a priest in 1823. He became the canon of Saint-Rombaut in Malines in 1838.

which he recorded interesting facts and events. Here is what he wrote on 17 June 1815:

> Saturday 17. Waterloo is filled with soldiers. A Corps of 12 to 14 thousand men just arrived. They came from Hal. They were probably stationed in Flanders. [...] In the morning, long lines of carriages filled with wounded began to arrive. The English army is retreating from Quatre-Bras towards Mont-Saint-Jean. We are deeply worried. Father fears that this army might get pushed back towards Waterloo. We might get stuck in the middle of the fighting. We have decided, if it becomes too dangerous, to leave everything behind and take refuge in the forest. But what to do with our young brothers and sisters in the middle of a battle? [...] I was with the Mayor at around 6 or 7 when I saw four French royalist officers from Genk. They looked worried. Among these officers was the Count of Menard. The Duke of Wellington is staying at the house of widow Bodenghien, on the other side of the church. Their headquarters are there. We hosted a French officer, a royalist wearing the white cockade.[56]

Wellington wanted to face the French at Mont-Saint-Jean, a place that he had visited the year before. But to fight there, the British commander needed at least one Prussian corps to match the enemy's manpower.[57] The Prussians, who were located around Wavre, managed to confirm their presence the next day in the morning. The night before the battle of Waterloo was miserable for both sides. The French did not expect a battle for another few days and were far more concerned about the lack of food and sleeping outside in the torrential rain. Lieutenant Martin described the night before Waterloo:

> What a night! It seemed that the sky was wrapped with darkness and opened up on us. The rain was torrential and uninterrupted. To make things even better, our regiment was on a cultivated field that was entirely flooded. This is where we were supposed to rest our tired limbs; this where we were to find the sweetness of rest. No wood, no straw; nothing to eat, and no way to find anything. Sad position![58]

A mixture of paranoia and optimism was widespread in the French army. René Bourgeois wrote:

> We were convinced that the English army was going to use the night to retreat and nobody doubted that we would reach Brussels the next

---

56. Christophe Bourachot, *Napoléon: La dernière bataille* (Paris, 2014), pp. 572–6.
57. d'Arjuzon, *Wellington*, p. 278.
58. Martin, 'Waterloo: lettre d'un officier genevois du 45e', pp. 493–528.

day. Therefore, we were pleased to consider the campaign over and we thought that we were already the masters of this city, and Marshal Grouchy was supposed to be in Namur, and was going to reach Liege at the same time as Bonaparte would reach the Netherlands. So-called deserters, in fact spies, told us that the Belgian army was only waiting for a battle to join us entirely. But knowing them, we kept them to the rear. [...] Anyhow, as dawn appeared, the army made ready to move and we were very surprised to see that the English had not only kept their positions of the previous day, but that they were very disposed to defend them. Bonaparte, who had not wanted to let them go during the night, was very satisfied to find them when he woke up. He could not contain his joy and said to a few people around him: 'Ah! I have them, these English.'[59]

Pierre-Joseph Tellier, the sixteen-year-old Belgian civilian, was on the other side looking at the British soldiers:

Sunday 18. Soldiers passed by all morning. At around 10, it was very quiet around us. Everybody is stupefied by the forthcoming events. There are only two or three Hanoverian hussars in the village, and they have been used here as dispatch riders for weeks. [...] People took refuge in the forest.[60]

Napoleon was not expecting the British to make a stand,[61] and when he discovered that the enemy was ready for battle he was apparently delighted to be given the opportunity to deal the British a fatal blow. Some of his lieutenants, including Marshal Soult, were far less enthusiastic about the forthcoming fight, having been beaten by Wellington in the past. It was even reported that the French Emperor told Soult: 'Just because you have all been beaten by Wellington, you think he is a good general. I tell you Wellington is a bad general, the English are poor troops, and this affair is nothing more than eating breakfast.'[62] Not too much credit should be given to these words. Napoleon may simply have been trying to raise his commanders' morale

59. Bourgeois, *Relation fidèle et détaille de la dernière campagne de Buonaparte*, pp. 44–5.
60. Bourachot, *La dernière bataille*, pp. 572–6.
61. Coppens, *Waterloo, les mensonges*, pp. 125–31. The soldiers were equally convinced that the British were not willing to fight. Surgeon Bourgeois wrote, 'We were generally convinced that the British army would use the night to retreat further and everybody was convinced that we would reach Brussels the next day. We all considered the campaign finished and saw ourselves as the masters of the city.' Bourgeois, *Relation fidèle et détaillée de la dernière campagne de Buonaparte*, p. 5.
62. Edward Coss, *All for the King's Shilling: the British soldier under Wellington, 1808–1814* (Oklahoma, 2010), p. 44.

before the crucial battle. For the French, the dreadful weather of the previous night was still causing a major problem. Indeed, the mud slowed down the artillery considerably. The French launched the initial attack against Hougoumont wood at around 11.30. Bernard Coppens has recently argued that the French had no idea that the trees of Hougoumont hid a farm. He also claimed, convincingly, that Napoleon and his men relied on outdated maps containing several mistakes about the geography of Mont-Saint-Jean.[63] Captain Pierre Robinaux[64] took part in the initial assault on Hougoumont:

> The corps to which I belonged (2nd) headed for the farm of Hougou-mont, reinforced and defended by the English. It is located on a small hill overlooking all sides of the field, and at the bottom of this farm there is a large wood below, in which we were walking in tight columns; we were at the extreme left of the army. Count Reille, who was leading the 2nd corps, ordered us to take the position occupied by the English, capture the farm and hold this position during the battle, without losing or winning more ground. Immediately, the charge was ordered and we climbed with our bayonets towards the enemy, who opposed us strongly. The combat was fierce on both sides and the shooting was deadly and was carried on with ardour. Thirty minutes were enough for the French to take this formidable position; if we had had cavalry regiments, we would have captured many prisoners. Meanwhile, the strongest shooting was heard from the centre and the right of the army but we were still holding this important position.[65]

Robinaux was mistaken. The French never captured the position, despite several assaults during the afternoon. Fighting at close range, the British and the Dutch suffered heavy losses but managed to repel the enemy. Major Jean-Louis Baux,[66] another French officer, also fought at Hougoumont. His testimony was closer to the truth:

> I had no officers any more; more than sixty had died and I had to promote new ones. Non-commissioned officers acted as captains and, pressed by the circumstances when I had to leave the farm to go forwards, I had to

63. Coppens, *Waterloo, les mensonges*, pp. 147–61.
64. Pierre Robinaux was born in Grand-Lucé in 1783. He is famous for the diary that he kept during the Napoleonic Wars and until 1832. He died in 1854.
65. Pierre Robinaux, *Journal de route du capitaine Robinaux* (Paris, 1908), p. 208.
66. Jean-Louis Baux, born on 11 September 1780, joined the French army in 1798. He became an officer in 1805 and was awarded the Legion of Honour the same year. He fought in the Netherlands, Germany and Russia before going to Spain. Wounded during the battle of Waterloo, he served again in the French army afterwards and reached the rank of general in 1835. He died on 28 March 1849.

designate new platoon leaders and take them from among corporals. How to keep order in such circumstances? How could we face the attacks of a well-organised cavalry and the masses facing us?[67]

Meanwhile, French cannon began firing at British positions. Belgian civilians watched the battle from a distance:

At 11, we heard the cannon firing. Soon, the explosions became louder. We saw long lines that looked very black. Mont-Saint-Jean was covered with smoke. We could see very clearly the flashes made by cannon. I have always read eagerly about the war in Spain, about battles fought by Napoleon. Alas! I have right in front of my eyes one of those battles. France, England, Prussia and the Netherlands are fighting half-a-league from here!
   Urban and I went to the attic and removed a slate to get a better look at the battlefield. We can see very clearly the cannon shots. We hear the volleys. After lunch, many inhabitants get out of their houses or climb to the attics to have a look at the battle. We can still see the cannon, but the smoke hides the soldiers. Mama is extremely scared.[68]

At 13.00 d'Erlon's corps moved forward towards Wellington's centre and left wing. The British and the French met near a sunken road, where both sides opened fire. The situation quickly became crucial for the British so Lord Uxbridge launched two brigades of heavy cavalry against the French. Lieutenant Martin described this deadly episode of the battle:

Death was flying everywhere; whole ranks were destroyed by grapeshot but nothing could stop us. We continued with the same order, the same precision. Dead men were immediately replaced by those following; ranks were less numerous but stayed united. Finally, we arrived on the high ground. We were about to be rewarded for such bravery: already the English were giving ground, already their cannon were leaving at full speed. A narrow path, lined by fences, was the only obstacle separating them from us. Our soldiers did not wait for the order to cross it; they rushed, jumped over the fences and let the ranks get disorganised to run after the enemy. Fatal mistake! We were trying to reorganise them. We were stopping them to gather them ... Just while I was pushing one soldier, I saw him falling to my feet, hacked by a sabre; I turn quickly. English cavalry was charging us from everywhere and was cutting us into bits and pieces. I only had time to rush to the middle of the crowd to

67. SHD AT: MR1962. Lettre de Jean-Louis Baux au maréchal Soult, 16 April 1833.
68. Bourachot, *La dernière bataille*, pp. 572–6.

avoid the same fate. The noise, the smoke, the confusion, inseparable in such moments, had prevented us from seeing that several squadrons of English dragoons had gone through a ravine on our right and reformed in our rear to charge from behind.

It is very difficult, even for the best cavalry, to beat soldiers forming a square and fighting with bravery and self-control. When infantry is disorganised, it is a massacre without risk for the cavalry, no matter how brave the attacked soldiers are. Therefore it turned into a general massacre. The cavalry penetrated our middle; our batteries, seeing that we were lost and fearing that they would be taken as well, fired at the mêlée and killed many of our men. In the flow of the mêlée, we too fired our muskets at the enemy but killed many of our own men. Bravery was in vain. Despite incredible valour, our eagle, captured and recaptured, stayed for good in enemy hands. Our soldiers tried in vain to extend their arms to pierce with their bayonets cavaliers on extremely tall horses. Pointless courage: their hands let their muskets fall and left them at the mercy of the enemy, who slashed without pity even the children who served as the drummers and the fifers of the regiment who begged, in vain, for mercy.[69]

Soon, the French and British cavalry met. Octave Levavasseur[70] saw the destruction of the cuirassiers guarding d'Erlon's left flank by the enemy:

Suddenly, the head of the column stopped and the enemy cavalry poured against our backs. Our cavaliers were pressed against each other in the defile, so much so that our men were unable to defend themselves. I hear only the noise of sabres penetrating our cavaliers' cuirasses: the enemy is doing a dreadful slaughter. But General Colbert,[71] commanding the cavalry that had come to meet us, took the squadrons that were not engaged in the defile and, turning around the hill trapping us, he charged by surprise the enemy and closed the passage, cutting into pieces the cavaliers who had thrown themselves at us. This is how we got out. Thanks to my horse's speed, I was able to join the tail of Crabet's column, leaving behind two hundred cuirassiers who were massacred. Their horses formed a barrier that prevented the enemy from reaching us. I took the horse of an English officer, who had been killed in the mêlée four feet from me, and used it during the rest of the battle.[72]

---

69. Martin, 'Waterloo: lettre d'un officier genevois du 45e', pp. 493–528.
70. See note 223.
71. Pierre David de Colbert-Chabanais, born on 18 October 1774, was wounded at the battle of Waterloo.
72. Levavasseur, *Souvenirs*, pp. 299–300.

The first British and Dutch wounded were already brought back. Pierre-Joseph Tellier, the Belgian civilian met above, saw them:

> At around 3, wounded men began to arrive from the path of Mont-Saint-Jean. They cannot walk on the pavement, [which is] filled with boxes, ambulances carrying badly wounded men, supply carts, etc. Progressively, the number of wounded increases. Most come to our house and ask for a drink. To prevent them from entering, father positioned me with a barrel of beer on one side of the house. Fearing that all our beer might be used, he mixed it with water. After having a drink, these wounded men resumed their walk towards Brussels. They go as far as they can from the battlefield. At 3 or 4, we hear screams of 'Run away!'[73]

At around 16.00, movement on the British line was mistaken for a retreat. Ney, always eager, ordered a gigantic cavalry charge involving 9,000 horses. *Chef d'escadron* Dieudonné Rigau[74] was commanding a mixed unit of dragoons and cuirassiers at Waterloo. He took part in this doomed charge:

> When the battle began at eleven, we were in the front line. General Lhéritier[75] arrived but, while talking to me, was hit by a bullet that went through his shoulder. He was forced to retreat and this is when we lost our engineers. The 7th regiment, led by Colonel Léopold,[76] came and took up position to the rear left of the 1st regiment. Then two small cannon, commanded by a *maréchal-des-logis*, were positioned next to our squadrons. They had just started firing when the English cavalry charged them. Without orders, the two closest squadrons, under my authority, spontaneously charged in front of the artillery while screaming 'Forward! Forward!' They were followed by the other squadrons and by Léopold's regiment. We remained on the high ground of Mont-Saint-Jean, where the Lion now is, all day until the retreat was ordered and we charged the enemy cavalry again and again. Never was a cavalry mêlée so big or so compact. Our squadrons kept the English squares at bay on the road and in the villages. They were so exhausted by holding these formations that we could hear officers screaming and trying to pick up those men who had collapsed. Marshal Ney was later wrongly blamed for

---

73. Bourachot, *La dernière bataille*, pp. 572–6.
74. See page 87.
75. Général Baron Samuel-François Lhéritier, born on 6 August 1772, commanded a cavalry division and was indeed wounded at the battle of Waterloo. He died in 1829.
76. Charles Philippe Léopold, born in Kallstadt on 10 January 1775, joined the French army in 1791. He led the 7th regiment of *dragons* and was wounded at Waterloo. He died on 5 February 1858.

ordering this charge. In fact, this premature move, as I just said, happened spontaneously.[77]

British soldiers immediately formed squares to protect not only themselves but also the artillery troops and officers. Lacking infantry and artillery support, the French cavalry units suffered heavy losses and failed to break the British formations. Georges Létang,[78] a French dragoon, charged against the British squares:

> Without any order (and it was a great mistake), the squadron at the head of the column of Lhéritier's division charged against this infantry and was followed by other squadrons. But the distance between us and the English gave them time to form squares to face the charge. These squares waited for our cavalry, having decided to fire at close range only. [...] The idea that they might be exposed to intense fire grasped [the French], and, probably to escape such fire, the 1st squadron turned right and the other squadrons followed them. The charge having failed, all the squadrons gathered near the farm of Belle Alliance, still occupied by the English. Their fire killed or wounded many of our people in a few moments. General Lhéritier, the division commander, General Piquet, a brigade commander, and two squadron leaders of this regiment were among the wounded.[79]

The cavalry had failed against the British squares but the French, still hoping to gain the upper hand, launched a second infantry assault between Hougoumont and La Haye Sainte. At 18.30 the latter was finally captured after violent combat and heavy losses on both sides. Wellington, who had lost several valuable commanders and many men during the afternoon, was not in a comfortable position. Indeed, the fall of La Haye Sainte threatened the centre of the British-Dutch army. Fortunately for him, Bülow's Prussian IV Corps was now engaged with the right flank of the French army. Louis-Vivant Lagneau was close to Napoleon when the Prussians intervened:

> I was ten feet behind the Emperor and we were in-between his headquarters and the farm of Belle-Alliance, from where I had been chased, with the wounded, by Prussian skirmishers who had emerged from the wood on our right. The Emperor's attention was fixed on this point,

---

77. Rigau, *Souvenirs des guerres de l'empire*, pp. 111–12.
78. Georges Létang was born in Meulan on 2 May 1788. After having studied at the military school, he was promoted to the rank of sous-lieutenant in 1806 and lieutenant in 1810. He fought in Prussia and Poland, Spain, Germany and France. He died in 1864.
79. SHD AT. *Relation du chef d'escadron Létang.*

from where he was expecting Marshal Grouchy, who had been sent orders. They never reached the marshal.

The Emperor was counting on Grouchy, and he was looking at his watch all the time. He had told General Duhesme,[80] who was on the right wing and was asking for help, to hold because Grouchy would be there soon to assist him. [...] Napoleon still believed the battle won when we were chased from our ambulance. Indeed, he thought that the Prussians who were firing at the Belle-Alliance were being pushed by Grouchy's corps. It was around half past two or three o'clock. Unfortunately, it was the Prussians, and the Prussians alone, led by General Bulow.[81]

Plancenoit was captured at 18.00 by the Prussians. The Young Guard retook the village soon after 19.00, stabilising the right flank of the French army. At around 19.30 the Imperial Guard moved towards the centre of the British line. Other units joined in this last attempt to turn the tide in favour of the French but failed and panic spread along the French lines. By 20.30 the French army was routed and was chased off by the Prussians. A curious episode happened during the retreat. Joseph Tyrbas de Chamberet,[82] a French physician, described how Prince Jerome Bonaparte murdered a British prisoner:

Passing on horseback next to a prisoner and finding him too slow for his liking, he ordered him to hurry. Having perhaps not understood the prince's order, [the British soldier] did not obey. Immediately, the prince shot him with his pistol at close range. Then he turned his horse and addressed us in the rudest way: 'What are you doing there, Sirs? Instead of walking casually, you should treat that wounded man.'[83]

By around 21.00 Belgian civilians living around Mont-Saint-Jean knew the outcome of the battle:

We heard cannon shots and muskets from 11.30 until 8.30 in the evening without interruption. In the evening, at 9.30, an officer came to see the wounded. I heard him saying: 'We have pushed back the French towards Genappe.'[84]

---

80. Guillaume Duhesme, born on 7 July 1766, was a division general. He led the Young Guard at Waterloo. He was badly wounded by the Prussians at Plancenoit and died two days later.
81. Lagneau, *Journal d'un chirurgien de la Grande Armée*, pp. 299–300.
82. Joseph Tyrbas de Chamberet was born in Limoges on 20 September 1779. He served as a military physician in Italy and Spain and during the Hundred Days. He later became a professor and died in Paris in September 1870.
83. Joseph Tyrbas de Chamberet, *Mémoires d'un médecin militaire aux XVIIIe et XIXe siècles* (Paris, 2001), p. 164.
84. Bourachot, *La dernière bataille*, pp. 572–6.

Only three days after the battle of Waterloo, Colonel Simon Hortode[85] wrote to his wife:

> Mrs Hortode, rue Favart, n. 2, Paris
> Vervins, 21 June 1815

> Since Sunday, this is the first free moment that I have to write. This was a fatal day for us and I do not know which demon stole our rightful victory. I only left the battlefield at 10 in the evening, at the same time as the Emperor and his brother, who used me as his aide-de-camp during the day, especially during the last three hours. I was the only officer left with him.

> What can I say? Death did not want me and I live for you and for my country. Thank God, but I do not want to hide the harm: it is considerable, considerable! However, if everybody thinks like me, everything is not lost.

> Farewell my friends, I will go to sleep and undress for the first time in twelve days and I will write [again] tomorrow.

> My little Hungarian saved me, because I was one of the last to retreat. This good horse was badly wounded by a bayonet, and my shoulder and my chest were struck by spent musket balls. Two of my buttons were flattened but not pierced. You must admit that it was fortunate because our division suffered the most.

> Tell M. Audouin that the harm is great. Regards to our friends. I kiss you both.

> Hortode

> My two horses were saved but I lost my coat. General Bourgeois[86] is slightly wounded. Same for General Barrois,[87] etc. etc.

> I will reach Vervins today, 21 June, at 3 in the afternoon. Tomorrow, I will join the division three leagues from Laon. Farewell my dear.

> H.

> Naughty Wellington!!! He had to be beaten! And he ... *Bone Deus* [Good God in Latin]![88]

---

85. Simon Hortode, born in Angers on 30 November 1764, fought during the Revolutionary Wars and the Guadeloupe expedition but was captured by the British in 1806. He returned to France in 1814 and fought during the Hundred Days. He died on 12 July 1832.

86. General Charles Bourgeois, born on 12 March 1759, was leading the 2nd Infantry Brigade at the battle of Waterloo. He died in Paris on 11 July 1821.

87. General Pierre Barrois, born in 1774, fought during the Revolutionary Wars and for Napoleon. He was wounded at the battle of Waterloo but survived. He died in 1860.

88. Bourachot, *Les hommes de Napoléon*, pp. 662–3.

Ironically, Marshal Grouchy won the battle of Wavre against the Prussians on 19 June 1815, but this final victory did not change anything in the Emperor's situation, and Napoleon Bonaparte was forced to abdicate for the second time on 24 June 1815. Weeks after the battle of Waterloo, French soldiers were still trying to make sense of the defeat. Lieutenant Martin, like many others, had no global vision of the battle and was not even aware that the Prussians had attacked:

> Who can explain the sudden flight which followed such heroic courage? I cannot, I am still trying to figure it out. I know that retreat became essential, but who ordered it? Was it treason? Was it panic and terror as some have said? I do not know.[89]

This early letter, written not long after the battle, is particularly revealing because it shows how quickly the French veterans adopted a range of dubious arguments to justify their overwhelming defeat. According to them, the battle of Waterloo was not the triumph of Britain, Prussia and the Netherlands, but rather the victory of treason and betrayal. Having won so many campaigns for so long, French soldiers were unable to come to terms with the fact that they had been defeated. Louis Marchand,[90] an army surgeon, wrote in his memoirs:

> Beaten all day [the British and Dutch armies], [our] victory was guaranteed when treason and our generals' desertion allowed a Prussian division to sneak through a gap between our lines to attack our rear where we had no reserve to oppose them. This Prussian move caused our defeat and it is a mistake to attribute this battle's victory to the English, who were in full retreat.[91]

Jean Guillemin,[92] who served with the 3rd regiment of the grenadiers of the Guard during the battle of Waterloo, was equally eager to denounce Wellington in a letter to a friend:

Sorel-Moussel (Eure-et-Loir), 10 June 1835

General,

[...] If I dare to comment, I would like to say that the Duke of Wellington, who claims for himself and the English the victory of the battle,

---

89. Martin, 'Waterloo: lettre d'un officier genevois du 45e', pp. 493–528.
90. Christophe Bourachot, *Napoléon: la dernière bataille*, p. 626.
91. Bourachot, *Les hommes de Napoléon*.
92. Jean Claude Vincent Guillemin was born in 1777. He served as chef de bataillon of the Guard during the Hundred Days. He died in 1836.

could have been, without the Prussians, the prisoner of Waterloo instead of being its prince [...][93]

Claims that Wellington did not win the battle of Waterloo and that it was an unfair fight can still be heard in France today. Occasionally, some even write that Napoleon was the true winner of Waterloo.[94] Many myths and romantic pictures have developed over the years but the reality of the battle is a cold one: more than 65,000 soldiers on all sides were killed, wounded or captured on 18 June 1815. After the battle some letters were found on French bodies. They are moving reminders of the lives that were lost on that day. The first had been written by a woman to Corporal Mayrique:[95]

> My dear friend,
> I answer your letter of the 14th and I am very pleased to hear that you are well. I received your letter of the twenty-fourth of the month and I gave birth to a big and beautiful girl on the twenty-fifth. So far, I am very well and I hope the same for you. We will baptise her and we will wait for your return to legitimise her [...].
> I hope, my dear angel, that you will answer quickly. We gave her the names of your mother: Marie Anne-Josèphe. Nothing else for now, except that I kiss you with my whole heart, as do my father and mother and the whole family. I hope that you will answer quickly. I am forever your devoted friend. Elisabeth Queret.[96]

The second letter was sent by a woman to a voltigeur named Pierre Potier:[97]

> To Sir Pierre Potier,
> Voltigeur first battalion of the 29th regiment of line infantry
> Bouchain
> Sir,
> Having written a few weeks ago, it is surprising to see that I have not received an answer. Sir, these are not the promises that you made to me

93. Jean Guillemin, 'Lettre du commandant Guillemin, chef de bataillon au 3e grenadiers de la Garde, à M. le lieutenant général baron Haxo', in: *Carnet de la sabretache: revue militaire rétrospective* (1905), p. 114.
94. See, for example, the rather surreal Dimitri Casali, *Qui a gagné Waterloo ? Napoléon 2015* (Paris, 2015).
95. It is unfortunately impossible to identify Corporal Mayrique. The name is probably spelled wrongly and no unit is mentioned in the letter.
96. Léon Van Dormael, 'A propos du prochain voyage du S. N. à Waterloo', in: *Souvenir Napoléonien*, 269 (1974), pp. 29–30.
97. Pierre Potier, born on 6 June 1787, served in the French army from 1808. He was captured at Danzig in 1814 but was sent to France after the first fall of Napoleon. He was killed at the battle of Waterloo.

and I know that a few of your comrades have come back to see their loved ones. I hope that you will have a moment to visit me and this would please me greatly. This would allow you, as well as me, to save money. These are my feelings. Your entirely devoted friend, Augustine Maillart.

PS: My mother and my sister Adélaïde send their regards.[98]

The third letter was written by a corporal named A. Viset.[99] Still in its envelope, it never reached its destination:

Miss,

I am happy to know how you feel. You demonstrate that you think clearly, as only an educated woman does. Believe me when I say that I scrutinised you and looked at your behaviour before becoming interested in you. I honour you! I only saw in you a simple life that encourages my devotion. The military uniform is a burden. But I could leave it, as it is my right. I am attracted to you and I want to settle down with you. I do not have much money but I do have bread [probably meaning that he has wealth]. But my idea is not to work the land. I would like to open a little shop. We will see what to do when we are in a more peaceful situation. I beg you to find a place to meet, where we can express our love with our hearts and mouths.

Miss, if this letter is not sealed with two burning hearts, it is because I was not able to find wax. But a loving heart closes this envelope with a simple button taken off his uniform. Your devoted servant and friend: A. Viset, corporal.

PS. The dragoons have arrived. I had to hurry, which is why I wrote badly.[100]

For the fortunate ones who survived, the war was finally over. In a letter to his mother, Lieutenant Martin summarised the common feeling of relief:

This now [is] the end of my letter and my story. It is a long one, it is true, but I am sure that my mother will find it interesting. I am still young and have, for the last three years, faced many hazards. But during this short time, during which millions of men have died, so many dangers have threatened me! And I escaped everything. I am truly tempted to believe that I am protected by the sky. Indeed, from Lutzen, where I

---

98. Van Dormael, 'A propos du prochain voyage', pp. 29–30.
99. We have been unable to identify Corporal Viset. Soldiers and non-commissioned officers of the Hundred Days are particularly hard to find. Registers were not especially well kept and a few even disappeared.
100. Van Dormael, 'A propos du prochain voyage', pp. 29–30.

started my career, to Mont-Saint-Jean, where I just ended it, I have been in all the right places; I have been everywhere where I could be hit. So many opportunities to [turn up my] toes, and I escaped with a few scratches!

But, God be praised! I hope that this is over now.[101]

## Defeat and Occupation

News of the defeat soon reached Paris and triggered an outpouring of rumours. Many soldiers and officers believed the Empire was not yet beaten and most expected another battle against the British and the Prussians. Alexandre Coudreux, who was on active duty but missed the fight on 18 June 1815, vowed to fight to the end after talking to survivors of the battle in a letter to his brother:

25 June 1815: [...] The first news of the army is disheartening. Yesterday, officers who were wounded on the nineteenth and twentieth of this month arrived and tried to comfort us. The army of General Grouchy, after having completely beaten the Prussians,[102] retired in good order behind the Sambre river and we were hoping that the four armies who were defeated at Waterloo still had enough men to stop the enemy. The extraordinary events which happened in Paris will probably help our unfortunate nation! In any case, we are determined to fight to the death for the noble cause that is our independence. [...] The 30th line infantry regiment lost half of its men. It was at the forefront of General Gérard. All the senior officers were killed ...[103]

Despite this display of bravado, Coudreux never fought again for Napoleon. In fact, Louis XVIII regained his throne and reached Paris on 8 July 1815. The Allies, convinced that France was too unstable to leave the King unsupported, dispatched up to a million foreign soldiers to occupy the country. The Prussians reached Brittany and occupied Paris with the British, while the Spanish took control of the area around the Pyrenees. France would not experience another occupation on such a scale until the invasion by Nazi Germany in 1940.[104] The presence of enemy soldiers on French soil was a humiliation for many Frenchmen. Emile Labretonnière, a French civilian encountered above, cynically described the entry of British troops to Paris:

---

101. Martin, 'Waterloo: lettre d'un officier genevois du 45e', pp. 493–528.
102. Marshal Grouchy's victory on 20 June 1815.
103. Coudreux, *Lettres du commandant Coudreux*, p. 282.
104. Jacques Hantraye, '1813–1818: les premières occupations de la période contemporaine en France', in: *Revue Historique des Armées*, 239 (2005), pp. 50–6.

Oh! It was really like being beaten twice to be vanquished by such a badly dressed army as the English one. It is acceptable to be fired at by beautiful grenadiers such as the Russian and Prussian guards, who look both manly and soldierly, or to be slashed by old Hussars of Brandenburg or Silesia, who are real light cavaliers. But how can you be a good soldier with such a small sugar-bread [the British shako] on your head, with this red uniform cut without grace or taste, or with these grey pants, sticking to these crooked knees? [...] I must nonetheless say something positive about the English. On the 50,000 chests I saw passing under my eyes, I saw no ribbons, none of these jewels that all other European armies wear. I only saw, rarely, a few officers wearing a medal hanging from a violet ribbon, an order of which I do not know the name.[105] British armies only need to love their nation, the glory of Albion, to fight with admirable valour.[106]

The experience of occupation varied greatly from one region to another. Prussian troops regularly brutalised French civilians and committed several atrocities. The lack of primary sources makes it impossible to count the number of rapes and murders but it is certain that they happened on a regular basis. Jacques Hantraye even described this display of violence and the inevitable hostility roused in the French population as a key factor in setting the tone for Franco-German relations in 1870 and after.[107] British troops seem to have behaved more correctly. More respectful and disciplined, they seem to have provoked far less hostility. Their uniforms never ceased to intrigue Frenchmen. On 3 August 1815 Alexandre Coudreux asked his brother: 'How is it going with the foreign troops? [...] Are Scottish dresses already in fashion in Touraine? The Scottish costume is a fine one ...'[108] Some did complain about the behaviour of British troops, possibly made worse by the consumption of fine French wines:

During that time, the arch of triumph[109] lost its trophies and its bas-reliefs were torn down. The horses of Venice,[110] which had ridden victoriously from Corinth to Paris, were strangled with crude ropes. There,

---

105. He is probably referring to the Army Gold Medal, also known as the Peninsular Gold Medal, issued in 1810.
106. Labretonnière, *Macédoine. Souvenirs du quartier latin*, pp. 287–8.
107. Hantraye, '1813–1818: les premières occupations de la période contemporaine en France', pp. 50–6.
108. Coudreux, *Lettres du commandant Coudreux*, p. 287.
109. He is talking about the Arc of the Place du Carrousel, not the more famous Arc de Triomphe across the Champs Elysées.
110. A copy of the horses of Saint Mark's Basilica in Venice.

an English officer, who had climbed up the monument, was laughing and posing in the chariot [...] This is the painful sight I was looking at from the museum while the Austrian cavalry was guarding the Carrousel's avenues.[111]

John Hobhouse was also in Paris in 1815. His correspondence shows that he had a radically different view of the British army's behaviour in the French capital:

Saturday, July 15 [1815]

[...] Marshal Blucher allows his subordinates every vengeance and pillage, which he seems inclined to direct against the town collectively, as well as individuals. The bridge of Jena had been mined by his order, and would have been blown up in spite of the king's remonstrance, had not the duke of Wellington placed a sentry upon it, who was ordered to quit his post preparatory to lighting the train, and actually saved this monument by adhering to his declaration that he could not leave the place until he was relieved by his corporal. [...] I understand that the Duke of Wellington is exceedingly concerned at these excesses, but says very naturally, that he cannot prevent them, unless he should draw out his army to fight the Prussian marshal.[112]

The presence of foreign soldiers on French soil was particularly bitter for veterans of the Napoleonic Wars. They saw this occupation as a humiliation and many were involved in fights or conflicts. Some, like Captain Hourquin from Verdun, even tried to kill Prussian soldiers. He was fortunately stopped and had to apologise in front of the whole Prussian regiment.[113] Places where alcohol was served, such as taverns or at local parties, were particularly at risk of fights between French and foreign soldiers. Even Wellington was not safe. Recognised alongside Blücher as the man who defeated Napoleon, he became a symbol of hatred for French nationalists. In July 1816 rumours surfaced about a possible attack. He was also reported on several occasions to be dead. In February 1818 he was supposed to have died after having eaten with Talleyrand.[114] A real attempt on Wellington's life took place on 10 February 1818 when a shot was fired at him but missed. Two men were tried for this

111. Labretonnière, *Macédoine. Souvenirs du quartier latin*, p. 294.
112. Hobhouse, *The substance of some letters*, p. 313.
113. Yann Guerrin, *La France après Napoléon: Invasions et occupations 1814–1818* (Paris, 2014), pp. 50–1.
114. Charles Maurice de Talleyrand-Périgord was the French Minister of Foreign Affairs for the Imperial Regime and a key player at the Congress of Vienna. By 1818 he was not in office but nonetheless had considerable influence.

attack but were found innocent by a French tribunal.[115] Interestingly, Napoleon, in his will, gave 10,000 francs to one of the men who attempted to murder the Duke of Wellington:

> 5. 10,000 francs to the subaltern officer Cantillon,[116] who has undergone a trial upon the charge of having endeavoured to assassinate Lord Wellington, of which he was pronounced innocent. Cantillon has as much right to assassinate that oligarchist as the latter had to send me to perish upon the rock of St Helena. Wellington, who proposed this outrage, attempted to justify it by pleading the interest of Great Britain. Cantillon, if he had really assassinated that lord, would have pleaded the same excuse, and been justified by the same motive, the interest of France, to get rid of this general, who, moreover, by violating the capitulation of Paris, had rendered himself responsible for the blood of the martyrs Ney, Labédoyère, etc. and for the crime of having pillaged the museums, contrary to the text of the treaties.

After years of occupation, the Allies left the country for good in 1818.[117] France was finally at peace and free, but she still had a long way to go to achieve stability.

---

115. Pierre-Joseph Cantillon, born in Wavre in 1788, was a sergeant in the Grenadiers of the Imperial Guard. He died after 1857.
116. The whole text can be found online in English at the following address: https://www.napoleon.org/en/history-of-the-two-empires/articles/napoleons-last-will-and-testament/ [consulted 24 February 2017].
117. Guerrin, *La France après Napoléon*, pp. 171–4.

*Chapter 6*

# Captivity in Great Britain

## Capture and Transportation to Britain

Our previous book explored briefly the controversy surrounding French prisoners in Britain during the Napoleonic Wars. Using personal letters, we argued that British prisons and prison-ships had little to do with the death factories portrayed in the French historiography and public memory.[1] This topic is important enough to deserve a more detailed investigation. Indeed, Britain is too often accused of the wilful negligence, at best, of French prisoners of war, and at worst, of genocidal tendencies. This chapter will first take a look at the circumstances in which French soldiers were captured and brought back to Britain, before exploring their life in captivity.

During the first years of the conflict between France and Britain, French soldiers were mainly taken prisoner in the colonies or following naval battles against the Royal Navy. Being made a prisoner of war was humiliating and left a stain on the military record. Not all soldiers were willing to describe the circumstances in which they had been taken prisoner, but there are, fortunately, exceptions. Soldiers and officers who had fought hard and deemed their honour safe were more likely to explain why they had surrendered. Obviously, telling the story was also a way for them to cast a positive light on an otherwise embarrassing moment. Joseph de Bonnefoux[2] was on board the *Belle Poule* when an attack was launched against three ships that were presumed to be merchant vessels coming from India. Unfortunately for the French, the ships actually belonged to the Royal Navy and were returning from the battle of Trafalgar. A deadly battle followed:

> Risking his life a thousand times, the commander showed himself, alone, and made a signal to indicate that he wanted to negotiate. It would have been a crime to continue firing on such a worthy man. The deepest silence followed the sound of the guns. Then, moved, our generous enemy took his bull-horn and, in our language, said the following words: 'Brave Frenchmen, all my guns are loaded; resistance is futile; surrender; I beg you in the name of humanity.' [. . .] The name of the ship to which

1. Wilkin and Wilkin, *Fighting for Napoleon*, pp. 161–8.
2. See page 24.

we surrendered was the *Ramilies*; the name of her magnanimous commander Pickmore.[3] He shed a few philanthropic tears when he came on
board and saw the carnage.[4]

Most French soldiers had never met or interacted with British people before
being captured and were eager to describe the enemy's behaviour in writing.
*Adjudant-commandant* Louis Mathieu Dembowski[5] took part in the Saint-
Domingue expedition and was captured with his wife and his young child on
board the *Clorinde*[6] while trying to break the British blockade on 1 December
1803. Initially he feared for the lives of his family, but his feelings towards his
captors evolved over the next few days. Dembowski was an officer and was
treated accordingly by the British:

> 12 *frimaire* [year XII. 4 December 1803]. Good food and excellent
> company, quite good music and they play quite correctly French songs.
> All of that made for a good day yesterday and provided us with a good
> night's sleep. The same for today. This life is monotonous but far better
> than our time on the *Clorinde*. The good manners of the captain and his
> officers make us forget that we are prisoners, a state tormenting me …
>
> 18 *frimaire* [10 December 1803] at 6 in the morning. We saw a large
> English convoy […] We dined with a few officers of the convoy who
> came to see the captain. […] We gave our names in writing to our com-
> rades headed for England and, from there, to France. We wanted to give
> news but the officers told us that all letters for France stay in England
> until peace is agreed. […]
>
> 22 *frimaire* [14 December 1803]. We are now in Port-Royal. Captain
> Dunn is leaving for Kingston and has promised to talk favourably about
> us to the admiral. He will maybe manage to have us sent to the United
> States. It is our wish, even if it is inconvenient. But prisoners sent from
> here to England, despite the fact that their transportation is done by the
> English, are sometimes left for a long time on the road and are often
> forced by political circumstances to stay in England without being sent

---

3. Francis Pickmore, born in 1756, was a naval officer and served later as the governor of
   Newfoundland. He died on 24 February 1818.
4. Jobbé-Duval, *Mémoires du Baron de Bonnefoux*, p. 183.
5. Louis Mathieu Dembowski was born in Gora (Poland) on 24 August 1768. He served in the
   Polish Legion of the French army from 1795. He took part in the Saint-Domingue
   expedition and was captured but quickly freed. He fought in Prussia in 1806 and in Spain.
   Promoted to the rank of general, he was wounded during a duel and died of his wounds in
   Valladolid on 18 July 1812.
6. The *Clorinde* was launched in 1800 but was captured by the Royal Navy on 30 November
   1803. The ship was used by the British before being broken up in 1817.

back to France on parole. Those sent to the United States are very happy, because they have no obstacle in going back to France. [...]

We are back, charmed to have been received so well. We met Captain Dunn who, on this occasion, did more for us than ever. He talked to the admiral, as I would have, and obtained, after a lunch to which we were invited, the promise to let us go to France by the United States. [...][7]

Lower ranks were far from enjoying such dignified treatment. Rochay, an infantryman already encountered in Chapter 2, was captured at the battle of Trafalgar and brought back to Britain:

On 24 *Brumaire* [15 November 1805] we left Gibraltar with five ships of the line loaded with war prisoners and we sailed for England.

On 12 *Frimaire* [3 December 1805] the ship *Mars*, on which I was, arrived alone in Portsmouth, harbour of England. The other ships got lost and reached Plymouth.

On 13 [4 December 1805] we were transported on board a ship where we stayed for eight days, before being transferred to the prison ship *St-Thomaso*. This is where I began to realise that I was a prisoner. There were around a thousand prisoners, cramped in together, and bad food. Finally, on 16 *Brumaire*, two hundred and fifty of us left this prison ship to be transferred to a land prison. We disembarked at Porchester [Portchester] and were sent the same day to Pitesfeld [Petersfield].

On 17 [8 December 1805], slept in Alton, a market town. On 18, slept in Basingtock [Basingstoke], town. On 19, slept in Marlow, city. On 20, slept in Reading, city. On 21, Chesham. On 23, slept in Amstaly, market town. On 24, slept in Dunstall [Dunstable], market town. On 25, slept in Bogdon, town. On 26, arrived at Normancross, our final destination, 53 leagues from Porsmouth [Portsmouth].[8]

From 1808 most soldiers brought to Britain were captured during the Peninsular War. In fact, 75 per cent of all French prisoners kept in Britain between 1803 and 1814 were taken in Spain or Portugal. Sergeant Major Beaujot,[9] fighting in the 26th line infantry regiment, fell into enemy hands on 27 September 1810:

A shot fired from 10 to 12 feet away broke my left leg. [...] I fell and was immediately surrounded by English soldiers who robbed me. One took

7. Louis Dembowski, 'Voyage de retour de Saint-Domingue en France de l'adjudant-commandant Dembowksi', in: *Carnet de la Sabretache: revue militaire rétrospective* (1914), pp. 1–7.
8. Rochay, 'Du Piémont aux Antilles et à Trafalgar', p. 510.
9. See page 99.

my bag, the other my watch, the third my belt. I begged this last one to take me to safety. [...] At that moment, a volley fired by French skirmishers forced the Englishman who had robbed me to leave me in a ravine, where he abandoned me. [Beaujot was left with other wounded French and British soldiers for two days.] We saw with indescribable happiness a detachment of English dragoons and Hanoverian Hussars under the command of General Crawfurt [Craufurd].[10] I need here to pay homage to the humanity not only of the general, but also of the English officers and soldiers. The soldiers distributed with kindness what they had, either wine, rum or biscuits.[11]

Jules Boucquel de Beauval[12] was also captured during the Peninsular War. First taken by the Spanish, he was later handed over to the British:

> Our crossing, hampered by bad weather, was even more difficult because we were deprived of hammocks and lodged in steerage like [slaves] brought to the market. We were subjected to every movement of the ship; our food was the same as that given to the sailors, but compared to what was provided by *don pedro* [the Spanish], this could be considered good.[13]

Louis François Gille[14] endured a similar ordeal. Captured by the Spanish, he was sent to the notorious island of Cabrera, where French soldiers were subjected to inhumane conditions by their captors. Indeed, only a third of the French prisoners survived imprisonment on Cabrera. So appalling were the conditions that a British ship offered clothes to the prisoners:

10. Robert Craufurd, born on 5 May 1764, was a Scottish major general who served in India. He commanded a light division. Craufurd was mortally wounded during the siege of Ciudad Rodrigo on 23 January 1812.
11. Charles-Rémy Beaujot, *Relation de la captivité du capitaine Beaujot, ancient sergent-major sous l'empire français* (Liège, 1856), p.
12. Jules Boucquel de Beauval was born in 1785 to a noble family from Artois. He fled with his family during the Revolution but came home in 1802. He joined the army and was sent to the Old Guard of the Imperial Guard. He fought at Ulm and Austerlitz and became an officer in 1807. He was transferred to the 63rd regiment of line infantry the same year and served in Spain, where he was captured by the Spanish. Sent to Tiverton, he escaped and managed to go back to France. He fought again in the following years but supported the monarchy during the Hundred Days. He continued serving in the army after the Napoleonic Wars and reached the rank of colonel.
13. Philippe Poisson, *Pontons et prisons sous le Premier Empire* (Paris, 1998), p. 58.
14. Louis François Gille, born in 1788, was conscripted when he was eighteen. He was captured by the Spanish during the battle of Bailen in 1808. Handed over to the British, he was released after the fall of Napoleon in 1814. He had a distinguished civilian career afterwards and died in 1863.

A few days later the same brig entered the bay; the officers disembarked and had bundles transferred to the home of the island's commander. The bundles contained blue shirts, trousers made of canvas and sailors' wool shirts. This was the result of a collection made by English sailors. The French commander thanked the English in the name of all the prisoners and the next day we shared the clothes.[15]

Other Frenchmen experienced Spanish prisons and British charity. Captain François was one of them:

3 February 1810: In the morning, three dogs who lived on board were killed and eaten. At around nine, a sailor jumped in the water and swam towards the English admiral. Everybody was watching him. A Spanish canoe tried to chase him but English sailors jumped in a canoe and were able to pull this unfortunate man out of the water. Under the gaze of the Spanish, they brought him to their ship and we saw that they gave him goods and bread. He was also given a drink. He handed over letters addressed to the admiral. Everywhere English people were giving him goods. He left on the Spanish canoe and shared with his comrades the biscuits that the English had given him. At around seven in the evening, a sailor swam to us to say that forty of his comrades had also gone to the English admiral's ship. Hunger drove them. This sailor told us that eight negroes were on board and that the crew was considering cutting their throats to eat them the next day.[16]

Months later, along with hundreds of other French prisoners, Louis François Gille was given to the British and transferred to England. The French were delighted and relieved to face far better conditions of detention:

Once on board the English ship, we were extremely pleased to notice a striking contrast with our previous fate. The cruelties inflicted by the ferocious Spanish were replaced by English soldiers' and sailors' caring attention. These good people displayed all sorts of consideration. They carried several of our ill or wounded comrades. Our belongings were brought by them and they did everything for us.

The *Britannia*, the name of the ship on which I had just arrived, was a beautiful three-masted vessel made ready to receive troops. The greatest cleanliness was everywhere. We were comfortable and I could only applaud this new situation. Since I had to renounce freedom, I was happy to have escaped the Spanish, with whom our existence was never safe.

15. Louis Gille, *Mémoires d'un conscrit de 1808: les prisons de Cabrera* (Paris, 1892), p. 245.
16. François, *Journal du capitaine François*, pp. 610–11.

Healthier and plentiful food replaced the inadequate rations of dried cod and biscuits given to us by the Spanish. Our officers were the only ones to be in a less beneficial position, because they were treated like us. Their self-esteem was piqued by this equality.[17]

On 20 September 1810 Louis François Gille saw England for the first time in his life. This new country with its lush vegetation was a welcome change from the Mediterranean landscape:

I had not seen anything as pleasurable for so long. I greatly admired the variety of the landscape. It was no longer the dark rocks that border Spain around the Mediterranean, it was nature in all its glory. [...] The coast was covered with vegetation, a few trees here and there, shadowing pretty countryside houses. [...] It was hard to believe. I saw fishmongers wearing black velvet robes and hats decorated with flowers and feathers. I could not believe that luxury was brought to such a level in England but I soon saw other examples.[18]

Philippe Beaudoin, encountered above, was also intrigued by Britain. Approaching his final destination, he wrote several observations about the country in his diary:

Belfast – there is in this city a big tower and a great bell tower, as well as a beautiful castle next to the city, on the right when entering, surrounded by trees that hide it from the harbour. At the entrance of the city, on the left, there is a very long bridge separating the suburbs from the city centre. This place is a beautiful harbour, with plenty of buildings. Around the city, there are beautiful country houses; moreover, there is a beautiful shop on the side of the harbour.

[...] On 15 *prairial* year XII [4 June 1806] there was a celebration for the king of England. [...] After the ceremony, they carried 'Bonaparte' around on a donkey in the streets. After this walk, in the evening, they burned the effigy with torches while telling me that they hoped to do the same to the man. But my answer irritated them.

[...] We arrived in Glasgow at six in the evening. Big city, beautiful and very populated. [...] There are not many beautiful women. In general, they have mouths shaped like ovens.[19]

The initial excitement did not last long. Soldiers and non-commissioned officers were about to start a dull life in prison, if they were lucky, or in

---

17. Gille, *Mémoires d'un conscrit*, pp. 252–3.
18. Gille, *Mémoires d'un conscrit*, pp. 255–6.
19. Philippe Beaudoin, *Carnet d'étapes: expédition de Saint-Domingue* (Paris, 2000), pp. 91–4.

prison-ships. For most, captivity would last years and would only end after the fall of Napoleon in 1814.

## Life in Britain

During the Revolutionary and Napoleonic Wars the growing number of prisoners forced the Admiralty to rethink its prison system. A Transport Office was established in August 1794 for 'conducting the transport business which has hitherto been transacted by the Navy Office; it had also the care of the prisoners of war'.[20] To detain the French, various strongholds and camps were either renovated or opened in England, including Portchester Castle, Forton near Plymouth, and Falmouth. The British also used Fort George, a fortress in Scotland, but refused to send French soldiers to Ireland, considering it too dangerous. These few camps quickly proved insufficient. Indeed, an enquiry led by the Admiralty in 1796 showed that the number of prisoners exceeded prison capacity. Portchester had reached its limit of 2,000 prisoners, Forton had 6,300, while Mill prison (Plymouth) was supposed to hold 3,300 but already had 3,513. There are only a few descriptions of British prisons during the Revolutionary Wars and the first years of Bonaparte as First Consul. One report, commissioned and published by the French republic on 24 January 1798, was damning:

> [...] Your commission has just finished a difficult task; it retraced the crimes that you have already experienced; ask for vengeance, in the name of humanity, against the English government [...] to rescue the life of twenty-two thousand republicans packed in the jails of England.
>
> [...] Ever since the war began, they have outraged our prisoners. Disregarding the agreements, they put in the same prisons officers and their subalterns, which led to unfortunate scenes and disciplinary problems. When we protested against this abuse, agents of Saint James laughed and answered: 'You are republicans, you want equality; you need therefore to be treated equally.' Soon, they feared reprisals and separated our officers.
>
> [...] We could write much about the acts of cruelty that those unfortunate men endure in those unhealthy prisons. Some are trapped in old ships, others in barracks built with badly jointed planks, through which penetrate cold and humidity from all sides. They have no straw; they lie in the mud and in waste. Their treatment is outrageous; if they are exposed to the wild rabble, mud is thrown in their faces; they are struck,

---

20. Thomas Walker, *The depot for prisoners at Norman Cross Huntingdonshire, 1796 to 1816* (London, 1913), p. 7.

they are shot for the slightest pretext ... These facts are damning; they
are found in many pieces of evidence given to your commission ...[21]

The report also reproduced a letter describing one particular atrocity committed in Plymouth:

> We were packed in together, seventy-two men in a shed of seventeen feet
> square by ten, several of which were built at the bottom of a mountain,
> from where water pours in and spreads across our cells, where the lack of
> air, hammocks, straw and bread are mild pains compared to the atrocious
> treatment inflicted on a daily basis by agents, officers, soldiers, guardians
> and others, who fire at prisoners on the slightest pretext.
>
> One day, in Plymouth, a prisoner was aimed at by a soldier and killed.
> They sent for the commissar With. He came and lifted the body. We
> asked for justice. He said: 'He is French.' And then he left.[22]

While this report was probably exaggerated, it was clear that improvements
were needed. The Admiralty soon adopted different measures to improve
detention conditions. A new prison, at Norman Cross (near Peterborough),
was built between 1796 and 1797; prison-ships were also used to address over-
crowding in camps and fortresses. This last solution proved convenient, especially since the authorities had been made aware that some 4,000 prisoners
captured in the West Indies were on their way to Britain.[23] By December 1799
no fewer than 25,646 French prisoners were detained: 10,128 in Portsmouth,
7,477 in Forton and 3,038 in Norman Cross, while the rest were divided
between Liverpool, Chatham, Stapleton, Edinburgh and Yarmouth. Soldier
Rochay described the prison at Norman Cross, where he died soon after. This
is the last entry in his diary:

> *Description of Normancross*: Normancross is located on a hill, a mile from
> ... and 3 miles from Pitercara [Peterborough]. It was built to serve as a
> prisoner-of-war camp. It is surrounded by a double fence. Prisons are
> distributed in four fields. Each field is surrounded by a third fence and
> holds four barracks where the prisoners live. Each barrack holds five
> hundred men.
>
> In the centre of these four fields is a guardroom where there are little
> cannon, which can fire at the four fields at the same time in case of revolt.
> At all times there is a garrison of two thousand men to guard the

21. François Riou, *Rapport fait par Riou, au nom de la commission spéciale, composée des représentants Quirot, Leclerc (de Maine, Loire)* (Paris, 1798), p. 5.
22. Riou, *Rapport fait par Riou*, p. 5.
23. Walker, *The depot for prisoners at Norman Cross*, pp. 10–16.

prisoners. It is relieved every six months. Their barracks are also built of wood and located within the perimeter of the first fence.[24]

Following the signing of the Treaty of Amiens in 1802, French prisoners were freed and repatriated. When war resumed the next year, the influx of captured enemy soldiers rose once again. In 1805 the authorities ordered the construction of a stone prison on Dartmoor. Another detention centre was opened in Perth in August 1812. Adelbert Doisy de Villargennes[25] described the prison at Forton:

> A prison it was in reality, but resembling in all respects a huge collection of barracks where an admirable organisation had been established, with strict yet humane regulations. Here, no moans of despair were heard, no despondent looks observable on the countenances of the inmates, but on all sides resounded shouts of laughter, or snatches of patriotic songs. No doubt this philosophy of 'making the best of things' might in part be attributed to the happy disposition of my countrymen – long may they cherish it!
>
> I was led by my foster-brother to a snug little corner occupied by him and a comrade, containing an apparently good bed and other small articles of furniture, partly purchased with their own money. The next compartment was a kitchen, shared by two hundred men, and from which drifted odours not in the least indicative of a famished population. I remained to dinner. I shall not say that the meal was sumptuous, but there was plenty of good food.[26]

Prisoners had to wear colourful uniforms to make them instantly recognisable in case of an escape. Louis François Gille, who explained what happened on his first day in the prison of Portchester, was visibly shocked by the uniform:

> On 28 September 1810, two months after leaving Cabrera, we disembarked below the walls of Portchester. We walked only fifteen to twenty steps to reach the gate, where we entered. [...] In the courtyard we saw a great number of men in yellow clothes. It was the first time I had seen such clothes. I could not suppress a laugh on seeing the costumes

---

24. Rochay, 'Du Piémont aux Antilles et à Trafalgar', p. 511.
25. Adelbert Doisy de Villargennes, born in 1792, served in the French navy from the age of fifteen. He served during the Peninsular War and became a midshipman. In 1809 he was promoted to the rank of sub-lieutenant in the 26th regiment of line infantry. He later served in Germany and then went back to Spain, where he was captured and sent to England. Adelbert Doisy de Villargennes survived the experience of captivity, came home and died in 1879.
26. Adelbert Doisy de Villargennes, *Reminiscences of army life* (Cincinnati, 1884), pp. 69–70.

that the English gave to their prisoners. [...] We went via the supply store where we each received a jacket, a vest and trousers made of yellow canvas, and a canvas shirt with blue and white stripes; [we were also given] a canvas hammock, a mattress weighing around two pounds, a wool blanket and arm-long pieces of rope.[27]

Life in prison was undoubtedly dull and revolved around a strict routine. Joseph Quantin[28] described a typical day at Portchester:

At six in the morning during summer, at seven in the winter, a bell, on top of a mast, tells the prisoners that their guards are here. Accompanied by soldiers, they indeed arrive soon after. They open the door (of the tower and the barracks) and count the prisoners, who are pushed by the soldiers who have entered inside, one by one. When it snows or rains, this operation, which lasts about an hour, seems very long for the men, who are lightly dressed.

At nine in the morning, the bell rings again. It is time for the market. The English put up stalls next to the fence, on the prisoners' side. During that time, they also distribute bread through two counters built inside the fence near the kitchen. [...] At noon, the bell rings to announce the departure of the English merchants, who are replaced by the French; they install their own shops, where are displayed products made by the prisoners. Also at noon they distribute soup and beef.

By the end of the day, the infernal sound of the bell precedes the guards and the soldiers, who bring the prisoners inside and close the doors of the tower and the barracks. When everybody is inside, the bell rings for the last time and invites prisoners to turn off their lights. Sentries on the ramparts are ordered to fire anywhere a light is seen.[29]

Unsurprisingly, prisoners were eager to write and receive letters to escape boredom and gain news of their homeland. Fortunately, a sophisticated system allowing prisoners to write and receive money had been organised by the authorities, as Joseph Quantin explained:

We received letters and even money quite easily from France. Every month, the English agent announced inside the prison the names of those who had received letters or money. Those who had something

---

27. Gille, *Mémoires d'un conscrit*, pp. 257–8.
28. Joseph Quantin was born in Paris and served in the Napoleonic army from 1807. He was captured in Spain and sent to Cadiz and then Cabrera. He was later handed over to the British and transferred to England. He survived the Napoleonic Wars.
29. Joseph Quantin, *Trois ans de séjour en Espagne dans l'intérieur du pays, sur les pontons, à Cadix, et dans l'île de Cabrera* (Paris, 1823), pp. 114–16.

were transported by joy but those who searched the list in vain were really sad.[30]

A few of the letters written from British prisons have survived. They reflect the fears and anxieties of the French soldiers in captivity. The following letter was written by Henri-Joseph Albert[31] from the prison at Stapleton:

Prison of Stapelton [Stapleton], near Bristol, 17 August 1811

My dear father and mother,

I have been a prisoner for five years in England and I have not received once a letter from you. I have, however, written many letters but I have to assume that they did not arrive or that your answers were lost. Be the judge of my sadness. Do I have to fear that something unfortunate has happened to you? This thought exacerbates my deplorable situation and makes the burden of my captivity even greater. How could I believe that you have forgotten me? You are incapable of this as your love for me has always been without boundaries and it is impossible that mere distance triggered such a change. I therefore hope that the present will bring one of your letters, since it is now very easy to write.

I count on your exactitude to give me this satisfaction. There is no greater [satisfaction] (after freedom) than to correspond with those who have brought you into this world. Troubles seem not as great and we have the pleasure of knowing that someone still cares about us in the world.

I will not try to move you by detailing the troubles that I face. I am too afraid to cause sorrow. I cannot, however, hide the fact that I am currently in the greatest misery. This is why I beg you to send me help if you can. I would owe you a second life because I do not think I can survive for much longer in such an atrocious position. Be moved by my sad fate. Heaven will reward you for your kindness and my gratitude will be eternal if you do for me this act of humanity.

Let us hope, my dear father and mother, that happier times will follow this one and will bring me home. While waiting for this fortunate moment, I wish you happiness and help. These are the wishes with which I kiss you thousands and thousands of times for life.

Your respectful son

Henry Joseph Albert

PS: If you want to send money and you have not had the opportunity before, ask for Mr Pérégaux, banker, street Chaussée d'Antin, Paris. He

---

30. Quantin, *Trois ans de séjour en Espagne*, pp. 130–1.
31. Henri-Joseph Albert was born in Soiron on 9 April 1784. He was conscripted into the 26th line regiment infantry in 1805. He was captured on a French ship by the British.

is very safe as most prisoners here receive money from him. Compliments to my brothers, sister, uncles, aunts, all our relatives and friends. Please tell me if my brothers are still with you.

My address is Henry Joseph Albert, soldier in the 26th regiment of line infantry N. 5444 prisoner at Stapleton near Bristol, England.[32]

Jean-François Giet,[33] also in Stapleton, had the following letter written for him by a friend, or perhaps by someone paid for his literary skills. Certainly the signature was different from the rest of the text:

From the prisoner of war [camp] of Stapleton in England, 6 March 1812

My dear Uncle,

Despite all my efforts to receive news from you and from my family since I have been captive in England, I have been unsuccessful. This is, however, the third [letter] that I send and perhaps this one will reach you directly and I will be happy to receive one from you. Dear uncle, I am pleased to say that I am perfectly healthy and hope that you are the same.

In my two first [letters], I asked for money to help with my captivity. This would be very helpful and I beg you to satisfy my legitimate request as soon as you receive this letter. You can give a sum of money to the director of the post of Malmedy, who will send it to Mr Peregaux La fitte Banker in Paris, rue de mon blanc, chaussée d'antin n. 6. He will send this to my address: Mr Jean-François Giet, soldier in the 36th regiment of line infantry, 1st Battalion, 2nd Company, prisoner of war in Stapleton, near Bristo [Bristol] in England. Do not be afraid of losing it [the money] because my comrades in misfortune receive letters from this banker every day. For the news that I ask for in such haste, put the address as mentioned above and do not forget to stamp the letter.

Give my letter to my mother and send her my affection and to my brothers.

One of my friends is with me and is named Lionnard Gabriel[34] from Removal. He asks that you write to his family. You would please him greatly.

---

32. AEL: FFP 1045. Letter from Henri-Joseph Albert to his parents, 17 August 1811.
33. Jean-François Giet, born in Malmedy on 24 May 1784, was called up for military duty in year XIII but tried to hide. He was arrested and sent to the 36th regiment of line infantry, 1st battalion, 2nd company, on 11 July 1808. He was captured by the British in Lisbon on 1 April 1809. AEL: FFP 1062. Letter from the War Minister of 3 February 1812 and individual papers of 14 April 1813.
34. Leonard-Louis Gabril, of Butgenbach, conscripted in year VII into the 89th half-brigade. He was captured in 1803 by the British. AEL: FFP 1062. Letter from the War Ministry, 6 June 1810.

If you can, my dear uncle, give me news in your letter; it would make me happy.

I am and will be for ever your devoted nephew Jean François Giet.[35]

Jean-Nicolas Terwagne[36] was kept at the prison at Valleyfield, Scotland. His letter suggests that life in the north was not very different from that in English camps:

In Scotland Valley Field, 30 September 1812

My dear father,

I received your letter of 6 April 1810. I can tell you that I am still in good health. I hope the same for you and all the family. My father, I ask for your help. When you receive this letter, send a bit of money to help me. In this adversity, this is the fourth letter that I have written without receiving an answer. I have reasons to believe that you are negligent since you have my address. Instead of writing one letter, write a few, so one might arrive. I believe that you have forgotten me completely because you should have sent news and money as soon as you had received my address. All my friends who are with me in the same prison receive news very often and they are from the same country as me. The son of Mossoux of Warsez received news from his father through the address I gave you. I can tell you that I have never been ill since I left home and have not been wounded.

I ask you to send news of the country and all the people I knew when I was there. My respect to my brothers and sisters, my father I beg you to answer and to tell me how things are. Nothing else to say at the moment.

I end this by kissing you from the deepest of my heart and I am, for life, your obedient son Nicolas Terwagne.

Here is my address: to Mister Jean Nicolas Terwagne of the 26th Regiment of Line, prisoner of war at Valley-feild [sic] in Scotland.

Here is the address to send money: Sir Périgaud Lafite and company Bankers in Paris. You must send 50f and, at the same time, write a letter to the bankers. [...] You will know that this letter is written by me because this is my handwriting.[37]

The conditions in British prisons were variable and uneven. Following major British victories, either on land or at sea, the prisons faced an increased influx

---

35. AEL: FFP 1045. Letter from Jean-François Giet to his uncle, 6 March 1812.
36. Jean-Nicolas Terwagne, born in Amay on 15 July 1784, was conscripted in the 26th regiment of line infantry on year XIII. He was captured in the Martinique on 24 February 1809 and was sent to Valley Field. AEL: Archives communales d'Amay.
37. AEL: FFP 1045. Letter from Jean-Nicolas Terwagne to his father, 30 September 1812.

of new prisoners and forced the Transport Office to move the captured soldiers around:

> After a few days' stay at Gosport, I was moved, along with several other transferred prisoners, on parole to Odiham, a small town in Hampshire; there, nothing occurred worth recording. The number of prisoners of war had, about this period, been considerably augmented by the taking of the Isle of France, Martinique and Guadeloupe. The towns required to receive officers on parole in England were found to be so inconveniently crowded that the government decided to quarter some of us in Scotland, where none had hitherto been sent. (Political reasons precluded Ireland from having any share in the distribution of prisoners.) Odiham furnished its contingent, and I was one of the party thus transported to Caledonia, where we landed at Leith on 1 October 1811. From Edinburgh we started for our destination, Selkirk, the county town of Selkirkshire, thirty-six miles south of Edinburgh. On the way, we halted a few hours at Penay, where about two thousand of our soldiers and sailors were confined: the organisation and regulations of the prison appeared to us modelled on those we had admired at Gosport.[38]

Official circles were weary of such prisons, regrouping thousands of potentially dangerous enemy soldiers. Louis François Gille was one of those prisoners who dreamed of a violent escape:

> We really wanted to escape and free all the French prisoners to force England to accept all the conditions imposed by France. The 70,000 Frenchmen in England were more than enough to realise this project, especially in a country lacking regular troops and whose strength was made up of a few militia regiments. And the war that we had planned was a war of partisans. We would have avoided any serious battle, but harassed troops dispatched to intercept us and acted against villages and towns ... Weapons and ammunition were available with a bit of audacity. Portchester could give us 800 muskets and two cannon. We were 7,000 French and that was enough to take Forton prison, where at least 3,000 Frenchmen were held. It was only two leagues from here. In less than an hour 10,000 men could be reunited ... But to follow this plan, we needed to know not only that France was willing to follow, but also that the troops based in Boulogne were ready to distract English maritime forces based in the Channel. However, the closing down of the camp in Boulogne destroyed our plans.[39]

38. Doisy de Villargennes, *Reminiscences of army life*, pp. 74–5.
39. Gille, *Mémoires d'un conscrit*, pp. 277–8.

Life in British camps was often monotonous for conscripts and low-ranking soldiers, but officers had more freedom and more opportunities to socialise with the local population. Jules Boucquel de Beauval explained how officers were confined to parole towns:

> The word of an officer prisoner of war is like a tacit agreement between him and the local authorities; he promises to follow a set of rules in exchange for free movement. The officer pawns his honour to enjoy the same freedom as common citizens. [...] We were forbidden from leaving our houses in the morning before one specific hour and had to be back before another. A bell rang in the morning to give the morning signal and again in the evening, as for workers in a factory, but this was not all ... One guinea [was] promised to any English person who arrested an officer violating this curfew. One guinea! What a bait for such greedy people![40]

In a few cases, officers were even offered the chance to go back to France in exchange for promising that they would not fight Britain again. Those who were confined to the parole towns were given a small sum of money by the Transport Office and were forbidden from going more than a mile from the town centre.[41] This treatment had its limitations but was far from unpleasant. Jules Boucquel de Beauval used his time to learn English and chase local women:

> I spent a year in Tiverton, intensively studying the English language and practising music. These two occupations were soon followed by a third and far more appealing one: the desire to please an interesting English woman, Miss W—, intelligent and beautiful, charming, and an orphan. It was necessary, as in a theatre play, to go behind her guardian's back. This man was not jealous of his ward, but in all of Tiverton he was the one who most hated the French.
>
> Everything was good until one day this man discovered how well disposed his niece was towards me. From then on, I was burdened with worries and threats. He even asked that I be sent to Wales (which is the Siberia of England).[42]

Boucquel de Beauval was not an exception. Several French officers interacted with local women and married in Britain. Others had interesting encounters

---

40. Poisson, *Pontons et prisons sous le Premier Empire*, p. 58.
41. Patrick Le Carvèse, 'Les prisonniers français en Grande-Bretagne de 1803 à 1814: première partie', *Napoleonica*, 8 (2010), pp. 3–29.
42. Poisson, *Pontons et prisons sous le Premier Empire*, p. 60.

during their captivity in England. Captain Gabriel Heuillet,[43] a veteran of the Imperial Guard, was wounded while fighting against the Prussians at Plancenoit and handed over to the British. While in captivity, he met the famous General Cambronne and had the opportunity to discuss the legendary words supposedly spoken at the end of the battle of Waterloo. He later summarised Cambronne's answer in a letter to a friend:

Sir and dear friend

My leg was wounded (during the defence of Planchenoit [Plancenoit]) and I was captured by the Prussians. I was brought to Brussels, where I met Battalion Commander de Bar, Herminier, Count Lobau, Colonel Gentil and Colonel Carré. The next day, when I was about to embark on the Ostend canal for England, I heard my name and, turning, I recognised General Cambronne, who was supposed to have died of a head wound: 'Hello, Heuillet,' he said, 'are you a prisoner?' 'I'm afraid so, but, in our position it is nice to meet old friends.' Soon, we arrived at Plymouth and we were left as parole prisoners in a city called Ashburton [Devon]. It is there that we learned from the English newspapers that General Cambronne had answered the English call for the French to surrender with these words: 'The Guard dies and does not surrender!' As we were dining together, we congratulated him for these glorious words that immortalised him and reflected so positively on the Imperial Guard. 'I am sorry,' he answered, 'but I did not say those words: I said something else … and not what is reported.' We begged him to lie nonetheless for the army's honour but he refused to do so.[44]

Officers had more freedom but also encountered hostile behaviour as a result. This was sometimes a problem, as Joseph de Bonnefoux found out while living near Thames:

This [Thames] was a town of manufacturers and was populated with workers who were not related to local families. [...] These turds [the workers] were full of hostile feelings against France, inspired by the newspapers, which they used against us vulnerable prisoners. They did not miss an opportunity to insult us or throw stones at us. Local people

---

43. Gabriel Heuillet was born in Sainte-Croix-Volvestre on 12 September 1780. He served as a drummer from 1794, became a corporal in 1799 and a lieutenant in 1807. In 1813 he became a captain in the Old Guard and he later served under the orders of General Cambronne. He was wounded at the battle of Waterloo and sent to captivity in England. Heuillet continued serving in the French army until 1835 and died in 1857.

44. Gabriel Heuillet, 'Extrait d'une lettre du capitaine Heuillet, du 2e chasseurs de la Garde', in: *Carnet de la Sabretache: revue militaire rétrospective* (1905), pp. 121–2.

living in this peaceful town were disgusted by these distasteful scenes, but they almost all feared the workers.[45]

It is often forgotten that French prisoners were also sent to Canada. While none of the French held captive in North America left a written testimony, we know a little about them through the diary of a US citizen named Benjamin Waterhouse,[46] who was captured during the war of 1812 and sent to Canada:

> We found that there were about two hundred French prisoners in Nova Scotia. Some had been there ever since 1803. Few of them were confined to prison. The chief of them lived in or near the town of Halifax, working for the inhabitants, or teaching dancing, or fencing, or their own language. Some of them were employed as butchers and cooks; others as nurses in the hospital; and they were everywhere favoured for their complaisance, obedience and good humour. They had the character of behaving better towards the British officers and inhabitants than the Americans, and I believe with reason; for our men seem to take a delight in plaguing, embarrassing and alarming those who were set over them. A Frenchman always tried to please, while many Americans seemed to take equal delight in letting the Nova Scotians know that they longed to be at liberty to fight them again. I confess I do not wonder that the submissive, smiling Frenchmen made more friends at Halifax than the ordinary run of American seamen.[47]

As this chapter has shown, British land prisons were not luxurious places but offered nonetheless acceptable conditions. Prison-ships, on the other hand, were far less enviable. *Pontons*, as they are known in French, had already been used by the British before the Revolutionary Wars to incarcerate criminals. During the Napoleonic Wars these derelict vessels, about fifty of them, were to be found at Chatham, Portsmouth and Plymouth. Britain was not the only nation to use them; Spain had its own fleet of prison-hulks in Cadiz and Cabrera, and even the French incarcerated soldiers from Austria, Russia and Prussia on similar prison-ships.[48] British prison-ships hosted not only French sailors but also infantry soldiers and even passengers of French ships captured by the Royal Navy. In theory, officers were not supposed to be sent

---

45. Jobbé-Duval, *Mémoires du Baron de Bonnefoux*, p. 200.
46. Benjamin Waterhouse, born in 1754, was an American physician who served with the United States during the war of 1812. He was captured by the British and sent to Canada, where he lived with French prisoners of war. He later became a professor at Harvard Medical School and died on 2 October 1846.
47. Benjamin Waterhouse, *A journal of a young man of Massachusetts* (Boston, 1816), p. 17.
48. Le Carvèse, 'Les prisonniers français en Grande-Bretagne', pp. 3–29.

to the ships, unless they had attempted to escape. It is estimated that about 40 per cent of French prisoners of war in Britain were kept on unseaworthy ships.[49] The prison-ships were dreaded by the French. Louis François Gille, who had been on board a Spanish prison-ship, had a moment of panic when he arrived in Portsmouth:

> On 26 [September 1810] we disembarked at Spithead where we were supposed to be quarantined, but the next day we entered the harbour of Portsmouth. We saw the prison-ships and the sight of them made me shake. The memory of those in Cadiz and the suffering I experienced on board the *Vencedor* was bringing back the most sinister memories. It is easy to understand how happy I felt when we learned that we would disembark the next day to be transferred to a land prison.[50]

There are many testimonies illustrating how filthy and miserable these places were. Sergeant Major Philippe Beaudoin, who was transferred from a land prison to a prison-hulk, explained:

> From Sheerness to Chatham river, 3 leagues. – There are nine prison ships with Frenchmen. Their names are: first, the *Bristol*; the *Glory*, a three-decker; the *Prince Couronne*; the *Buckingham*; the *Samson*, where bad subjects are brought; the *Rochester*; the *Souwick*; the *Resistible*; and the *Trusty*, for those who are ill. There are, in this depot, six thousand five or six hundred [prisoners]. Moreover, there is the *Bahama*, filled with Danes.
>
> The differences between land prisons and prison-ships are very important. There is no space to walk; we are on top of each other; nobody comes to see us; we are like abandoned men. There is no work but only chores, hoisting our water for our needs and not as much as we need. We are itchy during winter, and wash the spot where we sleep during summer. In a word, you only need to see them to understand that they are places of horror.
>
> [...] It is unfortunate that I do not know enough to describe the crimes of a nation [Britain] that wants to oppress the whole of Europe. They want to be seen as a well-behaved nation but there is no bandit or savage with such villainous traits as them. Daily they practise their cruelty on us, their unfortunate prisoners. In these situations, they are warriors, the cowards! Our men are incapable of defending themselves.
>
> Half of the time, they give us supplies that dogs would refuse. The bread is not baked and could be glued to the wall. The meat looks like it

49. Le Carvèse, 'Les prisonniers français en Grande-Bretagne', pp. 3–29.
50. Gille, *Mémoires d'un conscrit*, pp. 256–7.

has been dragged in the streets for a league. Moreover, twice a week we are given rotten salted fish: on Wednesday, herrings, on Saturday, cod. We refused it several times; their response was to give us nothing and they said that it was good enough for French people.

[...] I cannot take revenge but I hope that our Emperor will take care of this haughty nation. I do not think there is a Frenchman who hates them more than me; I want to take revenge before I die, this is what I want.[51]

Letters written from prison-ships were not optimistic either. Henri-Joseph Detongres[52] seems to have been in a difficult situation when he wrote:

Plimouth [Plymouth] in England, 10 February 1810

My dear father and mother

I have been unable to send news for a very long time but, after having endured many difficulties, I am now able to write. I left for Martinique three years ago and we stayed there for two years but the English took the colony a year ago and I have been a prisoner of war ever since. I do not have to tell you that my situation is really miserable. You will not have any difficulty believing it and I beg you to send help as soon as you receive this letter because I need it. You can find out my address but for more safety go to the post office and enquire as how to send something safely. I cannot write in more details now, and you will do the same when you answer. Send my regards to my cousin Brou and tell me what happened to my cousin Bayard. Charliere, of Sainte-Foi, is in the same prison as me. I end this letter, my dear father and mother, by telling you that I am your devoted son.

Henry Détangue [Detongres]

[...] Prisoner on-board the *Généreux*, Plimouth [Plymouth], England[53]

It is true that British prison-ships were far from exemplary conditions, but it must be highlighted that most modern French studies relay myths designed to damage Britain's reputation. For example, Jean-Claude Damamme wrote the following:

It is time to begin our descent to hell. Devils wore Spanish or English uniforms. [...] Disembarked at Bordeaux going home to Avignon, one

---

51. Beaudoin, *Carnet d'étapes: expédition de Saint-Domingue*, pp. 101–3.

52. Henri-Joseph Detongres, born in Herstal on 18 July 1788, was conscripted into the 26th line infantry regiment on 17 July 1807. He was captured by the British and brought from Martinique to England.

53. AEL: FFP 1045. Letter from Henri-Joseph Detongres to his parents, 10 February 1810.

survivor of prison-ships – those of Cadiz (but his remarks would have been the same for the English equivalent) said: 'Do not think that these horrible treatments, which are revolting to nature, are only found in half-savage countries such as Spain or Portugal. The English, our neighbours, our rivals in civilisation, economy and industry, reached a point that even the Spanish replicated timidly. The *pontons* of Plymouth were places of torture, graves a thousand times more frightening than the floating prisons of Cadiz. I thought I had reached the last resort of human misery but my comrades in England were even worse than me.'[54] In fact, the quote used by Damamme, which he did not reference, came from a book written by a soldier who had not even seen the inside of a British prison, nor even been to Britain.[55] Fabricated stories of alleged British crimes appeared during the last years of the eighteenth century and became widespread at the end of the First Empire. This propaganda campaign was followed by dramatic narrations by survivors who had returned from British prisons after 1815. Famous books, such as *Mes pontons* by Louis Garneray, or *L'Angleterre vue à Londres et dans ses provinces, pendant un séjour de dix années dont six comme prisonnier de guerre* by Pillet, have portrayed British prison-ships in the worst possible light.[56] Describing captivity as another deadly struggle between the French and the British was a way to rehabilitate ex-prisoners after the Napoleonic Wars. Instead of being passive spectators of a conflict fought by their fellow-countrymen, French prisoners were fighting their own war within British camps and prisons. This phenomenon is not unique to the period studied in this book. French civilians living in the territories invaded by the Germans during the First World War also tried to darken the Occupation to attract sympathy and legitimise their experience in the post-war world.[57] While books accusing Britain of deliberate cruelty against prisoners are often used in the historiography, other testimonies are systematically left out. US citizen Benjamin Waterhouse was brought from Canada to the prison-ships of Chatham. Here is how he described them:

> There were thirteen prison ships beside our own, all ships of the line, and one hospital ship, moored near each other. They were filled,

54. Jean-Claude Damamme, *Les soldats de la Grande Armée* (Paris, 2002), p. 282.
55. The quote is from Sébastien Blaze, *Mémoires d'un apothicaire* (Paris, 1828).
56. Louis Garneray, *Mes pontons, neuf années de captivité* (Paris, 1933) and René-Martin Pillet, *L'Angleterre vue à Londres et dans ses provinces, pendant un séjour de dix années, dont six comme prisonnier de guerre* (Paris, 1815).
57. Philipp Siegert and Bérénice Zunino, *Den Krieg neu denken? Penser la guerre autrement?* (Berlin, 2016).

principally, with Frenchmen, Danes and Italians. We found on our arrival twelve hundred Americans, chiefly men who had been impressed on board British men of war, and who had given themselves up, with a declaration that they would not fight against their own countrymen, and they were sent here and confined, without any distinction made between them and those who had been taken in arms. The injustice of the thing is glaring. During the night the prisoners were confined on the lower deck and on the main deck, but in the day time they were allowed the privilege of the 'pound', so called, and the fore-castle; which was a comfortable arrangement compared with the black holes of the *Regulus* and *Malabar*. There were three officers on board our ship, namely, a lieutenant, a sailing master, and a surgeon, together with sixty marines and a few invalid or superannuated seamen to go in the boats. The whole was under the command of a commodore, while Captain Hutchinson, agent for the prisoners of war, exercised a sort of control over the whole; but the butts and bounds of their jurisdiction I never knew. The commodore visited each of the prison ships every month, to hear and redress complaints, and to correct abuses, and to enforce wholesome regulations. All written communications and all intercourse by letter passed through the hands of Capt. Hutchinson. If the letters contained nothing of evil intent, they were suffered to pass; but if they contained anything which the agent deemed improper, they were detained. Complaints were sometimes made when those who wrote them thought they ought not [be censored].[58]

Doisy de Villargennes went one step further. Writing after the Napoleonic Wars, the French officer felt compelled to denounce the abundance of myths about British prisons:

Our first impulse was to go and look at and converse with our countrymen, many of whom had already been in captivity for years. Here truth and justice compel me to combat an erroneous belief in regard to the harsh treatment of prisoners of war, which was propagated with a purpose at the time, and upheld by those of our men who were so unfortunate as to be confined in the *pontons* – *id est*, vessels out of commission, at anchor in the roads. There, indeed, they had a hard fate to bear: wretched food, little exercise, extremely strict and occasionally cruel discipline – such was their lot; but we ascertained that none were sent to the *pontons* but refractory and incorrigible disturbers of the peace at

---

58. Waterhouse, *A journal of a young man of Massachusetts*, pp. 48–9.

Gosport prison, and also the crews of privateers indiscriminately, as the British government deemed such as having been captured in an illegal mode of warfare.[59]

In fact, historian Patrick Le Carvèse proved in a recent study that French prisoners were more likely to survive confinement in a prison-ship than a land prison.[60] If stories of mass casualties must be dismissed as myths, there is little doubt that life on board those derelict ships was monotonous. Prisoners found various strategies to cope with their state. According to Benjamin Waterhouse, the French soldiers spent much of the time gambling:

I have already mentioned that we had Frenchmen in this prison-ship. Instead of occupying themselves with forming a constitution, and making a code of laws, and defining crimes, and adjusting punishments, and holding courts, and pleading for, and against the person arraigned, these Frenchmen had erected billiard tables, and *rowletts* [in fact roulette], or wheels of fortune, not merely for their own amusement, but to lure the Americans to hazard their money, which these Frenchmen seldom failed to win.

These Frenchmen exhibited a considerable portion of ingenuity, industry and patience, in their little manufactories of bone, of straw and of hair. They would work incessantly to get money by selling these trifling wares; but many of them had a much more expeditious method of acquiring cash, and that was by gaming at the billiard tables, and the wheel of fortune. Their skills and address at these apparent games of hazard were far superior to the Americans'. They seemed to be calculated gamesters; their vivacity, their readiness and their everlasting professions of friendship were nicely adapted to inspire confidence in the unsuspecting American Jack Tar, who has no legerdemain about him. Most of the prisoners were in the way of earning a little money; but almost all of them were deprived of it by the French gamesters. Our people stood no chance with them, but were commonly stripped of every cent whenever they set out seriously to play with them. How often have I seen a Frenchman capering and singing and grinning, in consequence of his stripping one of our sailors of all his money.[61]

Sex was also a major preoccupation. In 1814 August-Dominique Dauphin, a surgeon, wrote a study of the main diseases from which French soldiers

59. Doisy de Villargennes, *Reminiscences of army life*, p. 68.
60. Le Carvèse, 'Les prisonniers français en Grande-Bretagne', pp. 3–29.
61. Waterhouse, *A journal of a young man of Massachusetts*, p. 55.

suffered while in captivity in England. He noted how masturbation was common:

> Overindulgence, masturbation, forced privation, were the causes of this morbific ailment. There is an intimate correlation between vocal, genital and respiratory organs.[62]

Unable to approach women, French soldiers found other ways to fuel their fantasies. Benjamin Waterhouse was reading a satirical work by Jonathan Swift when he was approached by French prisoners:

> While I was shaking my sides laughing at the comical characterful depictions of the witty Dean of St Patrick, the Frenchmen would come around me to know what the book contained, which so much tickled my fancy; they thought it was an obscene book, and wished someone to translate it to them: but all they could get out of me was the words '*John Bull* and *Louis Baboon!*'[63]

Unsurprisingly, homosexuality was common in British prisons. Sexual relations between men were usually kept secret in other circumstances but were so habitual in captivity that few men felt compelled to write about it. Lieutenant Mesonant[64] explained:

> Theft is not common on board prison-ships but there is another vice, more common, and generally quite widespread among men that five, seven and nine years of the most rigorous captivity have demoralised by depraving them of all pleasure associated with freedom ... If this vice is already so shameful as it is, and it is not even permissible to name it, it is made even worse by the vile and dishonest way in which it is practised in this horrible place, where misery breaches the last boundaries of shame and indecency. The active ones often display unnatural brutality; the passive ones are not ashamed to sell their favours for a price that I hate to put in writing, such as money, a ration of herrings, etc., or to hold an auction. There is no radical cure to these vices. [...] But prisoners do not hesitate to whip the backs of those who are guilty whenever they can, and they are spared even less than thieves. And then they are sent to the prison of misery [*raffalés*, an unusual slang word used mostly by criminals]. However, is this vice not excusable for those who are at an

---

62. Auguste-Dominique Dauphin, *Considérations sur quelques maladies qui ont principalement exercé leurs ravages parmi les Français prisonniers en Angleterre, depuis l'an 1803 jusqu'à juillet 1814* (Paris, 1815), p. 34.
63. Waterhouse, *A journal of a young man of Massachusetts*, p. 58.
64. Mesonant served in the 45th regiment of line infantry.

age of intense passions and who are locked for two decades in the pit of privations and are almost deprived of the hope of being released? And this hope is getting further and further away. Anyway! It is only one more drop in the torrent of afflictions brought by war.[65]

The diary of Philippe Beaudoin contains two pages about an incident that happened to him while on a prison-ship. This episode ended in bloodshed:

Unpleasant adventure that happened to me on 20 December 1811

Loose morals in this infernal prison. A fencing master named the 'beautiful Marseille' was an expert in this art and felt confident enough to flatter me, several times, as one would flatter a woman. The first time he showed up, I asked why he behaved like this and asked the purpose of this flattery. He answered that if I satisfied his desires, he would make me better at fencing. Knowing how things are in prison, I understood immediately what he wanted. At first, I thanked him very honestly for everything and said that I was good enough with weapons. As for your desires, you probably take me for someone else since I hate people like you. If it was in my power, I would burn all the people who misunderstand nature. Therefore, you have to stop pursuing me. Ask others rather than me because I promise that if you persist, I will slap you as a reward. This threat only made him laugh and he said that I did not look mean. I answered: 'I must agree that I am not to be feared, but try your nonsense again and see if I do not hold to my word.' A few minutes later he came back and tried again. Immediately, I slapped his face, but he managed to block my blow, took it for a joke and left. He came back two hours later. Thinking perhaps that he could be more successful another way, he came from behind and touched my buttock with his hand. I turned angrily and, saying nothing, slapped him so hard that he was knocked down. He was not joking any more and angrily tried to hit me back but failed. Then, he asked for a duel, which was agreed for the sake of duty and tranquillity. Two buttoned foils and we undressed. We began to fight in front of all the prisoners. Several French officers tried to separate us, saying that we were already unhappy in our prison without making it worse. But their prayers were in vain. I answered that I would rather die than let such a grave insult pass, and he was so angry at my blow that he was no less determined than I was. We fought for fifteen minutes at least without being able to make any impact. Witnesses, seeing that we were getting tired, ordered us to stop and rest. After four or five minutes we resumed with the same fervour. We both knew the

65. Poisson, *Pontons et prisons sous le Premier Empire*, p. 74.

game, the reason for which we prolonged this. However, after another ten to twelve minutes, after two feints, half a circle and a quarter, he exaggerated his parry ... I wounded him near the nipple. Luckily for him he partly parried the blow, or he would have been killed on the spot. I am relieved that his wound was not fatal because English laws are very strict. I would have been hanged. This is how it ended. He stayed at the hospital for a month or two. This is the danger you face in prison. Since this episode, nobody has approached me. As soon as the officers heard the reason for which I fought, I was summoned and congratulated for my behaviour in prison. They said that I was right not to give in to this monster.[66]

Escaping from prison-ships and land prisons was difficult but not impossible. A few recorded cases exist in the archives. Jules Boucquel de Beauval was one of those who managed to leave England in secret:

There are nine of us; three navy officers to supervise the navigation; six army officers to check the deck and the crew. Two Englishmen were persuaded to take us to the coast, 10 leagues from Tiverton. The way to the coast was not without dangers but [we travelled] without accident and really fast. We left the city at the beginning of the evening, hidden by fog. We waited in the fields until nightfall and reached the coast before the night was over. A shipping boat was waiting for us ...[67]

The winds were unfavourable and de Beauval was forced to hide with his friends. The next day they tried again and managed to reach Cherbourg. Baron de Bonnefoux also tried to escape four times but failed. He was punished and sent to the 'black hole', which he described:

Finally, we were caught, strangled, brought on board the *Bahama*, where we faced the punishment reserved for deserting prisoners: ten days of black-hole [in English in the text]. This was a cell only six feet long in the ship's hold. Air came in only through a few holes and would not have been enough to keep a mouse alive. Fortunately, they forgot to search us, and using a few tools we made an opening in the wall and, once in a while, we used it to breathe and drink a bit more water. [...] They came once every twenty-four hours to bring bread, soup, water, and to change our box of faeces, which was with us during these twenty-four hours.[68]
    [...] And so was halted my career, just when I was primed to be a leader. We knew, indeed, that the emperor was without pity for prisoners

---

66. Archives Départementales du Loiret: 1J1696. Diary of Philippe Beaudoin.
67. Poisson, *Pontons et prisons sous le Premier Empire*, pp. 61–2.
68. Jobbé-Duval, *Mémoires du Baron de Bonnefoux*, pp. 226–7.

and that England was too keen on contradicting him to exchange us. We were aware that we would suffer in many different ways in captivity; Napoleon did not even grant half-pay to officers of his own army when they were captured, but our time [in English prisons] was not even added to our pension.[69]

At least 130,000 French soldiers were captured and brought to Britain between 1803 and 1814. The first fall of Napoleon was followed by a period of negotiations between the provisional French government and the British authorities to release prisoners of war in both countries. On 13 April 1814 France sent a strong signal by issuing a decree to free foreign soldiers held in the country. French envoys travelled to London in May 1814 to negotiate with the Transport Office the release of French prisoners held in Britain. Amusingly, the French asked for those who had behaved well to be released first, inviting the Transport Office to 'not hesitate to keep everywhere the bad ones [*les mauvaise têtes*] and all those who are known to have a dangerous influence on their comrades'.[70] In total, 111,000 soldiers survived the British prisons and came home in 1814. Some 13,000 (10 per cent) died in captivity.[71] This statistic does not agree with the theory that the British systematically tried to kill French prisoners. As this chapter argues, the British found it hard to cope with large influxes of enemy soldiers. Emergency measures, such as prison-ships, were introduced to reduce the number of soldiers held in camps. Conditions were hard, food was poor and prisoners were psychologically distressed but there was no deliberate policy to make their life miserable. On the contrary, British authorities took steps to build new camps and improve conditions. In fact, French soldiers detained in Britain were more likely to survive the Napoleonic Wars than their fellow-countrymen still on active service.

---

69. Jobbé-Duval, *Mémoires du Baron de Bonnefoux*, p. 184.
70. Quoted in Le Carvèse, 'Les prisonniers français en Grande-Bretagne', pp. 3–29.
71. Le Carvèse, 'Les prisonniers français en Grande-Bretagne', pp. 3–29.

# Conclusion

The battle of Waterloo was a seminal moment in modern history. It was not the last battle of the campaign but it effectively destroyed Napoleon's ambitions. After more than two decades of war, France was finally ready for peace. Louis XVIII, restored to his throne during the summer of 1815, immediately took steps to reform and stabilise the country. On a far-away island, Napoleon spent his last years with a small court of admirers. The ex-Emperor spent his free time looking back at his extraordinary career. In 1817 he worked with General Gaspard Gourgaud[1] on a history of the Hundred Days. Gourgaud, a difficult character, left the island of Saint-Helena at the beginning of 1818 and immediately released a book titled *Campagne de dix-huit cent quinze ou relation des opérations militaires qui ont eu lieu en France et en Belgique, pendant les Cent Jours*.[2] This book became influential among French veterans. A second book, written by General Comte Bertrand[3] with the help of the ex-Emperor, was published anonymously in France in 1820. *Mémoires pour server à l'histoire de France sous Napoléon*[4] offered an even more favourable version of the Hundred Days than Gourgaud's monograph. In this publication, Napoleon was absolved of all the mistakes committed at Waterloo. Instead, the crushing defeat was blamed on men such as Ney and Grouchy. After Napoleon's death on 5 May 1821 his reputation was protected by a web of counterfactual texts. Soon after his death, the *Mémorial de Sainte-Hélène*, by Emmanuel de Las Cases, was published in France.[5] This book, based on daily conversations with the Emperor in exile, was to fuel nostalgia for decades.

Napoleon was not the only one reflecting on his military career. After 1815 thousands of French veterans wrote about their time in the army. Most,

---

1. Gaspard Gourgaud, born in Versailles on 14 November 1783, fought in the Napoleonic Wars. He saved the life of the Emperor at the battle of Brienne in 1814. Gourgaud followed Napoleon on the island of Saint-Helena but returned to France in 1818. He died in 1852.
2. Gaspard Gourgaud, *Campagne de dix-huit cent quinze ou relation des opérations militaires qui ont eu lieu en France et en Belgique, pendant les Cent Jours* (Paris, 1818).
3. Henri Gratien, Comte Bertrand was born in 1773. He served in the French army during the French Revolutionary Wars and the Napoleonic Wars. After the Emperor's defeat at the battle of Waterloo, he followed Napoleon to Saint-Helena. He died on 31 January 1844.
4. Anonymous, *Mémoires pour servir à l'histoire de France sous Napoléon* (Paris, 1820).
5. Emmanuel de Las Cases, *Le mémorial de Sainte-Hélène* (Brussels and London, 1823).

but not all, did their best to protect Napoleon's reputation. Fifteen years after the Napoleonic Wars, the French public had largely forgotten the hardship of conscription or those who had perished in faraway countries. Helped by romantic songs and paintings, a cult of Napoleon emerged, while his work on the island of Saint-Helena gained him further ground. The French King Louis-Philippe and his *Président du Conseil* Adolphe Thiers, a historian of the French Consulate and Empire, saw an opportunity to capitalise on the ex-Emperor's prestige. Both men negotiated with the British and finally succeeded in returning Napoleon's body. In 1840 a French frigate reached Saint-Helena. Napoleon's body was brought back to France and reburied at Les Invalides on 15 December 1840. Napoleon's return crowned an era of myths and exaggerations. During this period of rapid colonialisation and fierce economical competition, the war between Napoleon's France and Britain became a nationalistic tool. Waterloo was seen as a stolen victory, an unfair turn of faith proving Britain's deceitful nature. Wellington was painted as a talentless commander and the British army as a minor player in a glorious period of history. Napoleon's exile – far from unreasonable considering the harm caused by the Emperor in Europe and his escape from the island of Elba – was denounced as another act of British cruelty. This animosity, based on the wars of 1793–1815, proved so resilient and remained so widespread that it became a tool of German propaganda in the occupied territories of France during the First World War. Indeed, German psychological warfare used Napoleon's myth to demonstrate the Franco-British alliance's counter-intuitive nature. The French government was even forced to answer the enemy's campaign of psychological warfare. For example, a caricature, reproduced in this book, represented Napoleon on top of his grave shouting 'Long live the English'. The exact same phenomenon happened during the Second World War, when German propagandists once again used the Emperor to stir up anti-British feelings.[6]

Today, the Franco-British wars of 1793–1815 remain controversial. In France Napoleon is still the most admired historical figure, along with Charles de Gaulle and Louis XIV. Waterloo is a powerful symbol and has crystallised the public's attention. Many French still refuse to see this battle as a British victory. Some represent it as a stroke of luck helped by Grouchy's incompetence and Ney's folly. Others, less numerous, dare to call it a meta-phorical or a factual French victory.[7] In any case, Napoleon is rarely blamed for Waterloo's outcome, while Wellington is never given the credit he deserves. This refusal to acknowledge historical facts has recently triggered

6. See Bernard Wilkin and Maude Williams, 'German wartime Anglophobic propaganda in France, 1914–1945', in: *War in History*, 24 (2017), pp. 28–43.
7. See, for example, Casali, *Qui a gagné Waterloo?*

diplomatic tensions. In 2004 Windsor Castle's Waterloo Chamber was renamed the 'Music Room' to accommodate Jacques Chirac.[8] For the 200th anniversary of the battle of Waterloo, the Belgian government was forced to cancel the release of a two euro coin representing the famous battlefield. This project was so violently attacked by the French that the Belgian government decided instead to strike a commemorative coin.[9] Things are different in Britain. Nelson and Wellington have been immortalised in the centre of London, where they fight their last battles against armies of pigeons. French bad faith is an object of amusement and has recently been ridiculed in a book by Stephen Clarke.[10] The British are, however, not immune to controversies and clichés when looking back at the Napoleonic Wars. In 2016 Boris Johnson's comparison between Napoleonic France and the European Union caused widespread outrage.[11] More importantly, the public memory has forgotten the campaigns in Calabria and Flanders. Gone are the complexities of the Peninsular War or the battles in Egypt. Britain's allies are also largely forgotten. The Belgian-Dutch army that fought at Waterloo or the fundamental role played by Austria, Russia and Prussia, to name only a few, are often afterthoughts. It must be repeated here that the events described in this book were only part of a bigger story. Focusing on key events such as Trafalgar or Waterloo has kept this period alive but has fostered a rather simplistic vision of the past.

As this book has attempted to demonstrate, the war between the French and the British was a complex marathon filled with ideological and logistical challenges. The French disliked the British but did not hate them. They respected their steadiness under fire but remained confident in their own ability to prevail. In the French mind, the British were sneaky, untrustworthy on the diplomatic stage and unconventional on the battlefield. If the French never accepted the defeat of 1815, they learned to tolerate the British. During the Occupation of 1815–1818, Wellington's army behaved correctly with civilians and veterans alike. Less than a hundred years after these events, the French and the British would fight side by side on the Western Front.

---

8. See CNN website: http://edition.cnn.com/2004/WORLD/europe/11/19/uk.chirac.daytwo 0700/ [consulted 23 February 2017].
9. See this article by Belgian National Television (RTBF): https://www.rtbf.be/info/belgique/ detail_la-piece-commemorative-de-la-bataille-de-waterloo-frappee-ce-lundi?id=9001014 [consulted 23 February 2017].
10. Stephen Clarke, *How the French won Waterloo (or think they did)* (2015).
11. See the *Sunday Telegraph*, 15 May 2016: http://www.telegraph.co.uk/news/2016/05/14/ boris-johnson-the-eu-wants-a-superstate-just-as-hitler-did/ [consulted 23 February 2017] or the *Guardian*, 16 May 2016: https://www.theguardian.com/politics/2016/may/16/tories-divided-by-boris-johnsons-eu-hitler-comparison [consulted 23 February 2017].

# Bibliography

## Archives

Archives de l'Etat à Liège, Fonds Français Préfecture: 1042, 1043, 1044, 1045
Archives Départementales du Loiret: 1J1696. Diary of Philippe Beaudoin
Service Historique de la Défense, Archives de la Marine
Service Historique de la Défense, Armée de Terre

## Newspapers

*Bulletin de l'armée d'Espagne* (1808)

## Printed Primary Sources

Anonymous, *Bulletin de la société académique de l'arrondissement de Boulogne-sur-Mer: tome sixième* (Boulogne-sur-Mer, 1903)

Anonymous, 'Fragments d'un journal d'un savant de la Commission d'Egypte', in: *Carnet de la Sabretache: revue militaire rétrospective* (1936), pp. 309–10

Jean-Baptiste Barrès, *Souvenirs d'un officier de la Grande Armée* (Paris, 1923)

Fernand Beaucour, 'Notes et souvenirs de J.-J. Bellavoine, soldat du camp de Boulogne', in: *Revue du Nord*, 50 (1968), pp. 435–47

Philippe Beaudoin, 'Carnet d'étapes du sergent-major Philippe Beaudoin', in: *Carnet de la Sabretache: revue militaire rétrospective* (1909), pp. 209–24

Philippe Beaudoin, *Carnet d'étapes: expédition de Saint-Domingue* (Paris, 2000)

Charles-Rémy Beaujot, *Relation de la captivité du capitaine Beaujot, ancient sergent-major sous l'empire français* (Liège, 1856)

Bertier, 'Lettre d'un lieutenant de l'artillerie des guides', in: *Carnet de la Sabretache: revue militaire rétrospective* (1896), pp. 446–8

Pierre Bertrand, *Précis de l'histoire physique civile et politique de la ville de Boulogne-sur-Mer, depuis les Morins jusqu'en 1814* (Boulogne-sur-Mer, 1815)

Sébastien Blaze, *Mémoires d'un apothicaire* (Paris, 1828)

Joseph Bonaparte, *Mémoires et correspondance politique et militaire du roi Joseph. Tome 2* (Paris, 1854)

Napoléon Bonaparte, *Correspondance générale publiée par la Fondation Napoléon. Tome I: les apprentissages, 1784–1797* (Paris, 2004)

Napoléon Bonaparte, *Correspondance générale publiée par la Fondation Napoléon: Tome 9* (Paris, 2013)

René Bourgeois, *Relation fidèle et détaille de la dernière campagne de Buonaparte, terminée par la bataille de Mont-Saint-Jean dite de Waterloo ou de la Belle-Alliance* (Paris, 1815)

Paul de Bourgoin, *Souvenirs militaires du Baron de Bourgoing: sénateur, ambassadeur d'Espagne, ancien pair de France, ministre plénipotentiaire en Russie et en Allemagne ... 1791–1815* (Paris, 1897)

Antoine Boussard d'Hauteroche, *La vie militaire en Italie sous le Premier Empire (campagne des Calabres), 1806–1809: souvenirs du sous lieutenant d'Hauteroche* (Saint-Etienne, 1894)

Louis-Joseph Bricard, *Journal du canonnier Bricard, 1792–1802, publié pour la première fois par ses petits-fils Alfred et Jules Bricard, avec une introduction de Lorédan-Larchey* (Paris, 1891)

Comte de C\*\*\*, *Séjour de dix mois en France, par un émigré, qui n'avoit pu sortir de Toulon en décembre 1793, & ne s'est sauvé de France que par l'élargissement des prisonniers de Paris, en août 1794* (London, 1794)

Jean Jacques Régis de Cambacérès, *Lettres inédites à Napoléon, 1802–1814. Tome Ier: Janvier 1802–juillet 1807* (Paris, 1973)

Neil Campbell, *Napoleon at Fontainebleau and Elba, being a Journal of occurrences in 1814–1815* (London, 1869)

Alexandre Coudreux, *Lettres du commandant Coudreux à son frère, 1804–1815* (Paris, 1908)

Paul-Louis Courier, *Lettres écrites de France et d'Italie* (Paris, ND)

Jérôme Croyet, *Paroles de grognards* (Paris, 2016)

Auguste-Dominique Dauphin, *Considérations sur quelques maladies qui ont principalement exercé leurs ravages parmi les Français prisonniers en Angleterre, depuis l'an 1803 jusqu'à juillet 1814* (Paris, 1815)

Louis Dembowski, 'Voyage de retour de Saint-Domingue en France de l'adjudant-commandant Dembowksi', in: *Carnet de la Sabretache: revue militaire rétrospective* (1914), pp. 1–7

Ernest Deseille, *L'année boulonnaise: éphémérides historiques intéressant le pays boulonnais* (Boulogne-sur-Mer, 1886)

Léon van Dormael, 'A propos du prochain voyage du S. N. à Waterloo', in: *Souvenir Napoléonien*, 29 (1974), pp. 29–30

Alfred-Auguste Ernouf, *Souvenirs d'un officier polonais, Scènes de la vie militaire en Espagne et en Russie* (Paris, 1877)

Charles François, *Le journal d'un officier français ou les cahiers du capitaine François: 1792–1815* (Tours, 1913)

Louis Garneray, *Mes pontons, neuf années de captivité* (Paris, 1933)

Louis Gille, *Mémoires d'un conscrit de 1808: les prisons de Cabrera* (Paris, 1892)

Robert Guillemard, *Mémoires, souvenirs: mémoires de Robert Guillemard* (Paris, 1826)

Jean Guillemin, 'Lettre du commandant Guillemin, chef de bataillon au 3e grenadiers de la Garde, à M. le lieutenant général baron Haxo', in: *Carnet de la Sabretache: revue militaire rétrospective* (1905), p. 114

Gabriel Heuillet, 'Extrait d'une lettre du capitaine Heuillet, du 2e chasseurs de la Garde', in: *Carnet de la Sabretache: revue militaire rétrospective* (1905), pp. 121–2

John Hobhouse, *The substance of some letters, written by an Englishman resident at Paris during the last reign of the Emperor Napoleon* (Philadelphia, 1816)

Julien Houssart, 'Copie du rapport de combat de Trafalgar écrit le surlendemain, à bord du «Neptune» anglais et remis à l'Amiral Villeneuve', in: *Carnet de la Sabretache: revue militaire rétrospective* (1905), pp. 291–8

Jacques-Louis Hulot, *Souvenirs militaires du baron Hulot, général d'artillerie, 1773–1843* (Paris, 1886)

François-Joseph Jacquin, *Carnet de route d'un grognard de la révolution et de l'empire* (Paris, 1960)

Emile Jobbé-Duval, *Mémoires du Baron de Bonnefoux* (Paris, 1900)

Antoine Jomini, *Guerre d'Espagne: extrait des souvenirs inédits du général Jomini* (Paris, 1892)

Emile Labretonnière, *Macédoine. Souvenirs du quartier latin: Paris à la chute de l'Empire et pendant les Cent-Jours* (Paris, 1863)

Louis-Vivant Lagneau, *Journal d'un chirurgien de la Grande Armée(L.-V. Lagneau), 1803–1815. Avec une introduction de M. Frédéric Masson* (Paris, 1913)

Loredan Larche, *Correspondance intime de l'armée d'Egypte interceptée par la croisière anglaise* (Paris, 1866)

Louis Lejoille, 'Documents inédits sur l'expédition d'Egypte', in: *Carnet de la Sabretache: revue militaire rétrospective* (1936), p. 305

Octave Levavasseur, *Souvenirs du général Levavasseur* (Paris, 1908)

Nicolas Marcel, *Campagnes du capitaine Marcel, du 69e de ligne, en Espagne et en Portugal (1808–1814)* (Paris, 1913)

Jacques Martin, 'Waterloo: lettre d'un officier genevois du 45e', in: *Carnet de la Sabretache: revue militaire rétrospective* (1895), pp. 493–528

Joseph de Naylies, *Mémoires sur la guerre d'Espagne: pendant les années 1808, 1809, 1810, et 1811* (Paris, 1817)

Jean-Auguste Oyon, 'Campagnes et souvenirs militaires de Jean-Auguste Oyon', in: *Carnets de la Sabretache: revue militaire rétrospective* (1913), pp. 101–9

Guillaume Peyrusse, *1809–1815, memorial et archives de M. le baron Peyrusse, trésorier général de la couronne pendant les cent-jours* (Carcassonne, 1869)

René-Martin Pillet, *L'Angleterre vue à Londres et dans ses provinces, pendant un séjour de dix années, dont six comme prisonnier de guerre* (Paris, 1815)

Philippe Poisson, *Pontons et prisons sous le Premier Empire* (Paris, 1998)

Joseph Quantin, *Trois ans de séjour en Espagne dans l'intérieur du pays, sur les pontons, à Cadix, et dans l'île de Cabrera* (Paris, 1823)

Jacques Rambaud, *Lettres inédites ou éparses de Joseph Bonaparte à Naples (1806–1808)* (Paris, 1911)

Jacques Resal and P. Allorant, *Un médecin dans le sillage de la Grande Armée: correspondance entre Jean Jacques Ballard et son épouse Ursule demeurée en France (1805–1812)* (Paris, 2013)

Dieudonné Rigau, *Souvenirs des guerres de l'empire: réflexions, pensées, maximes, anecdotes, lettres diverses, testament philosophique; suivis d'une notice sur le général Rigau* (Paris, 1846)

François Riou, *Rapport fait par Riou, au nom de la commission spéciale, composée des représentants Quirot, Leclerc (de Maine, Loire)* (Paris, 1798)

Pierre Robinaux, *Journal de route du capitaine Robinaux* (Paris, 1908)

Rochay, 'Du Piémont aux Antilles et à Trafalgar: souvenirs d'un fantassin', in: *Carnet de la Sabretache: revue militaire rétrospective*, 417 (1958), pp. 497–511

François Rousseau, *Kléber et Menou en Egypte depuis le départ de Bonaparte* (Paris, 1900)

François-Michel Royer, 'Impressions d'un Allobroge devant Toulon', in: *Carnet de la Sabretache: revue militaire rétrospective* (1899), pp. 146–9

Daniel Savary, 'Quelques documents sur l'expédition du Général Humbert en Irlande', in: *Carnet de la Sabretache, revue militaire rétrospective* (Paris, 1899), pp. 399–401

Poumiès de la Siboutie, *Souvenirs d'un médecin de Paris* (Paris, 1910)

Duret de Tavel, *Séjour d'un officier français en Calabre* (Paris, 1820)

Christian Tortel and P. Carlier, *Bonaparte de Toulon au Caire d'après 19 lettres de François Bernoyer* (Paris, 1996)

Joseph Tyrbas de Chamberet, *Mémoires d'un médecin militaire aux XVIIIe et XIXe siècles* (Paris, 2001)

Auguste-Alexandre de Vanssay, *Fragments de mémoires inédits écrits en 1817 sous le titre de 'Souvenirs militaires d'un officier de dragon': pendant les campagnes de la Grande armée des années 1804 à 1811, armée d'Espagne* (Mortagne, 1864)

Jean-Baptiste Vertray, *L'armée française en Egypte, 1798–1801: journal d'un officier de l'armée d'Egypte* (Paris, 1883)

Edouard de Villiers, *Journal et souvenirs sur l'expédition d'Egypte: 1798–1801* (Paris, 1899)

Jean Stanislas Vivien, 'Souvenirs de ma vie militaire (1795–1822)', in: *Carnet de la Sabretache: revue militaire rétrospective* (1905), pp. 667–8

François-Joseph Zickel, 'Lettres et souvenirs d'un officier de cavalerie légère', in: *Carnet de la Sabretache: revue militaire rétrospective* (1907), pp. 770–2

## Secondary Sources

Zeinab Abul-Magd, 'A crisis of images: The French, Jihad, and the plague in Upper Egypt, 1798–1801', in: *Journal of World History*, 2 (2012), pp. 315–43

Angebault, *Mémoires sur les campagnes d'Espagne* (Paris, 1997)

Edward Baines, *History of the wars of the French Revolution* (London, 1818)

Veronica Baker-Smith, *Wellington's hidden heroes: the Dutch and the Belgians at Waterloo* (London, 2015)

Christophe Bourachot, *Les hommes de Napoléon: témoignages 1805–1815* (Paris, 2011)

Nicolas Cadet, 'Violences de guerre et transmission de la mémoire des conflits à travers l'exemple de la campagne de Calabre de 1806–1807', in: *Annales historiques de la Révolution française*, 348 (2007), pp. 147–63

Dimitri Casali, *Qui a gagné Waterloo? Napoléon 2015* (Paris, 2015)

Jacques Chochois and M. Poultier, *Napoléon, le camp de Boulogne, et ... la Légion d'Honneur* (Boulogne-sur-Mer, 2003)

Margaret Chrisawn, *The Emperor's friend: Marshal Jean Lannes* (Westport, 2001)

Jean-Claude Damamme, *Les soldats de la Grande Armée* (Paris, 2002)

A. Demougeot, 'Les Anglais à Nice pendant la paix d'Amiens 1802–1803', in: *Recherches Régionales*, 1 (1963), p. 34

Jacques Hantraye, '1813–1818: les premières occupations de la période contemporaine en France', in: *Revue Historique des Armées*, 239 (2005), pp. 50–6

Patrick Hogan, '1798 remembered: casualties sustained by government forces during the Humbert episode, August–September, 1798: a re-appraisal', in: *Journal of the Galway Archaeological and Historical Society*, 50 (1998), pp. 1–9

Ian Germani, 'Combat and culture: imagining the battle of the Nile', in: *The Northern Mariner/ Le Marin du Nord*, 1 (2000), pp. 53–72

John Grainger, *The Amiens truce: Britain and Bonaparte 1801–1803* (Woodbridge, 2004)

H. Grueber, 'The "descente en Angleterre" medal of Napoleon I', in: *Royal Numismatic Society*, 7 (1907), pp. 434–9

Jean-Louis Guérette, *Un général de vingt-six ans, Henri Jardon 1768–1809* (Verviers, 1988)

Yann Guerrin, *La France après Napoléon: Invasions et occupations 1814–1818* (Paris, 2014)

Michael Hughes, *Forging Napoleon's Grande Armée: motivation, military culture, and masculinity in the French army, 1800–1808* (New York, 2012)

Edward Ingram, 'Illusions of victory: The Nile, Copenhagen, and Trafalgar revisited', in: *Military Affairs*, 48 (1984), pp. 140–3

C. Jeannin, *Le Général Travot, pacificateur de la Vendée* (Paris, 1862)

Andrew Lambert, 'The glory of England: Nelson, Trafalgar and the meaning of victory', in: *The Great Circle*, 28 (2006), pp. 3–12

Patrick Le Carvèse, 'Les prisonniers français en Grande-Bretagne de 1803 à 1814: première partie', in: *Napoleonica*, 8 (2010), pp. 3–29

Finley Milton, 'Prelude to Spain: The Calabrian insurrection, 1806–1807', in: *Military Affairs*, 40 (1976), pp. 84–7

Rémi Monaque and John Welsh, 'Was Nelson killed by Robert Guillemard?', in: *The Mariner's Mirror*, 88 (2002), pp. 469–74

Jennifer Mori, 'The British Government and the Bourbon restoration: The occupation of Toulon, 1793', in: *The Historical Journal*, 40 (1997), pp. 699–719

Karen Nakache, 'Des marins français à Aboukir: témoignages', in: *Cahiers de la Méditerranée*, 57 (1998), pp. 207–33

Grace Neville, 'Up close and personal: The French in Bantry Bay (1796) in the Bantry Estate Papers', in: *Proceedings of the Harvard Celtic Colloquium*, 26/27 (2006/2007), pp. 132–45

Robert Tignor, *Egypt: a short history* (Princeton, 2010)

Jean Tulard, *Bibliographie critique des mémoires sur le consulat et l'empire* (Paris, 1971)

Thomas Walker, *The depot for prisoners at Norman Cross Huntingdonshire, 1796 to 1816* (London, 1913)

René Wilkin, 'Le remplacement militaire dans le département de l'Ourthe', in: *Bulletin de l'Institut archéologique liégeois*, CXII (2001–2002)

Bernard Wilkin and René Wilkin, *Fighting for Napoleon* (Barnsley, 2015)

# Index